:ER EXAMINATION SERIES

THIS IS YOUR **PASSBOOK®** FOR ...

ACCOUNTANT

NATIONAL LEARNING CORPORATION®
passbooks.com

PASSBOOK® SERIES

THE *PASSBOOK® SERIES* has been created to prepare applicants and candidates for the ultimate academic battlefield – the examination room.

At some time in our lives, each and every one of us may be required to take an examination – for validation, matriculation, admission, qualification, registration, certification, or licensure.

Based on the assumption that every applicant or candidate has met the basic formal educational standards, has taken the required number of courses, and read the necessary texts, the *PASSBOOK® SERIES* furnishes the one special preparation which may assure passing with confidence, instead of failing with insecurity. Examination questions – together with answers – are furnished as the basic vehicle for study so that the mysteries of the examination and its compounding difficulties may be eliminated or diminished by a sure method.

This book is meant to help you pass your examination provided that you qualify and are serious in your objective.

The entire field is reviewed through the huge store of content information which is succinctly presented through a provocative and challenging approach – the question-and-answer method.

A climate of success is established by furnishing the correct answers at the end of each test.

You soon learn to recognize types of questions, forms of questions, and patterns of questioning. You may even begin to anticipate expected outcomes.

You perceive that many questions are repeated or adapted so that you can gain acute insights, which may enable you to score many sure points.

You learn how to confront new questions, or types of questions, and to attack them confidently and work out the correct answers.

You note objectives and emphases, and recognize pitfalls and dangers, so that you may make positive educational adjustments.

Moreover, you are kept fully informed in relation to new concepts, methods, practices, and directions in the field.

You discover that you arre actually taking the examination all the time: you are preparing for the examination by "taking" an examination, not by reading extraneous and/or supererogatory textbooks.

In short, this PASSBOOK®, used directedly, should be an important factor in helping you to pass your test.

ACCOUNTANT

DUTIES AND RESPONSIBILITIES

Under supervision, performs professional accounting work of moderate difficulty and responsibility internally in departments and agencies or in conducting field audits and investigations; works independently or with others in executing responsible accounting assignments following prescribed rules of procedures; performs related work.

EXAMPLES OF TYPICAL TASKS

Examines the accuracy of the returns of taxpayers who have filed under various tax laws, determines the correct liability, and assesses accordingly. Makes field investigations and audits of the books of various types of enterprises to determine conformance with tax laws or housing regulations. Prepares working papers, schedules, financial statements, payroll lists, and inventory records. Maintains cost records and prepares reports. Reviews requests for the allocation of capital funds. Assists in preparation and analyses of budgets. Performs difficult arithmetic computations. Assists in the audits of accounts of departments and agencies for receipts under franchises, leases and permits. Checks and verifies entries, footings and extensions for accuracy. Maintains control of accounts of funds and reserves. Prepares journal entries and adjusting entries. May supervise employees performing work of lower responsibility.

TESTS

The written test may include questions on accounting and auditing principles and practices; maintenance, examination and review of financial books, records and transactions; financial statements budgets and supporting documents and schedules, interpretation and understanding of financial written material; and related areas.

HOW TO TAKE A TEST

I. YOU MUST PASS AN EXAMINATION

A. WHAT EVERY CANDIDATE SHOULD KNOW

Examination applicants often ask us for help in preparing for the written test. What can I study in advance? What kinds of questions will be asked? How will the test be given? How will the papers be graded?

As an applicant for a civil service examination, you may be wondering about some of these things. Our purpose here is to suggest effective methods of advance study and to describe civil service examinations.

Your chances for success on this examination can be increased if you know how to prepare. Those "pre-examination jitters" can be reduced if you know what to expect. You can even experience an adventure in good citizenship if you know why civil service exams are given.

B. WHY ARE CIVIL SERVICE EXAMINATIONS GIVEN?

Civil service examinations are important to you in two ways. As a citizen, you want public jobs filled by employees who know how to do their work. As a job seeker, you want a fair chance to compete for that job on an equal footing with other candidates. The best-known means of accomplishing this two-fold goal is the competitive examination.

Exams are widely publicized throughout the nation. They may be administered for jobs in federal, state, city, municipal, town or village governments or agencies.

Any citizen may apply, with some limitations, such as the age or residence of applicants. Your experience and education may be reviewed to see whether you meet the requirements for the particular examination. When these requirements exist, they are reasonable and applied consistently to all applicants. Thus, a competitive examination may cause you some uneasiness now, but it is your privilege and safeguard.

C. HOW ARE CIVIL SERVICE EXAMS DEVELOPED?

Examinations are carefully written by trained technicians who are specialists in the field known as "psychological measurement," in consultation with recognized authorities in the field of work that the test will cover. These experts recommend the subject matter areas or skills to be tested; only those knowledges or skills important to your success on the job are included. The most reliable books and source materials available are used as references. Together, the experts and technicians judge the difficulty level of the questions.

Test technicians know how to phrase questions so that the problem is clearly stated. Their ethics do not permit "trick" or "catch" questions. Questions may have been tried out on sample groups, or subjected to statistical analysis, to determine their usefulness.

Written tests are often used in combination with performance tests, ratings of training and experience, and oral interviews. All of these measures combine to form the best-known means of finding the right person for the right job.

II. HOW TO PASS THE WRITTEN TEST

A. NATURE OF THE EXAMINATION

To prepare intelligently for civil service examinations, you should know how they differ from school examinations you have taken. In school you were assigned certain definite pages to read or subjects to cover. The examination questions were quite detailed and usually emphasized memory. Civil service exams, on the other hand, try to discover your present ability to perform the duties of a position, plus your potentiality to learn these duties. In other words, a civil service exam attempts to predict how successful you will be. Questions cover such a broad area that they cannot be as minute and detailed as school exam questions.

In the public service similar kinds of work, or positions, are grouped together in one "class." This process is known as *position-classification*. All the positions in a class are paid according to the salary range for that class. One class title covers all of these positions, and they are all tested by the same examination.

B. FOUR BASIC STEPS

1) Study the announcement

How, then, can you know what subjects to study? Our best answer is: "Learn as much as possible about the class of positions for which you've applied." The exam will test the knowledge, skills and abilities needed to do the work.

Your most valuable source of information about the position you want is the official exam announcement. This announcement lists the training and experience qualifications. Check these standards and apply only if you come reasonably close to meeting them.

The brief description of the position in the examination announcement offers some clues to the subjects which will be tested. Think about the job itself. Review the duties in your mind. Can you perform them, or are there some in which you are rusty? Fill in the blank spots in your preparation.

Many jurisdictions preview the written test in the exam announcement by including a section called "Knowledge and Abilities Required," "Scope of the Examination," or some similar heading. Here you will find out specifically what fields will be tested.

2) Review your own background

Once you learn in general what the position is all about, and what you need to know to do the work, ask yourself which subjects you already know fairly well and which need improvement. You may wonder whether to concentrate on improving your strong areas or on building some background in your fields of weakness. When the announcement has specified "some knowledge" or "considerable knowledge," or has used adjectives like "beginning principles of…" or "advanced … methods," you can get a clue as to the number and difficulty of questions to be asked in any given field. More questions, and hence broader coverage, would be included for those subjects which are more important in the work. Now weigh your strengths and weaknesses against the job requirements and prepare accordingly.

3) **Determine the level of the position**

Another way to tell how intensively you should prepare is to understand the level of the job for which you are applying. Is it the entering level? In other words, is this the position in which beginners in a field of work are hired? Or is it an intermediate or advanced level? Sometimes this is indicated by such words as "Junior" or "Senior" in the class title. Other jurisdictions use Roman numerals to designate the level – Clerk I, Clerk II, for example. The word "Supervisor" sometimes appears in the title. If the level is not indicated by the title, check the description of duties. Will you be working under very close supervision, or will you have responsibility for independent decisions in this work?

4) **Choose appropriate study materials**

Now that you know the subjects to be examined and the relative amount of each subject to be covered, you can choose suitable study materials. For beginning level jobs, or even advanced ones, if you have a pronounced weakness in some aspect of your training, read a modern, standard textbook in that field. Be sure it is up to date and has general coverage. Such books are normally available at your library, and the librarian will be glad to help you locate one. For entry-level positions, questions of appropriate difficulty are chosen – neither highly advanced questions, nor those too simple. Such questions require careful thought but not advanced training.

If the position for which you are applying is technical or advanced, you will read more advanced, specialized material. If you are already familiar with the basic principles of your field, elementary textbooks would waste your time. Concentrate on advanced textbooks and technical periodicals. Think through the concepts and review difficult problems in your field.

These are all general sources. You can get more ideas on your own initiative, following these leads. For example, training manuals and publications of the government agency which employs workers in your field can be useful, particularly for technical and professional positions. A letter or visit to the government department involved may result in more specific study suggestions, and certainly will provide you with a more definite idea of the exact nature of the position you are seeking.

III. KINDS OF TESTS

Tests are used for purposes other than measuring knowledge and ability to perform specified duties. For some positions, it is equally important to test ability to make adjustments to new situations or to profit from training. In others, basic mental abilities not dependent on information are essential. Questions which test these things may not appear as pertinent to the duties of the position as those which test for knowledge and information. Yet they are often highly important parts of a fair examination. For very general questions, it is almost impossible to help you direct your study efforts. What we can do is to point out some of the more common of these general abilities needed in public service positions and describe some typical questions.

1) General information

Broad, general information has been found useful for predicting job success in some kinds of work. This is tested in a variety of ways, from vocabulary lists to questions about current events. Basic background in some field of work, such as sociology or economics, may be sampled in a group of questions. Often these are principles which have become familiar to most persons through exposure rather than through formal training. It is difficult to advise you how to study for these questions; being alert to the world around you is our best suggestion.

2) Verbal ability

An example of an ability needed in many positions is verbal or language ability. Verbal ability is, in brief, the ability to use and understand words. Vocabulary and grammar tests are typical measures of this ability. Reading comprehension or paragraph interpretation questions are common in many kinds of civil service tests. You are given a paragraph of written material and asked to find its central meaning.

3) Numerical ability

Number skills can be tested by the familiar arithmetic problem, by checking paired lists of numbers to see which are alike and which are different, or by interpreting charts and graphs. In the latter test, a graph may be printed in the test booklet which you are asked to use as the basis for answering questions.

4) Observation

A popular test for law-enforcement positions is the observation test. A picture is shown to you for several minutes, then taken away. Questions about the picture test your ability to observe both details and larger elements.

5) Following directions

In many positions in the public service, the employee must be able to carry out written instructions dependably and accurately. You may be given a chart with several columns, each column listing a variety of information. The questions require you to carry out directions involving the information given in the chart.

6) Skills and aptitudes

Performance tests effectively measure some manual skills and aptitudes. When the skill is one in which you are trained, such as typing or shorthand, you can practice. These tests are often very much like those given in business school or high school courses. For many of the other skills and aptitudes, however, no short-time preparation can be made. Skills and abilities natural to you or that you have developed throughout your lifetime are being tested.

Many of the general questions just described provide all the data needed to answer the questions and ask you to use your reasoning ability to find the answers. Your best preparation for these tests, as well as for tests of facts and ideas, is to be at your physical and mental best. You, no doubt, have your own methods of getting into an exam-taking mood and keeping "in shape." The next section lists some ideas on this subject.

IV. KINDS OF QUESTIONS

Only rarely is the "essay" question, which you answer in narrative form, used in civil service tests. Civil service tests are usually of the short-answer type. Full instructions for answering these questions will be given to you at the examination. But in case this is your first experience with short-answer questions and separate answer sheets, here is what you need to know:

1) Multiple-choice Questions

Most popular of the short-answer questions is the "multiple choice" or "best answer" question. It can be used, for example, to test for factual knowledge, ability to solve problems or judgment in meeting situations found at work.

A multiple-choice question is normally one of three types—

- It can begin with an incomplete statement followed by several possible endings. You are to find the one ending which *best* completes the statement, although some of the others may not be entirely wrong.
- It can also be a complete statement in the form of a question which is answered by choosing one of the statements listed.
- It can be in the form of a problem – again you select the best answer.

Here is an example of a multiple-choice question with a discussion which should give you some clues as to the method for choosing the right answer:

When an employee has a complaint about his assignment, the action which will *best* help him overcome his difficulty is to
A. discuss his difficulty with his coworkers
B. take the problem to the head of the organization
C. take the problem to the person who gave him the assignment
D. say nothing to anyone about his complaint

In answering this question, you should study each of the choices to find which is best. Consider choice "A" – Certainly an employee may discuss his complaint with fellow employees, but no change or improvement can result, and the complaint remains unresolved. Choice "B" is a poor choice since the head of the organization probably does not know what assignment you have been given, and taking your problem to him is known as "going over the head" of the supervisor. The supervisor, or person who made the assignment, is the person who can clarify it or correct any injustice. Choice "C" is, therefore, correct. To say nothing, as in choice "D," is unwise. Supervisors have and interest in knowing the problems employees are facing, and the employee is seeking a solution to his problem.

2) True/False Questions

The "true/false" or "right/wrong" form of question is sometimes used. Here a complete statement is given. Your job is to decide whether the statement is right or wrong.

SAMPLE: A roaming cell-phone call to a nearby city costs less than a non-roaming call to a distant city.

This statement is wrong, or false, since roaming calls are more expensive.
This is not a complete list of all possible question forms, although most of the others are variations of these common types. You will always get complete directions for

answering questions. Be sure you understand *how* to mark your answers – ask questions until you do.

V. RECORDING YOUR ANSWERS

Computer terminals are used more and more today for many different kinds of exams.

For an examination with very few applicants, you may be told to record your answers in the test booklet itself. Separate answer sheets are much more common. If this separate answer sheet is to be scored by machine – and this is often the case – it is highly important that you mark your answers correctly in order to get credit.

An electronic scoring machine is often used in civil service offices because of the speed with which papers can be scored. Machine-scored answer sheets must be marked with a pencil, which will be given to you. This pencil has a high graphite content which responds to the electronic scoring machine. As a matter of fact, stray dots may register as answers, so do not let your pencil rest on the answer sheet while you are pondering the correct answer. Also, if your pencil lead breaks or is otherwise defective, ask for another.

Since the answer sheet will be dropped in a slot in the scoring machine, be careful not to bend the corners or get the paper crumpled.

The answer sheet normally has five vertical columns of numbers, with 30 numbers to a column. These numbers correspond to the question numbers in your test booklet. After each number, going across the page are four or five pairs of dotted lines. These short dotted lines have small letters or numbers above them. The first two pairs may also have a "T" or "F" above the letters. This indicates that the first two pairs only are to be used if the questions are of the true-false type. If the questions are multiple choice, disregard the "T" and "F" and pay attention only to the small letters or numbers.

Answer your questions in the manner of the sample that follows:

32. The largest city in the United States is
    A. Washington, D.C.
    B. New York City
    C. Chicago
    D. Detroit
    E. San Francisco

1) Choose the answer you think is best. (New York City is the largest, so "B" is correct.)
2) Find the row of dotted lines numbered the same as the question you are answering. (Find row number 32)
3) Find the pair of dotted lines corresponding to the answer. (Find the pair of lines under the mark "B.")
4) Make a solid black mark between the dotted lines.

VI. BEFORE THE TEST

Common sense will help you find procedures to follow to get ready for an examination. Too many of us, however, overlook these sensible measures. Indeed, nervousness and fatigue have been found to be the most serious reasons why applicants fail to do their best on civil service tests. Here is a list of reminders:

- Begin your preparation early – Don't wait until the last minute to go scurrying around for books and materials or to find out what the position is all about.
- Prepare continuously – An hour a night for a week is better than an all-night cram session. This has been definitely established. What is more, a night a week for a month will return better dividends than crowding your study into a shorter period of time.
- Locate the place of the exam – You have been sent a notice telling you when and where to report for the examination. If the location is in a different town or otherwise unfamiliar to you, it would be well to inquire the best route and learn something about the building.
- Relax the night before the test – Allow your mind to rest. Do not study at all that night. Plan some mild recreation or diversion; then go to bed early and get a good night's sleep.
- Get up early enough to make a leisurely trip to the place for the test – This way unforeseen events, traffic snarls, unfamiliar buildings, etc. will not upset you.
- Dress comfortably – A written test is not a fashion show. You will be known by number and not by name, so wear something comfortable.
- Leave excess paraphernalia at home – Shopping bags and odd bundles will get in your way. You need bring only the items mentioned in the official notice you received; usually everything you need is provided. Do not bring reference books to the exam. They will only confuse those last minutes and be taken away from you when in the test room.
- Arrive somewhat ahead of time – If because of transportation schedules you must get there very early, bring a newspaper or magazine to take your mind off yourself while waiting.
- Locate the examination room – When you have found the proper room, you will be directed to the seat or part of the room where you will sit. Sometimes you are given a sheet of instructions to read while you are waiting. Do not fill out any forms until you are told to do so; just read them and be prepared.
- Relax and prepare to listen to the instructions
- If you have any physical problem that may keep you from doing your best, be sure to tell the test administrator. If you are sick or in poor health, you really cannot do your best on the exam. You can come back and take the test some other time.

VII. AT THE TEST

The day of the test is here and you have the test booklet in your hand. The temptation to get going is very strong. Caution! There is more to success than knowing the right answers. You must know how to identify your papers and understand variations in the type of short-answer question used in this particular examination. Follow these suggestions for maximum results from your efforts:

1) Cooperate with the monitor

The test administrator has a duty to create a situation in which you can be as much at ease as possible. He will give instructions, tell you when to begin, check to see that you are marking your answer sheet correctly, and so on. He is not there to guard you, although he will see that your competitors do not take unfair advantage. He wants to help you do your best.

2) Listen to all instructions

Don't jump the gun! Wait until you understand all directions. In most civil service tests you get more time than you need to answer the questions. So don't be in a hurry. Read each word of instructions until you clearly understand the meaning. Study the examples, listen to all announcements and follow directions. Ask questions if you do not understand what to do.

3) Identify your papers

Civil service exams are usually identified by number only. You will be assigned a number; you must not put your name on your test papers. Be sure to copy your number correctly. Since more than one exam may be given, copy your exact examination title.

4) Plan your time

Unless you are told that a test is a "speed" or "rate of work" test, speed itself is usually not important. Time enough to answer all the questions will be provided, but this does not mean that you have all day. An overall time limit has been set. Divide the total time (in minutes) by the number of questions to determine the approximate time you have for each question.

5) Do not linger over difficult questions

If you come across a difficult question, mark it with a paper clip (useful to have along) and come back to it when you have been through the booklet. One caution if you do this – be sure to skip a number on your answer sheet as well. Check often to be sure that you have not lost your place and that you are marking in the row numbered the same as the question you are answering.

6) Read the questions

Be sure you know what the question asks! Many capable people are unsuccessful because they failed to *read* the questions correctly.

7) Answer all questions

Unless you have been instructed that a penalty will be deducted for incorrect answers, it is better to guess than to omit a question.

8) Speed tests

It is often better NOT to guess on speed tests. It has been found that on timed tests people are tempted to spend the last few seconds before time is called in marking answers at random – without even reading them – in the hope of picking up a few extra points. To discourage this practice, the instructions may warn you that your score will be "corrected" for guessing. That is, a penalty will be applied. The incorrect answers will be deducted from the correct ones, or some other penalty formula will be used.

9) Review your answers

If you finish before time is called, go back to the questions you guessed or omitted to give them further thought. Review other answers if you have time.

10) Return your test materials

If you are ready to leave before others have finished or time is called, take ALL your materials to the monitor and leave quietly. Never take any test material with you. The monitor can discover whose papers are not complete, and taking a test booklet may be grounds for disqualification.

VIII. EXAMINATION TECHNIQUES

1) Read the general instructions carefully. These are usually printed on the first page of the exam booklet. As a rule, these instructions refer to the timing of the examination; the fact that you should not start work until the signal and must stop work at a signal, etc. If there are any *special* instructions, such as a choice of questions to be answered, make sure that you note this instruction carefully.

2) When you are ready to start work on the examination, that is as soon as the signal has been given, read the instructions to each question booklet, underline any key words or phrases, such as *least, best, outline, describe* and the like. In this way you will tend to answer as requested rather than discover on reviewing your paper that you *listed without describing*, that you selected the *worst* choice rather than the *best* choice, etc.

3) If the examination is of the objective or multiple-choice type – that is, each question will also give a series of possible answers: A, B, C or D, and you are called upon to select the best answer and write the letter next to that answer on your answer paper – it is advisable to start answering each question in turn. There may be anywhere from 50 to 100 such questions in the three or four hours allotted and you can see how much time would be taken if you read through all the questions before beginning to answer any. Furthermore, if you come across a question or group of questions which you know would be difficult to answer, it would undoubtedly affect your handling of all the other questions.

4) If the examination is of the essay type and contains but a few questions, it is a moot point as to whether you should read all the questions before starting to answer any one. Of course, if you are given a choice – say five out of seven and the like – then it is essential to read all the questions so you can eliminate the two that are most difficult. If, however, you are asked to answer all the questions, there may be danger in trying to answer the easiest one first because you may find that you will spend too much time on it. The best technique is to answer the first question, then proceed to the second, etc.

5) Time your answers. Before the exam begins, write down the time it started, then add the time allowed for the examination and write down the time it must be completed, then divide the time available somewhat as follows:

- If 3-1/2 hours are allowed, that would be 210 minutes. If you have 80 objective-type questions, that would be an average of 2-1/2 minutes per question. Allow yourself no more than 2 minutes per question, or a total of 160 minutes, which will permit about 50 minutes to review.
- If for the time allotment of 210 minutes there are 7 essay questions to answer, that would average about 30 minutes a question. Give yourself only 25 minutes per question so that you have about 35 minutes to review.

6) The most important instruction is to *read each question* and make sure you know what is wanted. The second most important instruction is to *time yourself properly* so that you answer every question. The third most important instruction is to *answer every question.* Guess if you have to but include something for each question. Remember that you will receive no credit for a blank and will probably receive some credit if you write something in answer to an essay question. If you guess a letter – say "B" for a multiple-choice question – you may have guessed right. If you leave a blank as an answer to a multiple-choice question, the examiners may respect your feelings but it will not add a point to your score. Some exams may penalize you for wrong answers, so in such cases *only*, you may not want to guess unless you have some basis for your answer.

7) Suggestions
   a. Objective-type questions
      1. Examine the question booklet for proper sequence of pages and questions
      2. Read all instructions carefully
      3. Skip any question which seems too difficult; return to it after all other questions have been answered
      4. Apportion your time properly; do not spend too much time on any single question or group of questions
      5. Note and underline key words – *all, most, fewest, least, best, worst, same, opposite,* etc.
      6. Pay particular attention to negatives
      7. Note unusual option, e.g., unduly long, short, complex, different or similar in content to the body of the question
      8. Observe the use of "hedging" words – *probably, may, most likely,* etc.
      9. Make sure that your answer is put next to the same number as the question
      10. Do not second-guess unless you have good reason to believe the second answer is definitely more correct
      11. Cross out original answer if you decide another answer is more accurate; do not erase until you are ready to hand your paper in
      12. Answer all questions; guess unless instructed otherwise
      13. Leave time for review

   b. Essay questions
      1. Read each question carefully
      2. Determine exactly what is wanted. Underline key words or phrases.
      3. Decide on outline or paragraph answer

4. Include many different points and elements unless asked to develop any one or two points or elements
5. Show impartiality by giving pros and cons unless directed to select one side only
6. Make and write down any assumptions you find necessary to answer the questions
7. Watch your English, grammar, punctuation and choice of words
8. Time your answers; don't crowd material

8) Answering the essay question

Most essay questions can be answered by framing the specific response around several key words or ideas. Here are a few such key words or ideas:

M's: manpower, materials, methods, money, management
P's: purpose, program, policy, plan, procedure, practice, problems, pitfalls, personnel, public relations

   a. Six basic steps in handling problems:
      1. Preliminary plan and background development
      2. Collect information, data and facts
      3. Analyze and interpret information, data and facts
      4. Analyze and develop solutions as well as make recommendations
      5. Prepare report and sell recommendations
      6. Install recommendations and follow up effectiveness

   b. Pitfalls to avoid
      1. *Taking things for granted* – A statement of the situation does not necessarily imply that each of the elements is necessarily true; for example, a complaint may be invalid and biased so that all that can be taken for granted is that a complaint has been registered
      2. *Considering only one side of a situation* – Wherever possible, indicate several alternatives and then point out the reasons you selected the best one
      3. *Failing to indicate follow up* – Whenever your answer indicates action on your part, make certain that you will take proper follow-up action to see how successful your recommendations, procedures or actions turn out to be
      4. *Taking too long in answering any single question* – Remember to time your answers properly

IX. AFTER THE TEST

Scoring procedures differ in detail among civil service jurisdictions although the general principles are the same. Whether the papers are hand-scored or graded by machine we have described, they are nearly always graded by number. That is, the person who marks the paper knows only the number – never the name – of the applicant. Not until all the papers have been graded will they be matched with names. If other tests, such as training and experience or oral interview ratings have been given, scores will be combined. Different parts of the examination usually have different weights. For example, the written test might count 60 percent of the final grade, and a rating of training and experience 40 percent. In many jurisdictions, veterans will have a certain number of points added to their grades.

After the final grade has been determined, the names are placed in grade order and an eligible list is established. There are various methods for resolving ties between those who get the same final grade – probably the most common is to place first the name of the person whose application was received first. Job offers are made from the eligible list in the order the names appear on it. You will be notified of your grade and your rank as soon as all these computations have been made. This will be done as rapidly as possible.

People who are found to meet the requirements in the announcement are called "eligibles." Their names are put on a list of eligible candidates. An eligible's chances of getting a job depend on how high he stands on this list and how fast agencies are filling jobs from the list.

When a job is to be filled from a list of eligibles, the agency asks for the names of people on the list of eligibles for that job. When the civil service commission receives this request, it sends to the agency the names of the three people highest on this list. Or, if the job to be filled has specialized requirements, the office sends the agency the names of the top three persons who meet these requirements from the general list.

The appointing officer makes a choice from among the three people whose names were sent to him. If the selected person accepts the appointment, the names of the others are put back on the list to be considered for future openings.

That is the rule in hiring from all kinds of eligible lists, whether they are for typist, carpenter, chemist, or something else. For every vacancy, the appointing officer has his choice of any one of the top three eligibles on the list. This explains why the person whose name is on top of the list sometimes does not get an appointment when some of the persons lower on the list do. If the appointing officer chooses the second or third eligible, the No. 1 eligible does not get a job at once, but stays on the list until he is appointed or the list is terminated.

X. HOW TO PASS THE INTERVIEW TEST

The examination for which you applied requires an oral interview test. You have already taken the written test and you are now being called for the interview test – the final part of the formal examination.

You may think that it is not possible to prepare for an interview test and that there are no procedures to follow during an interview. Our purpose is to point out some things you can do in advance that will help you and some good rules to follow and pitfalls to avoid while you are being interviewed.

What is an interview supposed to test?
The written examination is designed to test the technical knowledge and competence of the candidate; the oral is designed to evaluate intangible qualities, not readily measured otherwise, and to establish a list showing the relative fitness of each candidate – as measured against his competitors – for the position sought. Scoring is not on the basis of "right" and "wrong," but on a sliding scale of values ranging from "not passable" to "outstanding." As a matter of fact, it is possible to achieve a relatively low score without a single "incorrect" answer because of evident weakness in the qualities being measured.

Occasionally, an examination may consist entirely of an oral test – either an individual or a group oral. In such cases, information is sought concerning the technical knowledges and abilities of the candidate, since there has been no written examination for this purpose. More commonly, however, an oral test is used to supplement a written examination.

Who conducts interviews?

The composition of oral boards varies among different jurisdictions. In nearly all, a representative of the personnel department serves as chairman. One of the members of the board may be a representative of the department in which the candidate would work. In some cases, "outside experts" are used, and, frequently, a businessman or some other representative of the general public is asked to serve. Labor and management or other special groups may be represented. The aim is to secure the services of experts in the appropriate field.

However the board is composed, it is a good idea (and not at all improper or unethical) to ascertain in advance of the interview who the members are and what groups they represent. When you are introduced to them, you will have some idea of their backgrounds and interests, and at least you will not stutter and stammer over their names.

What should be done before the interview?

While knowledge about the board members is useful and takes some of the surprise element out of the interview, there is other preparation which is more substantive. It *is* possible to prepare for an oral interview – in several ways:

1) Keep a copy of your application and review it carefully before the interview

This may be the only document before the oral board, and the starting point of the interview. Know what education and experience you have listed there, and the sequence and dates of all of it. Sometimes the board will ask you to review the highlights of your experience for them; you should not have to hem and haw doing it.

2) Study the class specification and the examination announcement

Usually, the oral board has one or both of these to guide them. The qualities, characteristics or knowledges required by the position sought are stated in these documents. They offer valuable clues as to the nature of the oral interview. For example, if the job involves supervisory responsibilities, the announcement will usually indicate that knowledge of modern supervisory methods and the qualifications of the candidate as a supervisor will be tested. If so, you can expect such questions, frequently in the form of a hypothetical situation which you are expected to solve. NEVER go into an oral without knowledge of the duties and responsibilities of the job you seek.

3) Think through each qualification required

Try to visualize the kind of questions you would ask if you were a board member. How well could you answer them? Try especially to appraise your own knowledge and background in each area, *measured against the job sought*, and identify any areas in which you are weak. Be critical and realistic – do not flatter yourself.

4) Do some general reading in areas in which you feel you may be weak

For example, if the job involves supervision and your past experience has NOT, some general reading in supervisory methods and practices, particularly in the field of human relations, might be useful. Do NOT study agency procedures or detailed manuals. The oral board will be testing your understanding and capacity, not your memory.

5) Get a good night's sleep and watch your general health and mental attitude

You will want a clear head at the interview. Take care of a cold or any other minor ailment, and of course, no hangovers.

What should be done on the day of the interview?

Now comes the day of the interview itself. Give yourself plenty of time to get there. Plan to arrive somewhat ahead of the scheduled time, particularly if your appointment is in the fore part of the day. If a previous candidate fails to appear, the board might be ready for you a bit early. By early afternoon an oral board is almost invariably behind schedule if there are many candidates, and you may have to wait. Take along a book or magazine to read, or your application to review, but leave any extraneous material in the waiting room when you go in for your interview. In any event, relax and compose yourself.

The matter of dress is important. The board is forming impressions about you – from your experience, your manners, your attitude, and your appearance. Give your personal appearance careful attention. Dress your best, but not your flashiest. Choose conservative, appropriate clothing, and be sure it is immaculate. This is a business interview, and your appearance should indicate that you regard it as such. Besides, being well groomed and properly dressed will help boost your confidence.

Sooner or later, someone will call your name and escort you into the interview room. *This is it.* From here on you are on your own. It is too late for any more preparation. But remember, you asked for this opportunity to prove your fitness, and you are here because your request was granted.

What happens when you go in?

The usual sequence of events will be as follows: The clerk (who is often the board stenographer) will introduce you to the chairman of the oral board, who will introduce you to the other members of the board. Acknowledge the introductions before you sit down. Do not be surprised if you find a microphone facing you or a stenotypist sitting by. Oral interviews are usually recorded in the event of an appeal or other review.

Usually the chairman of the board will open the interview by reviewing the highlights of your education and work experience from your application – primarily for the benefit of the other members of the board, as well as to get the material into the record. Do not interrupt or comment unless there is an error or significant misinterpretation; if that is the case, do not hesitate. But do not quibble about insignificant matters. Also, he will usually ask you some question about your education, experience or your present job – partly to get you to start talking and to establish the interviewing "rapport." He may start the actual questioning, or turn it over to one of the other members. Frequently, each member undertakes the questioning on a particular area, one in which he is perhaps most competent, so you can expect each member to participate in the examination. Because time is limited, you may also expect some rather abrupt switches in the direction the questioning takes, so do not be upset by it. Normally, a board member will not pursue a single line of questioning unless he discovers a particular strength or weakness.

After each member has participated, the chairman will usually ask whether any member has any further questions, then will ask you if you have anything you wish to add. Unless you are expecting this question, it may floor you. Worse, it may start you off on an extended, extemporaneous speech. The board is not usually seeking more information. The question is principally to offer you a last opportunity to present further qualifications or to indicate that you have nothing to add. So, if you feel that a significant qualification or characteristic has been overlooked, it is proper to point it out in a sentence or so. Do not compliment the board on the thoroughness of their examination – they have been sketchy, and you know it. If you wish, merely say, "No thank you, I have nothing further to add." This is a point where you can "talk yourself out" of a good impression or fail to present an important bit of information. Remember, *you close the interview yourself.*

The chairman will then say, "That is all, Mr. _____, thank you." Do not be startled; the interview is over, and quicker than you think. Thank him, gather your belongings and take your leave. Save your sigh of relief for the other side of the door.

How to put your best foot forward

Throughout this entire process, you may feel that the board individually and collectively is trying to pierce your defenses, seek out your hidden weaknesses and embarrass and confuse you. Actually, this is not true. They are obliged to make an appraisal of your qualifications for the job you are seeking, and they want to see you in your best light. Remember, they must interview all candidates and a non-cooperative candidate may become a failure in spite of their best efforts to bring out his qualifications. Here are 15 suggestions that will help you:

1) Be natural – Keep your attitude confident, not cocky

If you are not confident that you can do the job, do not expect the board to be. Do not apologize for your weaknesses, try to bring out your strong points. The board is interested in a positive, not negative, presentation. Cockiness will antagonize any board member and make him wonder if you are covering up a weakness by a false show of strength.

2) Get comfortable, but don't lounge or sprawl

Sit erectly but not stiffly. A careless posture may lead the board to conclude that you are careless in other things, or at least that you are not impressed by the importance of the occasion. Either conclusion is natural, even if incorrect. Do not fuss with your clothing, a pencil or an ashtray. Your hands may occasionally be useful to emphasize a point; do not let them become a point of distraction.

3) Do not wisecrack or make small talk

This is a serious situation, and your attitude should show that you consider it as such. Further, the time of the board is limited – they do not want to waste it, and neither should you.

4) Do not exaggerate your experience or abilities

In the first place, from information in the application or other interviews and sources, the board may know more about you than you think. Secondly, you probably will not get away with it. An experienced board is rather adept at spotting such a situation, so do not take the chance.

5) If you know a board member, do not make a point of it, yet do not hide it

Certainly you are not fooling him, and probably not the other members of the board. Do not try to take advantage of your acquaintanceship – it will probably do you little good.

6) Do not dominate the interview

Let the board do that. They will give you the clues – do not assume that you have to do all the talking. Realize that the board has a number of questions to ask you, and do not try to take up all the interview time by showing off your extensive knowledge of the answer to the first one.

7) Be attentive

You only have 20 minutes or so, and you should keep your attention at its sharpest throughout. When a member is addressing a problem or question to you, give him your undivided attention. Address your reply principally to him, but do not exclude the other board members.

8) Do not interrupt

A board member may be stating a problem for you to analyze. He will ask you a question when the time comes. Let him state the problem, and wait for the question.

9) Make sure you understand the question

Do not try to answer until you are sure what the question is. If it is not clear, restate it in your own words or ask the board member to clarify it for you. However, do not haggle about minor elements.

10) Reply promptly but not hastily

A common entry on oral board rating sheets is "candidate responded readily," or "candidate hesitated in replies." Respond as promptly and quickly as you can, but do not jump to a hasty, ill-considered answer.

11) Do not be peremptory in your answers

A brief answer is proper – but do not fire your answer back. That is a losing game from your point of view. The board member can probably ask questions much faster than you can answer them.

12) Do not try to create the answer you think the board member wants

He is interested in what kind of mind you have and how it works – not in playing games. Furthermore, he can usually spot this practice and will actually grade you down on it.

13) Do not switch sides in your reply merely to agree with a board member

Frequently, a member will take a contrary position merely to draw you out and to see if you are willing and able to defend your point of view. Do not start a debate, yet do not surrender a good position. If a position is worth taking, it is worth defending.

14) Do not be afraid to admit an error in judgment if you are shown to be wrong

The board knows that you are forced to reply without any opportunity for careful consideration. Your answer may be demonstrably wrong. If so, admit it and get on with the interview.

15) Do not dwell at length on your present job

The opening question may relate to your present assignment. Answer the question but do not go into an extended discussion. You are being examined for a *new* job, not your present one. As a matter of fact, try to phrase ALL your answers in terms of the job for which you are being examined.

Basis of Rating

Probably you will forget most of these "do's" and "don'ts" when you walk into the oral interview room. Even remembering them all will not ensure you a passing grade. Perhaps you did not have the qualifications in the first place. But remembering them will help you to put your best foot forward, without treading on the toes of the board members.

Rumor and popular opinion to the contrary notwithstanding, an oral board wants you to make the best appearance possible. They know you are under pressure – but they also want to see how you respond to it as a guide to what your reaction would be under the pressures of the job you seek. They will be influenced by the degree of poise you display, the personal traits you show and the manner in which you respond.

ABOUT THIS BOOK

This book contains tests divided into Examination Sections. Go through each test, answering every question in the margin. At the end of each test look at the answer key and check your answers. On the ones you got wrong, look at the right answer choice and learn. Do not fill in the answers first. Do not memorize the questions and answers, but understand the answer and principles involved. On your test, the questions will likely be different from the samples. Questions are changed and new ones added. If you understand these past questions you should have success with any changes that arise. Tests may consist of several types of questions. We have additional books on each subject should more study be advisable or necessary for you. Finally, the more you study, the better prepared you will be. This book is intended to be the last thing you study before you walk into the examination room. Prior study of relevant texts is also recommended. NLC publishes some of these in our Fundamental Series. Knowledge and good sense are important factors in passing your exam. Good luck also helps. So now study this Passbook, absorb the material contained within and take that knowledge into the examination. Then do your best to pass that exam.

———

Z

*********5915

03/07

/22 03:21PM

Accountant /

National Learning

Corporation.

anfcc

33305250989039

Expires 03/17/22

Thu

ATION SECTION

EXAMINATION SECTION
TEST 1

DIRECTIONS: Each question or incomplete statement is followed by several suggested answers or completions. Select the one that BEST answers the question or completes the Statement. *PRINT THE LETTER OF THE CORRECT ANSWER IN THE SPACE AT THE RIGHT.*

1. Gross income of an individual for Federal income tax purposes does NOT include   1._____

    A. interest credited to a bank savings account
    B. gain from the sale of sewer authority bonds
    C. back pay received as a result of job reinstatement
    D. interest received from State Dormitory Authority bonds

2. A cash-basis, calendar-year taxpayer purchased an annuity policy at a total cost of   2._____
$20,000. Starting on January 1 of 2015, he began to receive annual payments of $1,500.
His life expectancy as of that date was 16 years.
The amount of annuity income to be included in his gross income for the taxable year 2015 is

    A. none   B. $250   C. $1,250   D. $1,500

3. The transactions related to a municipal police retirement system should be included in   3._____
a(n)

    A. intra-governmental service fund
    B. trust fund
    C. general fund
    D. special revenue fund

4. The budget for a given cost during a given period was $100,000. The actual cost for the   4._____
period was $90,000. Based upon these facts, one should say that the responsible man-
ager has done a better than expected job in controlling the cost if the cost is

    A. variable and actual production equaled budgeted production
    B. a discretionary fixed cost and actual production equaled budgeted production
    C. variable and actual production was 90% of budgeted production
    D. variable and actual production was 80% of budgeted production

5. In the conduct of an audit, the *most practical* method by which an accountant can satisfy   5._____
himself as to the physical existence of inventory is to

    A. be present and observe personally the audited firm's physical inventory being
       taken
    B. independently verify an adequate proportion of all inventory operations performed
       by the audited firm
    C. mail confirmation requests to vendors of merchandise sold to the audited firm
       within the inventory year
    D. review beforehand the adequacy of the audited firm's plan for inventory taking, and
       during the actual inventory-taking stages, verify that this plan is being followed

Questions 6-7.

DIRECTIONS: The following information applies to Questions 6 and 7.

For the month of March, the ABC Manufacturing Corporation's estimated factory overhead for an expected volume of 15,000 lbs. of a product was as follows:

	Amount	Overhead Rate Per Unit
Fixed Overhead	$3,000	$.20
Variable Overhead	$9,000	$.60

Actual volume was 10,000 lbs. and actual overhead expense was $7,700.

6. The Spending (Budget) Variance was   6.___

    A. $1,300 (Favorable)   B. $6,000 (Favorable)
    C. $7,700 (Favorable)   D. $9,000 (Favorable)

7. The Idle Capacity Variance was   7.___

    A. $300 (Favorable)   B. $1,000 (Unfavorable)
    C. $1,300 (Favorable)   D. $8,000 (Unfavorable)

Questions 8-11.

DIRECTIONS: Answer Questions 8 through 11 on the basis of the information given below.

A bookkeeper, who was not familiar with proper accounting procedures, prepared the following financial report for Largor Corporation as of December 31, 2015. In addition to the errors in presentation, additional data below was not considered in the preparation of the report. Restate this balance sheet in proper form, giving recognition to the additional data, so that you will be able to determine the required information to answer Questions 8 through 11.

LARGOR CORPORATION
December 31, 2015

Current Assets			
Cash		$110,000	
Marketable Securities		53,000	
Accounts Receivable	$261,400		
Accounts Payable	125,000	136,400	
Inventories		274,000	
Prepaid Expenses		24,000	
Treasury Stock		20,000	
Cash Surrender Value of			
Officers' Life Insuranc Policies		105,000	$722 , 400
Plant Assets			
Equipment		350,000	
Building	200,000		
Reserve for Plant			
Expansion	75,000	125,000	
Land		47,500	522,500
TOTAL ASSETS			$1,244,900

Liabilities
Salaries Payable ... 16,500
Cash Dividend Payable ... 50,000
Stock Dividend Payable ... 70,000
Bonds Payable ... 200,000
    Less Sinking Fund ... 90,000 ... 110,000
    TOTAL LIABILITIES ... $246,500

Stockholders' Equity:
Paid In Capital
    Common Stock ... 350,000

Retained Earnings and Reserves
Reserve for Income Taxes ... 90,000
Reserve for Doubtful Accounts ... 6,500
Reserve for Treasury Stock ... 20,000
Reserve for Depreciation Equipment ... 70,000
Reserve for Depreciation Building ... 80,000
Premium on Common stock ... 15,000
Retained Earnings ... 366,900 ... 648,400 ... 998,400

TOTAL LIABILITIES & EQUITY ... $1,244,900

Additional Data

A. Bond Payable will mature eight (8) years from Balance Sheet date.

B. The Stock Dividend Payable was declared on December 31, 2015.

C. The Reserve for Income Taxes represents the balance due on the estimated liability for taxes on income for the year ended December 31.

D. Advances from Customers at the Balance Sheet date totaled $13,600. This total is still credited against Accounts Receivable.

E. Prepaid Expenses include Unamortized Mortgage Costs of $15,000.

F. Marketable Securities were recorded at cost. Their market value at December 31, 2015 was $50,800.

8. After restatement of the balance sheet in proper form and giving recognition to the additional data, the Total Current Assets should be   8._____

A. $597,400   B. $702,400   C. $712,300   D. $827,300

9. After restatement of the balance sheet in proper form and giving recognition to the additional data, the Total Current Liabilities should be   9._____

A. $261,500   B. $281,500   C. $295,100   D. . D. $370,100

10. After restatement of the balance sheet in proper form and giving recognition to the additional data, the net book value of plant and equipment should be   10._____

A. $400,000   B. B, $447,500   C. $550,000   D. $597,500

11. After restatement of the balance sheet in proper form and giving recognition to the additional data, the Stockholders Equity should be   11._____

A. $320,000   B. $335,000   C. $764,700   D. $874,700

12. When preparing the financial statement, dividends in arrears on preferred stock should be treated as a   12._____

    A. contingent liability   B. deduction from capital
    C. parenthetical remark   D. valuation reserve

13. The IPC Corporation has an intangible asset which it values at $1,000,000 and has a life expectancy of 60 years. The *appropriate* span of write-off, as determined by good accounting practice, should be _____ years.   13._____

    A. 17   B. 34   C. 40   D. 60

14. The following information was used in costing inventory on October 31:   14._____

October	1 -	Beginning inventory -	800 units	@	$1.20
	4 -	Received	200 units	@	$1.40
	16 -	Issued	400 units		
	24 -	Received	200 units	@	$1.60
	27 -	Issued	500 units		

Using the LIFO method of inventory evaluation (end-of-month method), the total dollar value of the inventory at October 31 was   14._____

    A. $360   B. $460   C. $600   D. $1,200

15. If a $400,000 par value bond issue paying 8%, with interest dates of June 30 and December 31, is sold in November 1 for par plus accrued interest, the cash proceeds received by the issuer on November 1 should be *approximately*   15._____

    A. $405,000   B. $408,000   C. $411,000   D. $416,000

16. The TOTAL interest cost to the issuer of a bond issue sold for more than its face value is the periodic interest payment   16._____

    A. *plus* the discount amortization
    B. *plus* the premium amortization
    C. *minus* the discount amortization
    D. *minus* the premium amortization

17. If shareholders donate shares of stock back to the company, such stock received by the company is *properly* classified as   17._____

    A. Treasury stock
    B. Unissued stock
    C. Other assets - investment
    D. Current assets - investment

18. Assume the following transactions have occurred: 18._____
    1. 10,000 shares of capital stock of Omer Corp., par value $50, have been sold and issued on initial sale @ $55 per share during the month of June
    2. 2,000 shares of previously issued stock were purchased from shareholders during the month of September @ $58 per share.

As of September 30, the stockholders' equity section TOTAL should be

    A. $434,000   B. $450,000   C. $480,000   D. $550,000

19. Mr. Diak, a calendar-year taxpayer in the construction business, agrees to construct a building for the Supermat Corporation to cost a total of $500,000 and to require about two years to complete. By December 31, 2015, he has expended $150,000 in costs, and it was determined that the building was 35% completed.
If Mr. Diak is reporting income under the completed contract method, the amount of gross income he will report for 2015 is

19.____

A. none   B. $25,000   C. $175,000   D. $350,000

20. When the Board of Directors of a firm uses the present-value technique to aid in deciding whether or not to buy a new plant asset, it needs to have information reflecting

20.____

     A. the cost of the new asset only
     B. the increased production from use of new asset only
     C. an estimated rate of return
     D. the book value of the asset

KEY (CORRECT ANSWERS)

1.	D	11.	D
2.	B	12.	C
3.	B	13.	C
4.	A	14.	A
5.	D	15.	C
6.	A	16.	D
7.	B	17.	A
8.	C	18.	A
9.	C	19.	A
10.	B	20.	C

TEST 2

DIRECTIONS: Each question or incomplete statement is followed by several suggested answers or completions. Select the one that BEST answers the question or completes the statement. *PRINT THE LETTER OF THE CORRECT ANSWER IN THE SPACE AT THE RIGHT.*

Questions 1-3.

DIRECTIONS: The following information applies to Questions 1 through 3.

During your audit of the Avon Company, you find the following errors in the records of the company:

1. Incorrect exclusion from the final inventory of items costing $3,000 for which the purchase was not recorded.
2. Inclusion in the final inventory of goods costing $5,000, although a purchase was not recorded. The goods in question were being held on consignment from Reldrey Company.
3. Incorrect exclusion of $2,000 from the inventory count at the end of the period. The goods were in transit (F.O.B. shipping point); the invoice had been received and the purchase recorded.
4. Inclusion of items on the receiving dock that were being held for return to the vendor because of damage. In counting the goods in the receiving department, these items were incorrectly included. With respect to these goods, a purchase of $4,000 had been recorded.

The records (uncorrected) showed the following amounts:
1. Purchases, $170,000
2. Pretax income, $15,000
3. Accounts payable, $20,000; and
4. Inventory at the end of the period, $40,000.

1. The *corrected* inventory is   1.____

    A. $36,000   B. $42,000   C. $43,000   D. $44,000

2. The *corrected* income for the year is   2.____

    A. $12,000   B. $15,000   C. $17,000   D. $18,000

3. The *correct* accounts payable liabilities are   3.____

    A. $16,000   B. $17,000   C. $19,000   D. $23,000

4. An auditing procedure that is *most likely* to reveal the existence of a contingent liability is   4.____

    A. a review of vouchers paid during the month following the year end
    B. confirmation of accounts payable
    C. an inquiry directed to legal counsel
    D. confirmation of mortgage notes

Questions 5-6.

DIRECTIONS: The following information is to be used in answering Questions 5 and 6.

Mr. Zelev operates a business as a sole proprietor and uses the cash basis for reporting income for income tax purposes. His bank account during 2015 for the business shows receipts totaling $285,000 and cash payments totaling $240,000. Included in the cash payments were payments for three-year business insurance policies whose premiums totaled $1,575. It was determined that the expired premiums for this year were $475. Further examination of the accounts and discussion with Mr. Zelev revealed the fact that included in the receipts were the following items, as well as the proceeds received from customers:

$15,000 which Mr. Zelev took from his savings account and deposited in the business account.

$20,000 which Mr. Zelev received from the bank as a loan which will be repaid next year.

Included in the cash payments were $10,000 which Mr. Zelev took on a weekly basis from the business receipts to use for his personal expenses.

5. The amount of net income to be reported for income tax purposes for calendar year 2006 for Mr. Zelev is   5.____

   A. $21,100   B. $26,100   C. $31,100   D. $46,100

6. Assuming the same facts as those reported above, Mr. Zelev would be required to pay a self-employment tax for 2006 of   6.____

   A. $895.05   B. $1,208.70   C. $1,234.35   D. $1,666.90

7. For the year ended December 31, 2015, you are given the following information relative to the income and expense statements for the Sungam Manufacturers, Inc.:   7.____
   Sales $1,000,000
      Sales Returns 95,000

Cost of Sales
Opening Inventories $200,000
Purchases During the Year   567,000
Direct Labor Costs   240,000
Factory Overhead   24,400
Inventories End of Year   235,000

On June 15, 2015, a fire destroyed the plant and all of the inventories then on hand. You are given the following information and asked to ascertain the amount of the estimated inventory loss.

Sales up to June 15 $545,000
Purchased to June 15   254,500
Direct Labor   233,000
Overhead   14,550
Salvaged Inventory   95,000
The *estimated* inventory loss is

   A. $95,000   B. $162,450   C. $189,450   D. $257,450

8. Losses and excessive costs with regard to inventory can occur in any one of several operating functions of an organization.
    The operating function which bears the GREATEST responsibility for the failure to give proper consideration to transportation costs of material acquisitions is

8.____

    A. accounting   B. purchasing
    C. receiving   D. shipping

Questions 9-17.

DIRECTIONS: Questions 9 through 17 are to be answered on the basis of the information given below.

   You are conducting an audit of the PAP Company, which has a contract to supply the municipal hospitals with specialty refrigerators on a cost-plus basis. The following information is available:

Materials purchased	$1,946,700
Inventories, January 1	
Materials	268,000
Finished Goods (100 units)	43,000
Direct Labor	2,125,800
Factory Overhead (40% variable)	764,000
Marketing Expenses (all fixed)	516,000
Administrative Expenses (all fixed)	461,000
Sales (12,400 units)	6,634,000
Inventories, March 31	
Materials	167,000
Finished Goods (200 units)	(omitted)
No Work In Process	

9. The *net income* for the period is

9.____

    A. $755,500   B. $1,237,500
    C. $1,732,500   D. $4,980,500

10. The *number* of units manufactured is

10.____

    A. 12,400   B. 12,500   C. 12,600   D. 12,700

11. The *unit cost* of refrigerators manufactured is *most nearly*

11.____

    A. $389.00   B. $395.00   C. $398.00   D. $400.00

12. The *total* variable costs are

12.____

    A. $305,600   B. $764,000
    C. $4,479,100   D. $4,937,500

13. The *total* fixed costs are

13.____

    A. $458,400   B. $1,435,400
    C. $1,471,800   D. $1,741,000

While you are conducting your audit, the PAP Company advises you that they have changed their inventory costing from FIFO to LIFO. You are interested in pursuing the matter further because this change will affect the cost of the refrigerators. An examination of material part 2-317 inventory card shows the following activity:

May 2 - Received 100 units @ $5.40 per unit
May 8 - Received 30 units @ $8.00 per unit
May 15 - Issued 50 units
May 22 - Received 120 units @ $9.00 per unit
May 29 - Issued 100 units

14. Using the FIFO method under a perpetual inventory control system, the *total* cost of the units issued in May is   14._____

    A. $690   B. $960   C. $1,590   D. $1,860

15. Using the FIFO method under a perpetual inventory control system, the *value* of the closing inventory is   15._____

    A. $780   B. $900   C. $1,080   D. $1,590

16. Using the LIFO method under a perpetual inventory control system, the *total* cost of the units issued in May is   16._____

    A. $1,248   B. $1,428   C. $1,720   D. $1,860

17. Using the LIFO method under a perpetual inventory control system, the *value* of the closing inventory is   17._____

    A. $612   B. $780   C. $1,512   D. $1,680

Questions 18-20.

DIRECTIONS: For Questions 18 through 20, consider that the EEF Corporation has a fully integrated cost accounting system.

18. Unit cost of manufacturing dresses was $7.00. Spoiled dresses numbered 400 with a sales value of $800. When it is not customary to have a Spoiled Work account, the *most appropriate* account to be credited is   18._____

    A. Work In Process   B. Cost of Sales
    C. Manufacturing Overhead   D. Finished Goods

19. Overtime premium for factory workers (direct labor) totaled $400 for the payroll period. This was due to inadequate plant capacity. The account to be *debited* is   19._____

    A. Work In Process   B. Cost of Sales
    C. Manufacturing Overhead   D. Finished Goods

20. A month-end physical inventory of stores shows a shortage of $175. The account to be *debited* to correct this shortage is   20._____

    A. Stores   B. Work In Process
    C. Cost of Sales   D. Manufacturing Overhead

KEY (CORRECT ANSWERS)

1.	A		11.	B
2.	A		12.	C
3.	C		13.	B
4.	C		14.	B
5.	A		15.	B
6.	D		16.	A
7.	B		17.	A
8.	B		18.	A
9.	A		19.	C
10.	B		20.	C

EXAMINATION SECTION
TEST 1

DIRECTIONS: Each question or incomplete statement is followed by several suggested answers or completions. Select the one that BEST answers the question or completes the statement. *PRINT THE LETTER OF THE CORRECT ANSWER IN THE SPACE AT THE RIGHT.*

1. The Donaldson Company's cash balance includes a sum of $1,200,000 appropriated by the Board of Directors for the purchase of new equipment.
   On its financial statements, this amount should be included on the

   A. balance sheet as a current asset
   B. balance sheet as a non-current asset, specifically identified
   C. balance sheet as a fixed asset, included as part of plant cost
   D. income statement as a non-operating expense

   1.____

2. The trial balance of the Davis Corporation as of June 30, 2016, the end of its fiscal year, included opposite the title *Estimated Federal Income Taxes Accrued* the amount of $35,000, which included the company's estimate of the Federal income tax it would have to pay for its 2016 fiscal year and the amount of an unpaid additional assessment for the 2013 fiscal year.
   This amount should appear on the balance sheet as a(n)

   A. general reserve
   B. reduction of current assets
   C. current liability
   D. allocation of retained income

   2.____

3. A weekly payroll check was issued to an hourly employee based upon 88 hours of work instead of the normal 38 hours. The time card was somewhat illegible, and the number looked like it could have been 88.
   The BEST control procedure to prevent such an error would be

   A. desk checking   B. a hash total
   C. a limit test   D. a code check

   3.____

4. In preparing a bank reconciliation, outstanding checks should be

   A. *deducted* from the balance per books
   B. *deducted* from the balance per bank statement
   C. *added* to the balance per books
   D. *added* to the balance per bank statement

   4.____

5. Independence is essential and is expected under the generally accepted auditing standards.
   The fact and appearance of integrity and objectivity are BEST maintained if

   A. the auditor is unbiased
   B. the auditor is aware of the problem of third party liability
   C. there is no financial relationship between the client and the auditor
   D. all financial relationships between the auditor and the client are reported in footnote form

   5.____

6. An audit program is a plan of action and is used to guide the auditor in planning his work.　　6.____
Such a program, if standardized, must be modified to

    A. observe limits that management places on the audit
    B. counteract internal control weaknesses
    C. meet the limited training of the auditor
    D. limit interference with work of the firm being audited

7. In auditing the *Owner's Equity* section of any company, the section related to a publicly-　　7.____
held corporation which uses a transfer agent and registrar would be more intricate than
the audit of a partnership.
Therefore, the procedure that an auditor should use in this case is to

    A. obtain a listing of the number of shares of securities outstanding
    B. make a count of the number of shareholders
    C. determine that all stock transfers have been properly handled
    D. count the number of shares of stock in the treasury

8. In recent years, it has become increasingly more important to determine the correct　　8.____
number of shares outstanding when auditing the owner's equity accounts.
This is TRUE because

    A. there has been more fraud with respect to securities issued
    B. there are increased complexities determining the earnings per share
    C. there are more large corporations
    D. the auditor has to test the amount of invested capital

9. In auditing corporation records, an auditor must refer to some corporate documents that　　9.____
are NOT accounting documents. The one of the following to which he is LEAST likely to
refer is

    A. minutes of the board of directors meeting
    B. articles of incorporation of the corporation
    C. correspondence with public relations firms and the shareholders
    D. the by-laws of the corporation

10. A generally accepted auditing procedure which has been required by AICPA require-　　10.____
ments is the observation of inventories.
Since it is impossible to observe the entire inventory of a large firm, the auditor may
satisfy this requirement by

    A. establishing the balance by the use of a gross profit percentage method
    B. using sampling procedures to verify the count made by the client
    C. accepting the perpetual inventory records, once he has established that the entries
       are arithmetically accurate
    D. accepting the management statement that the inventory is correct as to quantity
       where observation is difficult

11. Materiality is an important consideration in all aspects of an audit examination. Attention　　11.____
must be given to accounts with small and zero balances when examining accounts payable.
This does not conflict with the concept of materiality because

A. the size of a balance is no clue to possible understatement of a liability
B. the balance of the account is not a measure of materiality
C. a sampling technique may suggest examining those accounts under consideration
D. the total of the accounts payable may be a material amount and, therefore, no individual account payable should be eliminated from review

12. In establishing the amount of a liability recorded on the books, which of the following   12.____
types of evidence should an auditor consider to be the MOST reliable?

A. A check issued by the company and bearing the payee's endorsement which is included with the bank statement
B. Confirmation of an account payable balance mailed by and returned directly to the auditor
C. A sales invoice issued by the client with a delivery receipt from an outside trucker attached
D. A working paper prepared by the client's accountant and reviewed by the client's controller

13. Prior period adjustments as defined by APB Opinion #9 issued by the AICPA never flow   13.____
through the income statement.
The one of the following which is NOT one of the four criteria established by APB #9 for meeting the qualifications for treatment as a prior period adjustment is that the adjustment item

A. is not susceptible to reasonable extension prior to the current period
B. must be determined primarily by someone other than company management
C. can be specifically identified with and directly related to the business activities of a particular prior period
D. when placed in the current period would give undesirable results of operations

14. The subject caption which does NOT belong in a report of a financial audit and review of   14.____
operations of a public agency is

A. Audit Program
B. Description of Agency Organization and Function
C. Summary Statement of Findings
D. Details of Findings

15. At the inception of an audit of a public assistance agency, you ascertain that the one-year   15.____
period of your audit includes 240,000 serially numbered payment vouchers.
The sample selection which would enable you to render the MOST generally acceptable opinion on the number of ineligible persons receiving public assistance is

A. the number of vouchers issued in a one-month period
B. every hundredth voucher
C. a random statistical selection
D. an equal size block of vouchers from each month

16. Of the following, the one which BEST describes an internal control system is the 16.___

    A. division of the handling and recording of each transaction into component parts so as to involve at least two persons, with each performing an unduplicated part of each transaction

    B. expansion of the worksheet to include provisions for adjustments to the books of account prior to preparation of the financial statements

    C. recording of transactions affecting negotiable instruments in accordance with the principles of debit and credit, and giving these instruments special treatment if they are interest or non-interest bearing notes

    D. taking of discounts, when properly authorized by the vendor, as an incentive for prompt payment

17. During audits of small businesses, an accountant is less likely to find that these establishments have a system of internal control comparable to larger firms because small businesses GENERALLY 17.___

    A. can absorb the cost of small fraudulent acts which may be perpetrated

    B. benefit more than larger firms by prevention of fraud than by detection of fraud

    C. have limited staff and the costs of maintaining the system are high

    D. use a double entry system which serves as a substitute for internal control

18. In the performance of a financial audit, especially one where there is a need for a thorough knowledge of law, an accountant would BEST be advised to 18.___

    A. rely on the testimony of witnesses, as they may be found during the course of the audit, in preference to the written record

    B. rely on the presumption that the client's actions are illegal when the audit discloses meager facts or evidence

    C. be aware of the specific legal objectives he is attempting to attain by means of his audit

    D. be aware of different conclusions he can reach depending upon what facts are stressed or discounted in his audit

19. There are various types of budgets which are used to measure different government activities.
The type of budget which PARTICULARLY measures input of resource as compared with output of service is the _____ budget. 19.___

    A. capital   B. traditional
    C. performance   D. program

20. Bank balances are usually confirmed through the use of a standard bank confirmation form as authorized by the AICPA and the Bank Administration Institute.
In addition to bank balances, these confirmations ALSO confirm 20.___

    A. the credit rating of the client

    B. details of all deposits during the past month

    C. loans and contingent liabilities outstanding

    D. securities held by the bank as custodian for the client

KEY (CORRECT ANSWERS)

1.	B		11.	A
2.	C		12.	B
3.	C		13.	D
4.	B		14.	A
5.	C		15.	C
6.	B		16.	A
7.	A		17.	C
8.	B		18.	C
9.	C		19.	C
10.	B		20.	C

TEST 2

DIRECTIONS: Each question or incomplete statement is followed by several suggested answers or completions. Select the one that BEST answers the question or completes the statement. *PRINT THE LETTER OF THE CORRECT ANSWER IN THE SPACE AT THE RIGHT.*

Questions 1-3.

DIRECTIONS: Questions 1 through 3 are based on the classification of items into the appropriate section of a corporation balance sheet. The list of sections to be used is given below:

Current assets	Investments
Current liabilities	Long-term liabilities
Deferred credits	Paid-in capital
Deferred expenses	Plant assets
Intangible assets	Retained earnings

1. With respect to *Bonds Payable Due* in 2015, the PROPER classification is 1.____

   A. Investments B. Paid-in capital
   C. Retained earnings D. Long-term liabi

2. With respect to *Premium on Common Stock,* the PROPER classification is 2.____

   A. Intangible assets B. Investments
   C. Retained earnings D. Paid-in capital

3. With respect to *Organization Costs,* the PROPER classification is 3.____

   A. Intangible assets B. Investments
   C. Plant assets D. Current liabilities

4. J. Frost operates a small, individually owned repair service and maintains adequate double entry records. A review of his bank accounts and other available financial records yields the following information: 4.____
   Deposits made during 2015 per bank statements totalled $360,000. Deposits included a bank loan of $25,000 and an additional investment by Frost of $5,000. Disbursements during 2015 per bank statements totalled $305,000. This amount includes personal withdrawals of $28,500 and repayment of debt of $15,000.
   The Net Equity of J. Frost at January 1, 2015 was determined to be $61,000.
   Net Equity of J. Frost at December 31, 2015 was determined to be $67,000.
   Based upon the *Net Worth* method, Frost's net income for the year ended December 31, 2015 was

   A. $6,000 B. $29,500 C. $41,500 D. $55,000

Questions 5-8.

DIRECTIONS: Questions 5 through 8 are based on the following Balance Sheet, Income Statement, and Notes relating to the books and records of the Hartman Corporation.

BALANCE SHEET (000 omitted)

	September 30, 2015 Debit	Credit	September 30, 2016 Debit	Credit
Cash	$ 18		$ 31	
Accounts receivable	28		26	
Inventory	10		15	
Land	40		81	
Building and equipment (Net)	60		65	
Accounts payable		$ 10		$ 11
Notes payable - short-term		2		2
Bonds payable		50		50
Mortgage payable		20		46
Common stock		50		86
Retained earnings		24		23
	$156	$156	$218	$218

INCOME STATEMENT FOR FISCAL YEAR ENDING SEPTEMBER 30, 2016

Income :
Sales		$85
Cost of sales		40
Gross margin		$45

Expenses :
Depreciation	$ 5	
Loss on sale of fixed assets	2	
Other operating expenses	32	
Total expenses		$39
Net income		$ 6

NOTES:
1. Dividend declared during the year 2016, $7,000.
2. Acquired land; gave $36,000 common stock and cash for the balance.
3. Wrote off $1,000 accounts receivable as uncollectible.
4. Acquired equipment; gave note secured by mortgage of $26,000.
5. Sold equipment; net cost per books, $16,000, sales price $14,000.

5. The amount of funds provided from net income for the year ended September 30, 2016 is   5.____

   A. $6,000   B. $7,000   C. $13,000   D. $14,000

6. Financing and investing activities not affecting working capital are reported under the   6.____
   rules of APB #19. Notes 1 through 5 refer to various transactions on the books of the
   Hartman Corporation.
   Select the answer which refers to the numbers reflecting the concept mentioned here.

A. Notes 1, 3, and 5	B. Notes 2 and 4
C. Notes 2, 4, and 5	D. All five notes

7. Funds applied for the acquisition of the land are   7.____

    A. $5,000   B. $36,000   C. $41,000   D. None

8. The net change in working capital from 2015 to 2016 is   8.____

    A. $6,000   B. $16,000   C. $22,000   D. $35,000

9. Sales during July 2015 for the Magnum Corporation, operating in Los Angeles, were   9.____
$378,000, of which $150,000 were on account. The sales figures given include the total
sales tax charged to retail customers. (Assume a sales tax rate on all sales of 8%.)
The CORRECT sales tax liability for July 2015 should be shown as

    A. $3,024   B. $18,240   C. $28,000   D. $30,240

10. Of the following statement ratios, the one that BEST represents a measure of cost effi-   10.____
ciency is

    A. Acid Test Ratio
    B. Operating Costs to Net Sales Ratio
    C. Cost of Manufacturing to Plant Assets ratio
    D. Earnings Per Share

Questions 11-13.

DIRECTIONS: Answer Questions 11 through 13 on the basis of the following information.

An examination of the books and records of the Kay May Corporation, a machinery
wholesaler, reveals the following facts for the year ended December 31, 2015:

    a. Merchandise was sold and billed F.O.B. shipping point on December 31, 2015 at a
sales price of $7,500. Although the merchandise costing $6,000 was ready for ship-
ment on that date, the trucking company did not call for the merchandise until January
2, 2016. It was not included in the inventory count taken on December 31, 2015.

    b. Merchandise with a sales price of $5,500 was billed and shipped to the customer on
December 31, 2015. The merchandise costing $4,800 was not included in the inven-
tory count taken on that day. Terms of sale were F.O.B. destination.

    c. Merchandise costing $5,000 was recorded as a purchase on December 26, 2015.
The merchandise was not included in the inventory count taken on December 31,
2015 since, upon examination, it was found to be defective and was in the process of
being returned to the vendor.

    d. Merchandise costing $2,500 was received on December 31, 2015. It was included in
the inventory count on that date. Although the invoice was dated January 3, 2016, the
purchase was recorded in the December 2015 Purchases Journal.

    e. Merchandise costing $4,000 was received on January 3, 2016. It was shipped F.O.B.
destination, and the invoice was dated December 30, 2015. The invoice was recorded
in the December 2015 Purchases Journal, and the merchandise was included in the
December 31, 2015 inventory.

11. The net change to correct the inventory value as of December 31, 2015 is: 11.____

    A. *Increase $800*   B. *Increase $5,800*
    C. *Increase $6,800*   D. *Decrease $12,055*

12. The net change to correct the sales figure for the year 2015 is: 12.____

    A. *Increase $2,000*   B. *Decrease $5,500*
    C. *Decrease $7,500*   D. *Decrease $13,000*

13. The net change to correct the purchases figure for the year 2015 is: 13.____

    A. *Decrease $11,500*   B. *Decrease $4,000*
    C. *Decrease $5,000*   D. *Decrease $9,000*

Questions 14-18.

DIRECTIONS: Each of the following Questions 14 through 18 consists of a description of a transaction that indicates a two-fold effect on the Balance Sheet. Each of these transactions may be classified under one of the following categories:

    A.   Assets are Understated, Retained Earnings are Understated
    B.   Assets are Overstated, Retained Earnings are Overstated
    C.   Liabilities are Understated, Retained Earnings are Overstated
    D.   Liabilities are Overstated, Retained Earnings are Understated

    Examine each question carefully. In the correspondingly numbered space at the right, print the letter preceding the category above which BEST describes the effect of each transaction on the Balance Sheet as of December 31, 2015.

14. A major equipment purchase was made at the beginning of 2015. The equipment had an   14.____
estimated six-year useful life, and depreciation was overlooked at December 31, 2015.

15. Unearned Rental Income was properly credited when received early in the year. No year-   15.____
end adjustment was made to transfer the earned portion to an appropriate account.

16. Goods on hand at a branch office were excluded from the year-end physical inventory.   16.____
The purchase of these goods had been properly recorded.

17. Accrued Interest on Notes Receivable was overlooked as of December 31, 2015.   17.____

18. Accrued Federal Income Taxes for 2015 have never been recorded.   18.____

19. The following are account balances for the dates shown: 19.____

	Dec. 31, 2016	Dec. 31, 2015
Current Assets :		
Cash	$168,000	$ 60,000
Short-term investments	16,000	20,000
Accounts receivable (net)	160,000	100,000
Inventory	60,000	40,000
Prepaid expenses	4,000	0

Current Liabilities:

Accounts payable	110,000	80,000
Dividends payable	30,000	0

Given the above account balances, the CHANGE in working capital is a(n)

A. *increase* of $128,000
B. *decrease* of $128,000
C. *increase* of $188,000
D. *decrease* of $188,000

20. In conducting an audit of plant assets, which of the following accounts MUST be examined in order to ascertain that additions to plant assets have been correctly stated and reflect charges that are properly capitalized?   20.___

A. Accounts receivable
B. Sales income
C. Maintenance and repairs
D. Investments

_____

KEY (CORRECT ANSWERS)

1.	D	11.	A
2.	D	12.	B
3.	A	13.	D
4.	B	14.	B
5.	C	15.	D
6.	B	16.	A
7.	A	17.	A
8.	B	18.	C
9.	C	19.	A
10.	B	20.	C

_____

EXAMINATION SECTION

TEST 1

DIRECTIONS: Each question or incomplete statement is followed by several suggested answers or completions. Select the one that BEST answers the question or completes the statement. *PRINT THE LETTER OF THE CORRECT ANSWER IN THE SPACE AT THE RIGHT.*

1. The independent auditor's PRIMARY objective in reviewing internal control is to provide   1.____
   A. assurance of the client's operational efficiency
   B. a basis for reliance on the system and determination of the scope of the auditing procedures
   C. a basis for suggestions for improving the client's accounting system
   D. evidence of the client's adherence to prescribed managerial policies

2. If there is an increase in work-in-process inventory during a period,   2.____
   A. cost of goods sold will be greater than cost of goods manufactured
   B. cost of goods manufactured will be greater than cost of goods sold
   C. manufacturing costs (production costs) for the period will be greater than cost of goods manufactured
   D. manufacturing costs for the period will be less than cost of goods manufactured

Questions 3-4.

DIRECTIONS: Questions 3 and 4 are to be answered on the basis of the information given below about the Parr Company and the Farr Company.

The Parr Company purchased 800 of the 1,000 outstanding shares of the Farr Company's common stock for $80,000 on January 1, 2018. During 2018, the Farr Company declared dividends of $8,000 and reported earnings for the year of $20,000.

3. Using the equity method, the investment in Farr Company on the Parr   3.____
   Company's books should show a balance, at December 31, 2018, of
   A. $89,600   B. $86,400   C. $80,000   D. $73,600

4. If, instead of using the equity method, the Parr Company uses the cost   4.____
   method, the balance, at December 31, 2018, in the investment account, should
   be
   A. $96,000   B. $86,400   C. $80,000   D. $73,600

Questions 5-6.

DIRECTIONS: Questions 5 and 6 are to be answered on the basis of the information given below about the Fame Corporation.

The Fame Corporation has 50,000 shares of $10 par value common stock authorized, issued and outstanding. The 50,000 shares were issued at $12 per share. The retained earnings of the company are $60,000.

5. Assuming that the Fame Corporation reacquired 1,000 of its common shares at $15 per share and the par value method of accounting for treasury stock was used, the result would be that
   A. stockholders' equity would increase by $15,000
   B. capital in excess of par would decrease by at least $2,000
   C. retained earnings would decrease by $5,000
   D. common stock would decrease by at least $15,000

5.____

6. Assuming that the Fame Corporation reissued 1,000 of its common shares at $11 per share and the cost method of accounting for treasury stock was used, the result would be that
   A. book value per share of common stock would decrease
   B. retained earnings would decrease by $11,000
   C. donated surplus would be credited for $5,500
   D. a gain on reissue of treasury stock account would be charged

6.____

7. On January 31, 2018, when the Montana Corporation's stock was selling at $36 per share, its capital accounts were as follows:
   Capital Stock (par value $20; 100,000 shares issued) $2,000,000
   Premium on Capital Stock   800,000
   Retained earnings   4,550,000
   If the corporation declares a 100% stock dividend and the par value per share remains at $20, the value of the capital stock would
   A. remain the same   B. increase to $5,600,000
   C. increase to $5,000,000   D. decrease

7.____

8. In a conventional form of the statement of sources and application of funds, which one of the following would NOT be included?
   A. Periodic amortization of premium of bonds payable
   B. Machinery, fully depreciated and scrapped
   C. Patents written off
   D. Treasury stock purchased from a stockholder

8.____

22

Questions 9-11.

DIRECTIONS: Questions 9 through 11 are to be answered on the basis of the balance sheet shown below for the Argo, Baron and Schooster partnership.

Cash	$ 20,000
Other assets	180,000
Total	$200,000
Liabilities	$ 50,000
Argo Capital (40%)	37,000
Baron Capital (40%)	65,000
Schooster Capital (20%)	48,000
Total	$200,000

9. If George is to be admitted as a new 1/6 partner without recording goodwill or bonus, George should contribute cash of   9.____
   A. $40,000   B. $36,000   C. $33,333   D. $30,000

10. Assume that Schooster is paid $51,000 by George for his interest in the partnership.   10.____
   Which of the following choices shows the CORRECT revised capital account for each partner?
   A. Argo, $38,500; Baron, $66,500; George, $51,000
   B. Argo, $38,500; Baron, $66,500; George, $48,000
   C. Argo, $37,000; Baron, $65,000; George, $51,000
   D. Argo, $37,000; Baron, $65,000; George, $48,000

11. Assume that George had not been admitted as a partner but that the partnership was dissolved and liquidated on the basis of the original balance sheet. Non-cash assets with a book value of $90,000 were sold for $50,000 cash. After payment of creditors, all available cash was distributed.   11.____
   Which of the following choices MOST NEARLY shows what each of the partners would receive?
   A. Argo, $0; Baron, $13,333; Schooster, $6,667
   B. Argo, $0; Baron, $3,000; Schooster, $17,000
   C. Argo, $6,667; Baron, $6,667; Schooster, $6,666
   D. Argo, $8,000; Baron, $8,000; Schooster, $4,000

12. Which one of the following should be restricted to ONLY one employee in order to assure proper control of assets?   12.____
   A. Access to safe deposit box
   B. Placing orders and maintaining relationship with a principal vendor
   C. Collection of a particular past due account
   D. Custody of the petty cash fund

23

13. To assure proper internal control, the quantities of materials ordered may be omitted from that copy of the purchase order which is
    A. sent to the accounting department
    B. retained in the purchasing department
    C. sent to the party requisitioning the material
    D. sent to the receiving department

13.____

14. The Amey Corporation has an inventory of raw materials and parts made up of many different items which are of small value individually but of significant total value.
A BASIC control requirement in such a situation is that
    A. perpetual inventory records should be maintained for all items
    B. physical inventories should be taken on a cyclical basis rather than at year end
    C. storekeeping, production, and inventory record-keeping functions should be separated
    D. requisitions for materials should be approved by a corporate officer

14.____

15. In conducting an audit of plant assets, which of the following accounts MUST be examined in order to ascertain that additions to plant assets have been correctly stated and reflect charges that are properly capitalized?
    A. Accounts Receivable   B. Sales Income
    C. Maintenance and Repairs   D. Investments

15.____

16. Which one of the following is a control procedure that would prevent a vendor's invoice from being paid twice (once upon the original invoice and once upon the monthly statement)?
    A. Attaching the receiving report to the disbursement support papers
    B. Prenumbering of disbursement vouchers
    C. Using a limit or reasonable test
    D. Prenumbering of receiving reports

16.____

17. A "cut-off" bank statement is received for the period December 1 to December 10, 2017. Very few of the checks listed on the November 30, 2017 bank reconciliation cleared during the cut-off period.
Of the following, the MOST likely reason for this is
    A. kiting
    B. using certified checks rather than ordinary checks
    C. holding the cash disbursement book open after year end
    D. overstating year-end bank balance

17.____

18. "Lapping" is a common type of defalcation.
Of the audit techniques listed below, the one MOST effective in the detection of "lapping" is
    A. reconciliation of year-end bank statements
    B. review of duplicate deposit slips
    C. securing confirmations from banks
    D. checking footings in cash journals

18.____

19. Of the following, the MOST common argument against the use of the negative accounts receivable confirmation is that   19.____
    A. cost per response is excessively high
    B. statistical sampling techniques cannot be applied to selection of the sample
    C. client's customers may assume that the confirmation is a request for payment
    D. lack of response does not necessarily indicate agreement with the balance

Questions 20-21.

DIRECTIONS: Questions 20 and 21 are to be answered on the basis of the information in the Payroll Summary given below. This Payroll Summary represents payroll for a monthly period for a particular agency.

PAYROLL SUMMARY

| Employee | Total Earnings | Deductions | | | | Net Pay |
		FICA	Withhold. Tax	State Tax	Other	
W	450.00	26.00	67.00	18.00	6.00	333.00
X	235.00	14.00	33.00	8.00	2.00	178.00
Y	341.00	20.00	52.00	14.00	5.00	250.00
Z	275.00	16.00	30.00	6.00	2.40	220.60
Totals	1,301.00	76.00	182.00	46.00	15.40	981.60

20. Based on the data given above, the amount of cash that would have to be available to pay the employees on payday is   20.____
    A. $1,301.00   B. $981.60   C. $905.60   D. $662.60

21. Based on the data given above, the amount required to be deposited with a governmental depository is   21.____
    A. $334.00   B. $182.00   C. $158.00   D. $76.00

Questions 22-23.

DIRECTIONS: Questions 22 and 23 are to be answered on the basis of the information given below concerning an imprest fund.

Assume a $1,020 imprest fund for cash expenditures is maintained in your agency. As an audit procedure, the fund is counted and the following information results from that count.

Unreimbursed bills properly authorized	$345.00
Check from employee T. Jones	125.00
Check from Supervisor R. Riggles	250.00
I.O.U. signed by employee J. Sloan	100.00
Cash counted – coins and bills	200.00
TOTAL	$1,020.00

22. A PROPER statement of cash on hand based upon the data shown above should show a balance of 　　22.____
    A. $1,020　　　　B. $1,000　　　　C. $545　　　　D. $200

23. Based upon the data shown above, the account reflects IMPROPER handling of the fund because 　　23.____
    A. vouchers are unreimbursed
    B. the cash balance is too low
    C. employees have used it for loans and check-cashing purposes
    D. the unreimbursed bills should not have been authorized

Questions 24-25.

DIRECTIONS: Questions 24 and 25 are to be answered on the basis of the following information.

The following information was taken from the ledgers of the Past Present Corporation: Common stock had been issued for $6,000,000. This represented 400,000 shares of stock at a stated value of $5 per share. Fifty-thousand shares are in the treasury. These 50,000 shares were acquired for $25 per share. The total undistributed net income since the origin of the corporation was $3,750,000 as of December 31, 2017. Ten-thousand of the treasury stock shares were sold in January 2018 for $30 per share.

24. Based only on the information given above, the TOTAL stockholders' equity that should have been shown on the balance sheet as of December 31, 2017 was 　　24.____
    A. $2,000,000　　B. $6,000,000　　C. $8,500,000　　D. $9,750,000

25. Based only on the information given above, the Retained Earnings as of December 31, 2018 will be 　　25.____
    A. $2,000,000　　B. $3,750,000　　C. $3,800,000　　D. $4,050,000

Questions 26-29.

DIRECTIONS: Questions 26 through 29 are to be answered on the basis of the following information.
A statement of income for the Dartmouth Corporation for the 2018 fiscal year follows:

Sales	$89,000	
Cost of Goods Sold	20,000	
Gross Margin		$34,000
Expenses		20,000
Net Income Before Income Taxes		$14,000
Provision for Income Taxes (50%)		7,000
Net Income		$7,000

The following errors were discovered relating to the 2018 fiscal year:
- Closing inventory was overstated by $2,100
- A $3,000 expenditure was capitalized during fiscal year 2018 that should have been listed under Expenses. This was subject to 10% amortization taken for a full year.
- Sales included $3,500 of deposits received from customers for future orders.
- Accrued salaries of $850 were not included in Cost of Goods Sold.
- Interest receivable of $500 was omitted.

Assume that the books were not closed and that you have prepared a corrected income statement. Answer Questions 26 through 29 on the basis of your corrected income statement.

26. The gross margin after accounting for adjustments SHOULD BE   26.____
    A. $37,500   B. $35,400   C. $31,900   D. $27,550

27. The adjusted income before income taxes SHOULD BE   27.____
    A. $5,350   B. $9,550   C. $15,000   D. $15,850

28. The adjusted income after provision for a 50% tax rate SHOULD BE   28.____
    A. $7,925   B. $7,500   C. $4,500   D. $2,675

29. After making adjustments, sales to be reported for fiscal year 2018 SHOULD BE   29.____
    A. unchanged   B. increased by $3,500
    C. decreased by $3,500   D. reduced by $2,100

Questions 30-33.

DIRECTIONS: Questions 30 through 33 are to be answered on the basis of the following budget for the Utility Corporation for 2017:

Sales	$550,000
Cost of Goods Sold	320,000
Selling Expenses	75,000
General Expenses	60,000
Net Income	95,000

30. If sales are actually 12% above the budget, then ACTUAL sales will be   30.____
    A. $550,000   B. $562,000   C. $605,000   D. $616,000

31. If actual costs of goods sold exceed the budget by 10%, then the cost of goods sold will be   31.____
    A. $294,400   B. $320,000   C. $345,600   D. $352,000

32. If selling expenses exceed the budget by 10%, the INCREASE in the selling expenses will be   32.____
    A. $750   B. $3,750   C. $7,500   D. $8,333

33. If general expenses are under budget by 5%, they will amount to   33.____
   A. $3,000   B. $57,000   C. $60,000   D. $63,000

Questions 34-35.

DIRECTIONS: Questions 34 and 35 are to be answered on the basis of the following
              information.

The Yontiff Company began business on January 2, 2018. During the first month, credit sales totaled $100,000. During February, credit sales totaled $125,000. 70% of credit sales are paid during the month of sale, and the balance is collected during the following month.

34. During the month of January, cash collections on credit sales totaled   34.____
   A. $70,000   B. $95,000   C. $100,000   D. $125,000

35. During the month of February, cash collections on credit sales totaled   35.____
   A. $70,000   B. $87,500   C. $117,505   D. $125,000

Questions 36-38.

DIRECTIONS: Questions 36 through 38 are to be answered on the basis of the following
              information taken from the balance sheet of the F Corporation.

Common Stock $200 Par $1,400,000
Premium on Common Stock   115,000
Deficit   50,000

36. The number of shares of common stock outstanding is   36.____
   A. 200   B. 700   C. 7,000   D. 14,000

37. The total equity is   37.____
   A. $50,000   B. $115,000   C. $1,400,000   D. $1,465,000

38. The book value per share of stock is MOST NEARLY   38.____
   A. $160   B. $200   C. $209   D. $312

Questions 39-40.

DIRECTIONS: Questions 39 and 40 are to be answered on the basis of the following
              statement.

You are examining the expense accounts of a contractor and you discover that, although his payroll records show proper deductions from employees, he has never provided for the payroll tax expenses for these employees.

39. As a result of the oversight described in the above statement, the Costs of   39.____
   Construction in Progress as given on the balance sheet will be _____ on the
   balance sheet.
   A. understated   B. overstated   C. unaffected   D. omitted

40: As a result of the oversight described in the above statement, the balance sheet   40.____
    for the firm will reflect an
      A. overstatement of liabilities   B. understatement of liabilities
      C. overstatement of assets   D. understatement of assets

---

KEY (CORRECT ANSWERS)

1.	B	11.	D	21.	A	31.	D
2.	C	12.	D	22.	D	32.	C
3.	A	13.	D	23.	C	33.	B
4.	C	14.	C	24.	C	34.	A
5.	B	15.	C	25.	B	35.	C
6.	A	16.	A	26.	D	36.	C
7.	A	17.	C	27.	A	37.	D
8.	B	18.	B	28.	D	38.	C
9.	D	19.	D	29.	C	39.	A
10.	D	20.	B	30.	D	40.	B

29

TEST 2

DIRECTIONS: Each question or incomplete statement is followed by several suggested answers or completions. Select the one that BEST answers the question or completes the statement. *PRINT THE LETTER OF THE CORRECT ANSWER IN THE SPACE AT THE RIGHT.*

Questions 1-4.

DIRECTIONS: Questions 1 through 4 are to be answered on the basis of the following information.

In the audit of the Audell Co. for the calendar year 2017, the accountant noted the following errors:
- An adjusting entry for $10 for interest accrued on a customer's $4,000, 60-day, 6% note was not recorded at the end of December 2016. In 2017 the total interest received was credited to Interest Income.
- Equipment was leased on December 1, 2016 and rental of $300 was paid in advance for the next three months and charged to Rent Expense.
- On November 1, 2016, space was rented at $75 per month. The tenant paid six months rent in advance which was credited to Rent Income.
- Salary expenses in the amount of $60 were not recorded at the end of 2016.
- Depreciation in the amount of $80 was not recorded at the end of 2016.
- An error of $200 in addition on the year-end 2016 physical inventory sheets was made. The inventory was overstated.

1. The amount of the net adjustment to Net Income for 2016 is   1._____
   A. Credit $430   B. Debit $430   C. Credit $600   D. Credit $560

2. The net change in asset values at December 31, 2016 is   2._____
   A. Credit $70   B. Debit $70   C. Debit $110   D. Credit $60

3. The net change in liabilities at December 31, 2016 is   3._____
   A. Debit $360   B. Credit $430   C. Debit $560   D. Credit $360

4. The net change in Owner's Equity at December 31, 2016 is   4._____
   A. Debit $710   B. Debit $430   C. Credit $320   D. Credit $710

5. As of October 2, 2017, the Mallory Company's books reflect a balance of   5._____
   $2,104.75 in its account entitled, Cash in Bank. A comparison of the book entries with the bank statement showed the following:
   - A check in the amount of $76.25 outstanding at the end of September 2017 had not been returned.
   - One check, which was returned with the October bank statement, in the amount of $247 had been recorded in the October cash book as $274.
   - A total of $139 of checks issued in October had not been returned with the October bank statement.
   - A deposit of $65 was returned by the bank because of insufficient funds.

- The bank charged a service charge of $3.25 for the month of October which was not reported on the books until November.
- The bank had credited $247 representing a note collected in the amount of $250 which was not picked up on the books until November.
- A deposit of $305.50 was recorded on the books in October but not on the bank statement.

The balance in the bank as shown on the bank statement at October 31, 2017 is

A. $2,220.25   B. $2,104.75   C. $2,006.25   D. $2,315.25

Questions 6-8.

DIRECTIONS: Questions 6 through 8 are to be answered on the basis of the following information.

A company purchased three cars at $3,150 each on April 2, 2018. Depreciation is to be computed on a mileage basis. The estimated mileage to be considered is 50,000 miles, with a trade-in value of $650 for each car.

After having been driven 8,400 miles, car #1 was completely destroyed on November 23, 2017 and not replaced. The insurance company paid $2,500 for the loss.

As of December 31, 2017, of the two remaining cars, car #2 had been driven 10,300 miles and car #3 was driven 11,500 miles.

On July 10, 2018, after having been driven a total of 24,600 miles, car #2 was sold for $1,800.

Car #3, after having been driven a total of 27,800 miles, was traded in on December 28, 2018 for a new car (#4) that had a list price of $3,000. On the purchase of car #4, the dealer allowed a trade-in value of $1,850.

6.   The balance in the Allowance for Depreciation account at December 31, 2017 is   6.____
     A. $1,850   B. $910   C. $1,090   D. $1,110

7.   The depreciation expense for the calendar year 2018 is   7.____
     A. $1,530   B. $2,000   C. $2,500   D. $3,000

8.   The book value of the new car (car #4), using the income tax method, is   8.____
     A. $1,850   B. $3,000   C. $2,500   D. $2,910

Questions 9-10.

DIRECTIONS: Questions 9 and 10 are to be answered on the basis of the following information.

The Pneumatic Corp. showed the following balance sheets at December 31, 2017 and December 31, 2018:

	12/31/2017	12/31/2018
Cash	$6,700	$9,000
Accounts Receivable	12,000	11,500
Merchandise Inventory	31,500	32,000
Prepaid Expenses	800	1,000
Equipment	21,000	28,000
	$72,000	$81,500
Accumulated Depreciation	$4,000	$5,500
Accounts Payable	17,500	11,500
Common Stock - $5 Per Share	10,000	5,000
Premium on Common Stock	40,000	50,000
Retained Earnings	10,500	13,000
	$72,000	$81,500

Additional Information:
A further examination of the Pneumatic Corp.'s transactions for 2018 showed the following:
- Depreciation on equipment, $2,500
- Fully depreciated equipment that cost $1,000 was scrapped, and cost and related accumulated depreciation eliminated.
- Two thousand shares of common stock were sold at $6 per share.
- A cash dividend of $10,000 was paid.

9. A statement of funds provided and applied for the calendar year 2018 would show that net income provided funds in the amount of
    A. $2,500   B. $9,500   C. $15,000   D. $22,500

9.____

10. The funds applied to the acquisition of equipment during the calendar year 2018 amounts to
    A. $21,000   B. $28,000   C. $1,000   D. $8,000

10.____

11. A company's Wage Expense account had a $19,100 debit balance before any adjustment at the end of its December 31, 2017 fiscal year. The company employs five individuals who earn $15 per day and were paid on Friday for the five days ending on Friday, December 26, 2017. All employees worked during the week ending January 2, 2018.
The adjusted balance in the Wage Expense account at December 31, 2017 is
    A. $22,300   B. $19,100   C. $19,250   D. $19,325

11.____

Questions 12-13.

DIRECTIONS: Questions 12 and 13 are to be answered on the basis of the following information.

The Peach Corp.'s books reflect an account entitled "Allowance for Bad Debts" showing a credit balance of $1,510 as of January 1, 2017.
During 2017, it wrote off $735 of bad debts and increased the allowance for bad debts by an amount equal to ¼ of 1% of sales of $408,000.
During 2018, it wrote off $605 as bad debts and recorded $50 of a debt that had been previously written off.
An addition to the "Allowance for Bad Debts" was provided based upon ¼ of 1% on $478,000 of sales.

12. The balance in the "Allowance for Bad Debts" account at December 31, 2018 is   12.____
    A. $2,550   B. $2,435   C. $2,360   D. $2,240

13. The amount of the Bad Debt expense for the calendar year 2018 is   13.____
    A. $1,195   B. $1,405   C. $1,000   D. $1,510

14. The following ratio is based upon the 2018 financial statements of the Chino   14.____
    Corp.:
    Number of Times Bond Interest Earned: $28,000/$3,000 = 9.33 times
    Information relating to the corrections of the income data for 2018 follows:
    • Rental payment for December 2018 at $1,200 per month had been recorded in January 2019. No provision has been made for this expense on the 2018 books.
    • During 2018, merchandise shipped on consignment and unsold had been recorded as
         Debit – Accounts Receivable $4,000
         Credit – Sales   4,000
    (Note: The inventory of this merchandise was properly recorded.)
    If the described ratio, Number of Times Bond Interest Earned, was recomputed, taking into consideration the corrections listed above and ignoring tax factors in the calculations, the recomputed Number of Times Bond Interest Earned would be _____ times.
    A. 8.10   B. 7.60   C. 6.20   D. 5.10

Questions 15-16.

DIRECTIONS: Questions 15 and 16 are to be answered on the basis of the following information.

The Delancey Department Store, Inc. sells merchandise on the installment basis. The selling price of its merchandise is $500 and its cost is $325.

At the end of its fiscal year, an examination of its accounts showed the following:

Sales (Installment)	$500,000
Installment Accounts Receivable	280,000
Sales Commissions	15,000
Other Expenses	32,000

15. The net income for the fiscal year, before taxes, using the installment method of reporting income, is

    A. $30,000   B. $20,000   C. $15,000   D. $35,000

15.____

16. The balance in the Deferred Income Account at the end of the fiscal year is

    A. $110,000   B. $80,000   C. $76,000   D. $98,000

16.____

Questions 17-18.

DIRECTIONS: Questions 17 and 18 are to be answered on the basis of the following information.

The Merrimac Company sold 8,800 units of a product at $5 per unit during the calendar year 2018. In addition, it had the following transactions:

	Units	Unit Cost
Inventory – January 1, 2018	1,000	$2.80
Purchases – March	1,000	3.00
June	4,000	3.20
September	3,000	3.30
October	1,000	3.50

17. If we assume that selling and administrative expenses cost $8,800, the Net Income for the calendar year 2018, using the first-in first-out method of costing inventory, is

    A. $8,460   B. $7,360   C. $6,600   D. $4,070

17.____

18. If we assume that selling and administrative expenses cost $8,800, the Net Income for the calendar year 2018, using the last-in first-out method of costing inventory, is

    A. $4,550   B. $7,360   C. $6,600   D. $5,000

18.____

19. L. Eron and A. Pilott are partners who share income and losses in the ratio   19.____
    3:2, respectively. The balance in the Profit and Loss account on December 31,
    2018, prior to distribution to the partners, is $20,800. Before distributing any
    profits to the partnership in the agreed ratio, L. Eron is to be given credit for
    interest on his loan of $60,000, outstanding for the entire year, at 6% per
    annum. A. Pilott is to receive a bonus of 10% of the net income over $5,100,
    after deducting the bonus to himself and the interest to L. Eron.
    Giving consideration to all the above information, the total amount of net
    income to be credited to A. Pilott is
    A. $8,320   B. $2,080   C. $7,540   D. $15,700

Questions 20-21.

DIRECTIONS: Questions 20 and 21 are to be answered on the basis of the following
              information.

    Schneider and Samuels are partners with capital balances on December 31, 2018 of
$15,000 and $25,000, respectively. They share profits in a ratio of 2:1.
    Goroff is to be admitted to the partnership. He agrees to be admitted as a partner with a
cash investment to give him a one-third interest in the capital and profits of the business. All the
parties agree that the good will to be granted to Goroff should be valued at $6,000.

20. The required cash to cover Goroff's investment in a business partnership   20.____
    according to the terms stated is
    A. $20,000   B. $14,000   C. $6,000   D. $25,000

21. After his cash investment, and all other initial entries, the credit to Goroff's   21.____
    Capital account is
    A. $20,000   B. $14,000   C. $6,000   D. $25,000

22. The Marlin Corp. sold 7,800 units of its product at $25 per unit and suffered   22.____
    a net loss for its calendar year ending December 31, 2017 of $2,000. The fixed
    expenses amounted to $80,000 and the variable expenses $117,000. The
    Marlin Corp. believes that by expending $20,000 in an advertising campaign, it
    could increase its sales, retaining the $25 per unit selling price, to generate a
    profit.
    Assuming the above facts, the sales revenue for 2017 reflecting the break-even
    point is
    A. $195,000   B. $217,000   C. $250,000   D. $300,000

23. The Anide Corp., which keeps its books on the accrual basis, had the following   23.____
    transactions for its calendar year ending December 31, 2018.
    • April 15, 2018 – Authorized the issuance of $3,000,000 of 5.5%, 20 year bonds, dated
      May 1, 2018. Interest to be paid November 1 and May 1.
    • June 1, 2018 – Sold the entire issue at $2,965,150 plus accrued interest.
    • November 1, 2018 – Paid the interest due.
    The interest expense for the calendar year ending December 31, 2018 is
    A. $85,000   B. $165,000   C. $110,000   D. $97,300

Questions 24-26.

DIRECTIONS: Questions 24 through 26 are to be answered on the basis of the following information:

The following information was taken from a worksheet that was used in the preparation of the balance sheet and the profit and loss statement of the Hott Company for 2018.

The Balance Sheet Contained	Amount
Travel Expense Unpaid	$995
Legal and Collection Fees – Prepaid in Advance	672
Interest Received in Advance	469

The Profit and Loss Statement Contained	Amount
Travel Expenses	$7,343
Legal and Collection Fees	5,461
Interest Income	3,114

The proper adjusting and closing entries were made on the books of the company by the accountant and the described information was reported on the financial statements. The books are kept on an accrual basis.

On the basis of the above facts, the balance in each of the following accounts in the trial balance, *before adjusting and closing entries were made*, was as follows:

24.   Travel Expense Account   24._____
       A. $8,338   B. $7,343   C. $6,348   D. $995

25.   Legal and Collection Fees Account   25._____
       A. $672   B. $4,789   C. $5,461   D. $6,133

26.   Interest Income Account   26._____
       A. $3,583   B. $3,114   C. $2,645   D. $469

Questions 27-28.

DIRECTIONS: Questions 27 and 28 are to be answered on the basis of the following information.

The following is the stockholder's equity section of a corporation:
       Preferred Stock (7%, cumulative, non-participating,
       $100 par value, 5,000 shares issued and outstanding) $500,000

       Common Stock ($1.00 par value, 500,000, issued and
       outstanding)   500,000
                                                                                                             $1,000,000

       Deficit   (40,000)
                                                                                                               $960,000

27. Assuming two years' dividends in arrears on the preferred stock, the book value per share of common stock is   27.____
    A. 78¢   B. 80¢   C. 63¢   D. 94¢

28. Assuming two years' dividends in arrears on the preferred stock, the book value per share of preferred stock is   28.____
    A. $130   B. $114   C. $98   D. $140

Questions 29-30.

DIRECTIONS: Questions 29 and 30 are to be answered on the basis of the following information.

Regina Corporation on December 31, 2017 had the following stockholder's equity:

Common Stock ($10 par value, 10,000 shares authorized and outstanding)	$100,000
Retained Earnings	20,000
	$120,000

On December 31, 2017, the Astro Corp. purchased 9,000 shares of the Regina Corporation's outstanding shares, paying $14 per share.

29. The entry to eliminate Astro Corp.'s investment and the Regina Corporation's stockholder's equity on consolidation would show a debit or credit to an account called "Excess of Cost Over book Value" of   29.____
    A. Credit, $18,000   B. Debit, $18,000
    C. Debit, $15,000   D. Debit, $19,000

30. If the Regina Corporation had earnings for the calendar year 2018 of $10,000 and had paid out $8,000 of these earnings as dividends, and an entry to eliminate the Astro Corp.'s investment and the Regina Corporation's stockholder's equity were made, the minority stockholder's equity would be   30.____
    A. $15,600   B. $10,100   C. $12,200   D. $14,800

KEY (CORRECT ANSWERS)

1.	B	11.	D	21.	A
2.	A	12.	B	22.	C
3.	D	13.	A	23.	D
4.	B	14.	B	24.	C
5.	A	15.	A	25.	D
6.	C	16.	D	26.	A
7.	A	17.	B	27.	A
8.	D	18.	C	28.	B
9.	C	19.	C	29.	B
10.	D	20.	B	30.	C

TEST 3

DIRECTIONS: Each question or incomplete statement is followed by several suggested answers or completions. Select the one that BEST answers the question or completes the statement. *PRINT THE LETTER OF THE CORRECT ANSWER IN THE SPACE AT THE RIGHT.*

1. For the measurement of net income to be as realistic as possible, it is *desirable* that revenue be recognized at the point that   1.____
   A. cash is collected from customers
   B. an order for merchandise or services is received from a customer
   C. a deposit or advance payment is received from a customer
   D. goods are delivered or services are rendered to customers

2. An accounting principle must receive substantial authoritative support to qualify as "generally accepted." Many organizations and agencies have been influential in the development of generally accepted accounting principles, but the MOST influential leadership has come from the   2.____
   A. New York Stock Exchange
   B. American Institute of Certified Public Accountants
   C. Securities and Exchange Commission
   D. American Accounting Association

3. In which one of the following ways does the declaration and payment of a cash dividend affect corporate net income? It _____ net income.   3.____
   A. does not affect   B. reduces
   C. increases   D. capitalizes

4. Under which one of the following headings of the corporate balance sheet should the liability for a dividend payable in stock appear?   4.____
   A. Current Liabilities   B. Long Term Liabilities
   C. Stockholders' Equity   D. Current Assets

5. In which one of the following is "Working Capital" MOST likely to be found?   5.____
   A. Income Statement
   B. Analysis of Retained Earnings
   C. Computation of Cost of Capital
   D. Statement of Funds Provided and Applied

6. Which of the following procedures is NOT generally mandatory in auditing a merchandising corporation?   6.____
   A. Physical observation of inventory count
   B. Written circularization of accounts receivable
   C. Confirmation of bank balance
   D. Circularization of the stockholders

7. A company purchased office supplies during 2018 in the total amount of
   $1,400 and charged the entire amount to the asset account. An inventory of
   supplies taken on December 31, 2018 shows the cost of unused supplies to be
   $250.
   The entry to record this fact, assuming the books have not been closed,
   involves
      A. credit to capital   B. debit to supplies expense
      C. credit to supplies expense   D. debit to supplies on hand

   7.____

8. A corporation's records show $600,000 (credit) in net sales, $200,000 (debit)
   in year-end accounts receivable, and $2,000 (debit) in Allowance for Bad
   Debts. The company's aged schedule of accounts receivable indicates a
   probable future loss from failure to collect year-end receivables in the amount
   of $6,000.
   Of the following, the MOST correct entry to adjust the Allowance for Bad Debts
   at year-end is
      A. $1,000 credit   B. $4,000 credit
      C. $8,000 debit   D. $8,000 credit

   8.____

Questions 9-10.

DIRECTIONS: Questions 9 and 10 are to be answered on the basis of the following
information.

A company commenced business in 2018 and purchased inventory as follows:

March	100 units @	$5	$500
June	300	6	1,800
October	200	7	1,400
November	500	6	3,500
December	100	6	600
TOTAL	1,200		$7,800

**Units sold in 2018 amounted to 900

9. Under the LIFO inventory principal, the value of the remaining inventory is
     A. $1,700   B. $1,875   C. $2,145   D. $2,225

   9.____

10. Under the FIFO inventory principle, the value of the remaining inventory is
      A. $1,650   B. $1,875   C. $2,000   D. $2,025

    10.____

11. When doing a trial balance, assume that, as a result of a single error, the
    total of the credit balances is greater than the total of the debit balances.
    Which one of the following single errors could NOT be the cause of this
    discrepancy?
       A. Failure to post a debit   B. Posting a debit as a credit
       C. Failure to post a credit   D. Posting a credit twice

    11.____

Questions 12-13.

DIRECTIONS: Questions 12 and 13 are to be answered on the basis of the following information.

A and B are partners with capital balances of $20,000 and $30,000, respectively, at June 30, 2018, who share profits and losses, 40% and 60%, respectively. On July 1, 2018, C is to be admitted into the partnership under the following conditions:
- Partnership assets are to be revalued and increased by $10,000.
- C is to invest $40,000 but be credited for $30,000 while the remaining $10,000 is to be credited to A and B to compensate them for their pre-existing goodwill.

12. After C is admitt4ed and the proper entries are made, A's capital account will   12.____
have a credit balance of
    A. $24,500   B. $28,000   C. $30,200   D. $36,000

13. After the admission of C to the partnership, C's share of profits and losses   13.____
is agreed upon at 20%.
Assuming no other adjustments, the new percentage for profit and loss distribution to A will be
    A. 18%   B. 32%   C. 36%   D. 45%

14. A company reports as income for tax purposes $70,000 and its book income   14.____
before the provision for income taxes is $100,000.
Assuming a 50% tax rate, the PROPER tax expense to be recorded following tax allocation procedures is
    A. $33,000   B. $40,000   C. $50,000   D. $60,000

15. The relationship between the total of cash and current receivables to total   15.____
current liabilities is commonly referred to by accountants as the
    A. acid-test ratio   B. cross-statement ratio
    C. current ratio   D. R.O.I. ratio

16. On a statement of sources and application of funds, the depreciation expense   16.____
is normally shown as a(n)
    A. addition to operating income   B. subtraction from funds provided
    C. addition to funds applied   D. reduction from operating income

17. Company A owns 100% of the capital stock of Company B and reports on a   17.____
consolidated basis. During the year, Company A sold inventory to Company B at a profit of $100,000. One-half of this inventory has been sold at year-end by Company B to the public.
Which one of the following would be the MOST correct adjustment, if any, to make the consolidated retained earnings conform to generally accepted accounting principles?
    A. Decrease by $50,000   B. Increase by $50,000
    C. Increase by $100,000   D. No adjustment

18. X, Y, and Z are partners with capital of $11,000, $12,000, and $4,500. X has a   18.____
loan due from the partnership to him of $2,000. Profits and losses are shared
in the ratio of 4:5:1, respectively. The partnership has paid off all outside
liabilities, and its remaining assets consist of $9,000 in cash and $20,500 of
accounts receivable. The partners agree to disburse the $9,000 to themselves
in such a way that, even if one of the receivables is realized, no partner will
have been overpaid.
Under these conditions, which of the following MOST NEARLY represents the
amount to be paid to partner X?
  A. $1,960   B. $3,200   C. $4,800   D. $5,000

19. R Company needs $2,000,000 to finance an expansion of plant facilities. The   19.____
company expects to earn a return of 15% on this investment before considering
the cost of capital or income taxes. The average income tax rate for the R
Company is 40%.
If the company raises the funds by issuing 6% bonds at face value, the
earnings available to common stockholders after the new plant facilities are in
operation may be expected to increase by
  A. $65,000   B. $70,000   C. $108,000   D. $116,000

20. The budget for a given factory overhead cost was $150,000 for the year. The   20.____
actual cost for the year was $125,000.
Based on these facts, it can be said that the plant manager has done a better
job than expected in controlling this cost if the cost is a
  A. semi-variable cost
  B. variable cost and actual production was $83\frac{1}{3}\%$ of budgeted production
  C. semi-variable cost which includes a fixed element of $25,000 per period
  D. variable cost and actual production was equal to budgeted production

21. The Home Office account on the books of the City Branch shows a credit   21.____
balance of $15,000 at the end of a year and the City Branch account on the
books of the Home Office shows a debit balance of $12,000.
Of the following, the MOST likely reason for the discrepancy in the two
accounts is that
  A. merchandise shipped by the Home Office to the branch has not been
     recorded by the branch
  B. the Home Office has not recorde4d a branch loss for the first quarter of
     the year
  C. the branch has just mailed a check for $3,000 to the Home Office which
     has not yet been received by the Home Office
  D. the Home Office has not yet recorded the branch profit for the first quarter
     of the year

22. The concept of matching costs and revenues means that   22.____
  A. the expenses offset against revenues should be related to the same time
     period
  B. revenues are at least as great as expenses on the average
  C. revenues and expenses are equal
  D. net income equals revenues minus expenses for the same earning period

23. If the inventory at the end of the current year is understated, and the error is   23.____
not caught during the following year, the effect is to
    A. *overstate* the income for the two-year period
    B. *overstate* income this year and understate income next year
    C. *understate* income this year and overstate income next year
    D. *understate* income this year, with no effect on the income of the next year

KEY (CORRECT ANSWERS)

1.	D		11.	C
2.	B		12.	B
3.	A		13.	B
4.	C		14.	C
5.	D		15.	A
6.	D		16.	A
7.	B		17.	A
8.	D		18.	C
9.	A		19.	C
10.	C		20.	D

21.	D
22.	A
23.	C

ACCOUNTING
EXAMINATION SECTION
TEST 1

DIRECTIONS : Each question or incomplete statement is followed by several suggested answers or completions. Select the one that *BEST* answers the question or completes the statement. *PRINT THE LETTER OF THE CORRECT ANSWER IN THE SPACE AT THE RIGHT.*

Questions 1-5.

DIRECTIONS: Answer Questions 1 through 5 based on the information below.

When balance sheets are analyzed, working capital always receives close attention. Adequate working capital enables a company to carry sufficient inventories, meet current debts, take advantage of cash discounts and extend favorable terms to customers. A company that is deficient in working capital and unable to do these things is in a poor competitive position.

Below is a Trial Balance as of June 30, 2015, in alphabetical order, of the Worth Corporation:

	Debits	Credits
Accounts Payable		$ 50,000
Accounts Receivable	$ 40,000	
Accrued Expenses Payable		10,000
Capital Stock		10,000
Cash	20,000	
Depreciation Expense	5,000	
Inventory	60,000	
Plant & Equipment (net)	30,000	
Retained Earnings		20,000
Salary Expense	35,000	
Sales		100,000
	$190,000	$190,000

1. The Worth Corporation's Working Capital, based on the data above, is   1.____

    A. $50,000   B. $55,000   C. $60,000   D. $65,000

2. Which one of the following transactions increases Working Capital?   2.____

    A. Collecting outstanding accounts receivable
    B. Borrowing money from the bank based upon a 90-day interest-bearing note payable
    C. Paying off a 60-day note payable to the bank
    D. Selling merchandise at a profit

3. The Worth Corporation's Current Ratio, based on the above data, is   3.____

    A. 1.7 to 1   B. 2 to 1   C. 2.5 to 1   D. 4 to 3

4. Which one of the following transactions decreases the Current Ratio? 4.__

   A. Collecting an account receivable
   B. Borrowing money from the bank giving a 90-day interest-bearing note payable
   C. Paying off a 60-day note payable to the bank
   D. Selling merchandise at a profit

5. The payment of a current liability, such as Payroll Taxes Payable, will 5.__

   A. *increase* the current ratio but have no effect on the working capital
   B. *increase* the Working Capital, but have no effect on the current ratio
   C. *decrease* both the current ratio and working capital
   D. *increase* both the current ratio and working capital

6. During the year 2015, the Ramp Equipment Co. made sales to customers totaling 6.__
$100,000 that were subject to sales taxes of $8,000. Net cash collections totaled
$92,000. Discounts of $3,000 were allowed. During the year 2015, uncollectible accounts
in the sum of $2,000 were written off the books.
The net change in accounts receivable during the year 2015 was

   A. $10,500   B. $11,000   C. $13,000   D. $13,500

7. The Grable Co. received a $6,000, 8%, 60-day note dated May 1, 2015 from a customer. 7.__
On May 16, 2015, the Grable Co. discounted the note at 6% at the bank.
The net proceeds from the discounting of the note amounted to

   A. $5,954.40   B. $6,034.40   C. $6,064.80   D. $6,080.00

Question 8.

DIRECTIONS: Answer Question 8 based on the information below.

   In reviewing the customers' accounts in the Accounts Receivable Ledger for the entire
year 2014, the following errors are discovered
   1. A sale in the amount of $500 to the J. Brown Co. was erroneously posted to the K.
      Brown Co.
   2. A sales return of $100 from the Gale Co. was debited to their account
   3. A check was received from a customer, M. White and Co. in payment of a sale of
      $500 less 2% discount. The check was entered properly in the cash receipts book
      but was posted to the M. White and Co. account in the amount of $490

8. The difference between the controlling account and its related accounts receivable 8.__
schedule amounts to

   A. $90   B. $110   C. $190   D. $210

9. Assume that you are called upon to audit a cash fund. You find in the cash drawer post- 9.__
age stamps and I.O.U.'s signed by employees, totaling together $425.
In preparing a financial report, the $425 should be reported as

   A. petty cash   B. investments
   C. supplies and receivables   D. cash

10. On December 31, 2014, before adjustment, Accounts Receivable had a debit balance of   10.____
$60,000 and the Allowance for Uncollectible Accounts had a debit balance of $1,000. If
credit losses are estimated at 5% of Accounts Receivable and the estimated method of
reporting bad debts is used, then bad debts expense for the year 2014 would be reported
as

    A. $1,000   B. $2,000   C. $3,000   D. $4,000

Questions 11-12.

DIRECTIONS: Answer Questions 11 through 12 based on the information below.

Accrued salaries payable on $7,500 had not been recorded on December 31, 2014.
Office supplies on hand of $2,500 at December 31, 2014 were erroneously treated as
expense instead of inventory. Neither of these errors was discovered or corrected.

11. These two errors would cause the income for 2014 to be   11.____

    A. *understated* by $5,000   B. *overstated* by $5,000
    C. *understated* by $10,000   D. *overstated* by $10,000

12. The effect of these errors on the retained earnings at December 31, 2014 would be   12.____

    A. *understated* by $2,500   B. *overstated* by $2,500
    C. *understated* by $5,000   D. *overstated* by $5,000

Questions 13-14.

DIRECTIONS: Answer Questions 13 through 14 based on the information below.

Albano, Borrone, and Colluci operate a retail store under the trade name of ABC. Their
partnership agreement provides for equally sharing profits and losses after salaries of $5,000
to Albano, $10,000 to Borrone, and $15,000 to Colluci.

13. If the net income of the partnership (prior to salaries to partners) is $21,000, then   13.____
Albano's share of the profits, considering all aspects of the agreement, is determined to
be

    A. $2,000   B. $3,000   C. $5,000   D. $7,000

14. The share of the profits that apply to Borrone, similarly, is determined to be   14.____

    A. $2,000   B. $3,000   C. $5,000   D. $7,000

Questions 15-17.

DIRECTIONS: Answer Questions 15 through 17 based on the information below.

The Kay Company currently uses FIFO for inventory valuation. Their records for the year
ended June 30, 2015 reflect the following:

July 1, 2014 inventory	100,000 units @ $7.50
Purchases during year	400,000 units @ $8.00
Sales during year	350,000 units @ $15.00
Expenses exclusive of income taxes	$1,290,000
Cash Balance on June 30, 2014	$250,000
Income Tax Rate	45%

Assume the July 1, 2014 inventory will be the LIFO Base Inventory.

15. If the company should change to the LIFO as of June 30, 2015, then their income before taxes for the year-ended June 30, 2015, as compared with the income FIFO method, will be

    A. *increased b $50,000*
    C. *increased by $100,000*
    B. *decreased by $50,000*
    D. *decreased by $100,000*

15.__

16. Assuming the given tax rate (45%), the use of the LIFO method will result in an approximate tax expense for fiscal 2015 of

    A. $45,000   B. $50,000   C. $72,000   D. $94,500

16.__

17. Assuming the given tax rate (45%), the use of the LIFO inventory method compared with the FIFO method, will result in a change in the approximate income tax expense for fiscal 2015 as follows:

    A. *Increase of $22,500*
    C. *Increase of $45,000*
    B. *Decrease of $22,500*
    D. *Decrease of $45,000*

17.__

18. An accountant in an agency, in addition to his regular duties, has been assigned to train a newly appointed assistant accountant. The latter believes that he is not being given the training that he needs in order to perform his duties.
Accordingly, the most appropriate FIRST step for the assistant accountant to take in order to secure the needed training is to

    A. register for the appropriate courses at the local college as soon as possible
    B. advise the accountant in a formal memo that his apparent lack of interest in the training is impeding his progress
    C. discuss the matter with the accountant privately and try to discover what seems to be the problem
    D. secure such training informally from more sympathetic accountants in the agency

18.__

19. You have worked very hard and successfully helped complete a difficult audit of a large corporation doing business with your agency. Your supervisor gives you a brief nod of approval when you expected a more substantial degree of recognition. You are angry and feel unappreciated. Of the following, the *most appropriate* course of action for you to take would be to

    A. voice your displeasure to your fellow workers at being taken for granted by an unappreciative supervisor
    B. say nothing now and assume that your supervisor's nod of approval may be his customary acknowledgment of efforts well done
    C. let your supervisor know that he owes you something by repeatedly stressing the outstanding job you've done
    D. ease off on your work quality and productivity until your efforts are finally appreciated

19.__

20. You have been assisting in an audit of the books and records of businesses as a member   20.____
of a team. The accountant in charge of your group tells you to start preliminary work
independently on a new audit. This audit is to take place at the offices of the business.
The business officers have been duly notified of the audit date. Upon arrival at their
offices, you find that their records and files are in disarray and that their personnel are
antagonistic and uncooperative. Of the following, the *most desirable* action for you to
take is to

    A. advise the business officers that serious consequences may follow unless immediate cooperation is secured
    B. accept whatever may be shown or told you on the grounds that it would be unwise to further antagonize uncooperative personnel
    C. inform your supervisor of the situation and request instructions
    D. leave immediately and return later in the expectation of encountering a more cooperative attitude.

KEY (CORRECT ANSWERS)

1.	C	11.	C
2.	D	12.	A
3.	B	13.	A
4.	B	14.	D
5.	A	15.	B
6.	B	16.	C
7.	B	17.	B
8.	D	18.	C
9.	C	19.	B
10.	D	20.	C

TEST 2

DIRECTIONS : Each question or incomplete statement is followed by several suggested answers or completions. Select the one that *BEST* answers the question or completes the statement. *PRINT THE LETTER OF THE CORRECT ANSWER IN THE SPACE AT THE RIGHT.*

Questions 1-3.

DIRECTIONS: Answer Questions 1 through 3 based on the following.

The city is planning to borrow money with a 5-year, 7% bond issue totaling $10,000,000 on principal when other municipal issues are paying 8%.
      Present value of $ 1 - 8% - 5 years - .68058
      Present value of annual interest payments - annuity 8% - 5 years -3.99271

1. The funds obtained from this bond issue (ignoring any costs related to issuance) would be, approximately,   1.___

    A. $9,515,390   B. $10,000,000
    C. $10,484,610   D. $10,800,000

2. At the date of maturity, the bonds will be redeemed at   2.___

    A. $9,515,390   B. $10,000,000
    C. $10,484,610   D. $10,800,000

3. As a result of this issue, the *actual* interest costs each year as related to the 7% interest payments will   3.___

    A. be the same as paid ($700,000)
    B. be more than $700,000
    C. be less than $700,000
    D. fluctuate depending on the market conditions

4. Following the usual governmental accounting concepts, the activities of a municipal employee retirement plan, which is financed by equal employer and employee contributions, should be accounted for in a(n)   4.___

    A. agency fund
    B. intragovernmental service fund
    C. special assessment fund
    D. trust fund

Questions 5-7.

DIRECTIONS: Answer Questions 5 through 7 based on the following.

The Balance Sheet of the JLA Corp. is as follows:

Current assets	$50,000	Current liabilities	$20,000
Other assets	75,000	Common stock	75,000
Total	$125,000	Retained earnings	30,000
		Total	$125,000

5. The working capital of the JLA Corp. is

    A. $30,000   B. $50,000   C. $105,000   D. $125,000

5.____

6. The operating ratio of the JLA Corp. is

    A.   2 to 1   B. $2\frac{1}{2}$ to 1   C.   1 to 2   D. 1 to $2\frac{1}{2}$

6.____

7. The stockholders' equity is

    A. $30,000   B. $75,000   C. $105,000   D. $125,000

7.____

Question 8.

DIRECTIONS: Answer Question 8 based on the following figures taken from a set of books for the year ending June 30, 2015.

	Trial Balance Before Adjustments	Trial Balance After Adjustments
Commissions Payable	cr ---	cr $ 1,550
Office Salaries	dr $9,500	dr $10,680
Rental Income	cr $4,300	cr $ 4,900
Accumulated Depreciation	cr $7,000	cr $ 9,700
Supplies Expense	dr $1,760	dr $ 1,200

8. As a result of the adjustments reflected in the adjusted trial balance, the net income of the company before taxes will be

    A. *increased* by $4,270   B. *decreased* by $4,270
    C. *increased* by $5,430   D. *decreased* by $5,430

8.____

Question 9.

DIRECTIONS: Answer Question 9 based on the following facts concerning the operations of a manufacturer of office desks.

Jan.	1, 2014	Goods in Process Inventory	4,260 units	40% complete
Dec.	31, 2014	Goods in Process Inventory	3,776 units	25% complete
Jan.	1, 2014	Finished Goods Inventory	2,630 units	
Dec.	31, 2014	Finished Goods Inventory	3,180 units	

Sales consummated during the year-127,460 units

9. Assuming that all the desks are the same style, the number of equivalent complete units, manufactured during the year 2008 is:

    A. 127,250   B. 127,460   C. 128,010   D. 131,510

9.____

Questions 10-11.

DIRECTIONS: Answer Questions 10 through 11 based on the following.

On January 1, 2015, the Lenox Corporation was organized with a cash investment of $50,000 by the shareholders. Some of the corporate records were destroyed. However you were able to discover the following facts from various sources:

Accounts Payable at December 31, 2015 (arising from merchandise purchased)	$16,000
Accounts Receivable at December 31, 2015 (arising from the sales of merchandise)	18,000
Sales for the calendar year 2015	94,000
Inventory, December 31, 2015	20,000
Cost of Goods Sold is 60% of the selling price	
Bank loan outstanding - December 31, 2015	15,000
Expenses paid in cash during the year	35,000
Expenses incurred but unpaid as of December 31, 2015	4,000
Dividend paid	25,000

10. The *correct* cash balance is   10.___

    A. $5,600   B. $20,600   C. $38,600   D. $40,600

11. The stockholders' equity on December 31, 2015 is   11.___

    A. $23,600   B. Deficit of $26,400
    C. $27,600   D. $42,400

Questions 12-13.

DIRECTIONS: Answer Questions 12 and 13 based on the following facts developed from the records of a company that sells its merchandise on the installment plan.

Sales	Calendar Year 2014	Calendar Year 2015
Total volume of sales	$80,000	$100,000
Cost of Goods Sold	60,000	40,000
Gross Profit	$20,000	$ 60,000
Cash Collections		
From 2014 Sales	$18,000	$36,000
From 2015 Sales		22,000
Total Cash Collections	$18,000	$58,000

12. Using the deferred profit method of determining the income from installment sales, the gross profit on sales for the calendar year 2014 was   12.___

    A. $4,500   B. $18,000   C. $20,000   D. None

13. Using the deferred profit method of determining the income from installment sales, the gross profit on sales for the calendar year 2015 was   13.___

    A. $22,000   B. $22,200   C. $60,000   D. None

Questions 14-15.

DIRECTIONS: Answer Questions 14 through 15 based on the following data developed from an examination of the records of Ralston, Inc. for the month of April 2015.

Beginning inventory: 10,000 units @ $4.00 each

Purchases				sales			
April	10	20,000 units @ $5 each	April	13	15,000	units	@ $8 each
	17	60,000 units @ $6 each		21	50,000	units	@ $9 each
	26	40,000 units @ $7 each		27	50,000	units	@ $10 each

14. The gross profit on sales for the month of April, 2015, assuming that inventory is priced   14._____
on the FIFO basis, is

    A. $330,000   B. $355,000   C. $395,000   D. $435,000

15. The gross profit on sales for the month of April, 2015, assuming that inventory is priced   15._____
on the LIFO basis, is

    A. $330,000   B. $355,000   C. $395,000   D. $435,000

Question 16.

DIRECTIONS: Answer Question 16 based on the data presented for June 30, 2015.

Balance per Bank Statement	$24,019.00
Balance per General Ledger	20,592.64
Proceeds of note collected by the bank which had	
not been recorded in the Cash account	4,000.00
Interest on note collected by the bank (no book entries	
made)	39.40
Debit memo for Bank charges for the month of May	23.50
Deposit in Transit (June 30, 2015)	2,144.00
Customer's check returned by the bank due to lack of funds	150.00
Outstanding checks - June 30, 2015	1,631.46
Error in recording check made by our bookkeeper - check	
cleared in the amount of $463.00 but entered in the bank	
book for $436.00	

16. If we wish to reconcile the bank and book balance so that the bank balance and the book   16._____
balance are reconciled to a corrected balance, the corrected balance should be

    A. $20,592.64   B. $24,019.00   C. $24,531.54   D. $26,163.00

17. The Ateb Company has issued a $500,000 bond issue on January 1, 2014, at 8% inter-   17._____
est, payable semi-annually, sold at par, with interest payable on June 30 and December
31.
On September 30, 2014, at the close of the fiscal year of the Ateb Company, the interest expense accrual should reflect interest payable of, approximately,

    A. $10,000   B. $20,000   C. $40,000   D. $50,000

18. Assume that a new procedure requires that a particular and unvarying sequence of steps   18._____
be followed in order to yield the desired data. You are assigned to be in charge of subordinates working with this procedure.
Which one of the following is *most likely* to impress subordinates with the importance
of following the sequence of steps exactly as given?

    A. *Explain* the consequences of error if the procedure is not followed
    B. *Suggest* how rewarding would be the feeling of finding errors before the supervisor
       catches them
    C. *Indicate* that independent verification of their work will be done by other staff mem-
       bers
    D. *Advise* that upward career mobility usually results from following instructions
       exactly

19. It is essential for an experienced accountant to know approximately how long it will take him to complete a particular assignment because   19.___

    A. his supervisors will need to obtain this information only from someone planning to perform the assignment
    B. he must arrange his schedule to insure proper completion of the assignment consistent with agency objectives
    C. he must measure whether he is keeping pace with others performing similar assignments
    D. he must determine what assignments are essential and have the greatest priority within his agency

20. There are circumstances which call for special and emergency efforts by employees. You must assign your staff to make this type of effort.
Of the following, this special type of assignment is *most likely* to succeed if the   20.___

    A. time schedule required to complete the assignment is precisely stated but is not adhered to
    B. employees are individually free to determine the work schedule
    C. assignment is clearly defined
    D. employees are individually free to use any procedure or method available to them

---

KEY (CORRECT ANSWERS)

1.	A	11.	A
2.	B	12.	A
3.	B	13.	B
4.	D	14.	C
5.	A	15.	B
6.	B	16.	C
7.	C	17.	A
8.	B	18.	A
9.	A	19.	B
10.	B	20.	C

ACCOUNTING
EXAMINATION SECTION
TEST 1

DIRECTIONS : Each question or incomplete statement is followed by several suggested
answers or completions. Select the one that *BEST* answers the question or
completes the statement. *PRINT THE LETTER OF THE CORRECT ANSWER
IN THE SPACE AT THE RIGHT.*

Questions 1-5.

DIRECTIONS: Answer Questions 1 through 5 based on the information below.

When balance sheets are analyzed, working capital always receives close attention.
Adequate working capital enables a company to carry sufficient inventories, meet current
debts, take advantage of cash discounts and extend favorable terms to customers. A company that is deficient in working capital and unable to do these things is in a poor competitive
position.

Below is a Trial Balance as of June 30, 2015, in alphabetical order, of the Worth Corporation:

	Debits	Credits
Accounts Payable		$ 50,000
Accounts Receivable	$ 40,000	
Accrued Expenses Payable		10,000
Capital Stock		10,000
Cash	20,000	
Depreciation Expense	5,000	
Inventory	60,000	
Plant & Equipment (net)	30,000	
Retained Earnings		20,000
Salary Expense	35,000	
Sales		100,000
	$190,000	$190,000

1. The Worth Corporation's Working Capital, based on the data above, is   1.____

   A. $50,000   B. $55,000   C. $60,000   D. $65,000

2. Which one of the following transactions increases Working Capital?   2.____

   A. Collecting outstanding accounts receivable
   B. Borrowing money from the bank based upon a 90-day interest-bearing note pay-
       able
   C. Paying off a 60-day note payable to the bank
   D. Selling merchandise at a profit

3. The Worth Corporation's Current Ratio, based on the above data, is   3.____

   A. 1.7 to 1   B. 2 to 1   C. 2.5 to 1   D. 4 to 3

4. Which one of the following transactions decreases the Current Ratio?　　4.___

   A. Collecting an account receivable
   B. Borrowing money from the bank giving a 90-day interest-bearing note payable
   C. Paying off a 60-day note payable to the bank
   D. Selling merchandise at a profit

5. The payment of a current liability, such as Payroll Taxes Payable, will　　5.___

   A. *increase* the current ratio but have no effect on the working capital
   B. *increase* the Working Capital, but have no effect on the current ratio
   C. *decrease* both the current ratio and working capital
   D. *increase* both the current ratio and working capital

6. During the year 2015, the Ramp Equipment Co. made sales to customers totaling　　6.___
$100,000 that were subject to sales taxes of $8,000. Net cash collections totaled
$92,000. Discounts of $3,000 were allowed. During the year 2015, uncollectible accounts
in the sum of $2,000 were written off the books.
The net change in accounts receivable during the year 2015 was

   A. $10,500　　　　B. $11,000　　　　C. $13,000　　　　D. $13,500

7. The Grable Co. received a $6,000, 8%, 60-day note dated May 1, 2015 from a customer.　　7.___
On May 16, 2015, the Grable Co. discounted the note at 6% at the bank.
The net proceeds from the discounting of the note amounted to

   A. $5,954.40　　　　B. $6,034.40　　　　C. $6,064.80　　　　D. $6,080.00

Question 8.

DIRECTIONS:　Answer Question 8 based on the information below.

   In reviewing the customers' accounts in the Accounts Receivable Ledger for the entire
year 2014, the following errors are discovered
   1. A sale in the amount of $500 to the J. Brown Co. was erroneously posted to the K.
      Brown Co.
   2. A sales return of $100 from the Gale Co. was debited to their account
   3. A check was received from a customer, M. White and Co. in payment of a sale of
      $500 less 2% discount. The check was entered properly in the cash receipts book
      but was posted to the M. White and Co. account in the amount of $490

8. The difference between the controlling account and its related accounts receivable　　8.___
schedule amounts to

   A. $90　　　　　B. $110　　　　　C. $190　　　　　D. $210

9. Assume that you are called upon to audit a cash fund. You find in the cash drawer post-　　9.___
age stamps and I.O.U.'s signed by employees, totaling together $425.
In preparing a financial report, the $425 should be reported as

   A. petty cash　　　　　　　　　　B. investments
   C. supplies and receivables　　　　D. cash

10. On December 31, 2014, before adjustment, Accounts Receivable had a debit balance of 10.____
$60,000 and the Allowance for Uncollectible Accounts had a debit balance of $1,000. If
credit losses are estimated at 5% of Accounts Receivable and the estimated method of
reporting bad debts is used, then bad debts expense for the year 2014 would be reported
as

    A. $1,000   B. $2,000   C. $3,000   D. $4,000

Questions 11-12.

DIRECTIONS: Answer Questions 11 through 12 based on the information below.

Accrued salaries payable on $7,500 had not been recorded on December 31, 2014.
Office supplies on hand of $2,500 at December 31, 2014 were erroneously treated as
expense instead of inventory. Neither of these errors was discovered or corrected.

11. These two errors would cause the income for 2014 to be   11.____

    A. *understated* by $5,000   B. *overstated* by $5,000
    C. *understated* by $10,000   D. *overstated* by $10,000

12. The effect of these errors on the retained earnings at December 31, 2014 would be   12.____

    A. *understated* by $2,500   B. *overstated* by $2,500
    C. *understated* by $5,000   D. *overstated* by $5,000

Questions 13-14.

DIRECTIONS: Answer Questions 13 through 14 based on the information below.

Albano, Borrone, and Colluci operate a retail store under the trade name of ABC. Their
partnership agreement provides for equally sharing profits and losses after salaries of $5,000
to Albano, $10,000 to Borrone, and $15,000 to Colluci.

13. If the net income of the partnership (prior to salaries to partners) is $21,000, then   13.____
Albano's share of the profits, considering all aspects of the agreement, is determined to
be

    A. $2,000   B. $3,000   C. $5,000   D. $7,000

14. The share of the profits that apply to Borrone, similarly, is determined to be   14.____

    A. $2,000   B. $3,000   C. $5,000   D. $7,000

Questions 15-17.

DIRECTIONS: Answer Questions 15 through 17 based on the information below.

The Kay Company currently uses FIFO for inventory valuation. Their records for the year
ended June 30, 2015 reflect the following:

July 1, 2014 inventory	100,000 units @ $7.50
Purchases during year	400,000 units @ $8.00
Sales during year	350,000 units @ $15.00
Expenses exclusive of income taxes	$1,290,000
Cash Balance on June 30, 2014	$250,000
Income Tax Rate	45%

Assume the July 1, 2014 inventory will be the LIFO Base Inventory.

15. If the company should change to the LIFO as of June 30, 2015, then their income before taxes for the year-ended June 30, 2015, as compared with the income FIFO method, will be

 A. *increased* b $50,000
 B. *decreased* by $50,000
 C. *increased* by $100,000
 D. *decreased* by $100,000

16. Assuming the given tax rate (45%), the use of the LIFO method will result in an approximate tax expense for fiscal 2015 of

 A. $45,000   B. $50,000   C. $72,000   D. $94,500

17. Assuming the given tax rate (45%), the use of the LIFO inventory method compared with the FIFO method, will result in a change in the approximate income tax expense for fiscal 2015 as follows:

 A. *Increase* of $22,500
 B. *Decrease* of $22,500
 C. *Increase* of $45,000
 D. *Decrease* of $45,000

18. An accountant in an agency, in addition to his regular duties, has been assigned to train a newly appointed assistant accountant. The latter believes that he is not being given the training that he needs in order to perform his duties.
Accordingly, the most appropriate FIRST step for the assistant accountant to take in order to secure the needed training is to

 A. register for the appropriate courses at the local college as soon as possible
 B. advise the accountant in a formal memo that his apparent lack of interest in the training is impeding his progress
 C. discuss the matter with the accountant privately and try to discover what seems to be the problem
 D. secure such training informally from more sympathetic accountants in the agency

19. You have worked very hard and successfully helped complete a difficult audit of a large corporation doing business with your agency. Your supervisor gives you a brief nod of approval when you expected a more substantial degree of recognition. You are angry and feel unappreciated. Of the following, the *most appropriate* course of action for you to take would be to

 A. voice your displeasure to your fellow workers at being taken for granted by an unappreciative supervisor
 B. say nothing now and assume that your supervisor's nod of approval may be his customary acknowledgment of efforts well done
 C. let your supervisor know that he owes you something by repeatedly stressing the outstanding job you've done
 D. ease off on your work quality and productivity until your efforts are finally appreciated

20. You have been assisting in an audit of the books and records of businesses as a member 20.____
of a team. The accountant in charge of your group tells you to start preliminary work
independently on a new audit. This audit is to take place at the offices of the business.
The business officers have been duly notified of the audit date. Upon arrival at their
offices, you find that their records and files are in disarray and that their personnel are
antagonistic and uncooperative. Of the following, the *most desirable* action for you to
take is to

    A. advise the business officers that serious consequences may follow unless immedi-
ate cooperation is secured
    B. accept whatever may be shown or told you on the grounds that it would be unwise
to further antagonize uncooperative personnel
    C. inform your supervisor of the situation and request instructions
    D. leave immediately and return later in the expectation of encountering a more coop-
erative attitude.

_____

KEY (CORRECT ANSWERS)

1.	C	11.	C
2.	D	12.	A
3.	B	13.	A
4.	B	14.	D
5.	A	15.	B
6.	B	16.	C
7.	B	17.	B
8.	D	18.	C
9.	C	19.	B
10.	D	20.	C

_____

TEST 2

DIRECTIONS : Each question or incomplete statement is followed by several suggested answers or completions. Select the one that *BEST* answers the question or completes the statement. *PRINT THE LETTER OF THE CORRECT ANSWER IN THE SPACE AT THE RIGHT.*

Questions 1-3.

DIRECTIONS: Answer Questions 1 through 3 based on the following.

The city is planning to borrow money with a 5-year, 7% bond issue totaling $10,000,000 on principal when other municipal issues are paying 8%.
   Present value of $ 1 - 8% - 5 years - .68058
   Present value of annual interest payments - annuity 8% - 5 years -3.99271

1. The funds obtained from this bond issue (ignoring any costs related to issuance) would   1.____
    be, approximately,

    A. $9,515,390   B. $10,000,000
    C. $10,484,610   D. $10,800,000

2. At the date of maturity, the bonds will be redeemed at   2.____

    A. $9,515,390   B. $10,000,000
    C. $10,484,610   D. $10,800,000

3. As a result of this issue, the *actual* interest costs each year as related to the 7% interest   3.____
    payments will

    A. be the same as paid ($700,000)
    B. be more than $700,000
    C. be less than $700,000
    D. fluctuate depending on the market conditions

4. Following the usual governmental accounting concepts, the activities of a municipal   4.____
    employee retirement plan, which is financed by equal employer and employee contribu-
    tions, should be accounted for in a(n)

    A. agency fund
    B. intragovernmental service fund
    C. special assessment fund
    D. trust fund

Questions 5-7.

DIRECTIONS: Answer Questions 5 through 7 based on the following.

The Balance Sheet of the JLA Corp. is as follows:

Current assets	$50,000	Current liabilities	$20,000
Other assets	75,000	Common stock	75,000
Total	$125,000	Retained earnings	30,000
		Total	$125,000

5. The working capital of the JLA Corp. is   5.____

    A. $30,000   B. $50,000   C. $105,000   D. $125,000

6. The operating ratio of the JLA Corp. is   6.____

    A. 2 to 1   B. $2\frac{1}{2}$ to 1   C. 1 to 2   D. 1 to $2\frac{1}{2}$

7. The stockholders' equity is   7.____

    A. $30,000   B. $75,000   C. $105,000   D. $125,000

Question 8.

DIRECTIONS: Answer Question 8 based on the following figures taken from a set of books for the year ending June 30, 2015.

	Trial Balance Before Adjustments	Trial Balance After Adjustments
Commissions Payable	cr ---	cr $ 1,550
Office Salaries	dr $9,500	dr $10,680
Rental Income	cr $4,300	cr $ 4,900
Accumulated Depreciation	cr $7,000	cr $ 9,700
Supplies Expense	dr $1,760	dr $ 1,200

8. As a result of the adjustments reflected in the adjusted trial balance, the net income of the company before taxes will be   8.____

    A. *increased* by $4,270   B. *decreased* by $4,270
    C. *increased* by $5,430   D. *decreased* by $5,430

Question 9.

DIRECTIONS: Answer Question 9 based on the following facts concerning the operations of a manufacturer of office desks.

Jan. 1, 2014	Goods in Process Inventory	4,260 units	40% complete
Dec. 31, 2014	Goods in Process Inventory	3,776 units	25% complete
Jan. 1, 2014	Finished Goods Inventory	2,630 units	
Dec. 31, 2014	Finished Goods Inventory	3,180 units	

Sales consummated during the year-127,460 units

9. Assuming that all the desks are the same style, the number of equivalent complete units, manufactured during the year 2008 is: 9.____

    A. 127,250   B. 127,460   C. 128,010   D. 131,510

Questions 10-11.

DIRECTIONS: Answer Questions 10 through 11 based on the following.

On January 1, 2015, the Lenox Corporation was organized with a cash investment of $50,000 by the shareholders. Some of the corporate records were destroyed. However you were able to discover the following facts from various sources:

Accounts Payable at December 31, 2015 (arising from merchandise purchased)	$16,000
Accounts Receivable at December 31, 2015 (arising from the sales of merchandise)	18,000
Sales for the calendar year 2015	94,000
Inventory, December 31, 2015	20,000
Cost of Goods Sold is 60% of the selling price	
Bank loan outstanding - December 31, 2015	15,000
Expenses paid in cash during the year	35,000
Expenses incurred but unpaid as of December 31, 2015	4,000
Dividend paid	25,000

10. The *correct* cash balance is   10._____

    A. $5,600   B. $20,600   C. $38,600   D. $40,600

11. The stockholders' equity on December 31, 2015 is   11._____

    A. $23,600   B. Deficit of $26,400
    C. $27,600   D. $42,400

Questions 12-13.

DIRECTIONS: Answer Questions 12 and 13 based on the following facts developed from the records of a company that sells its merchandise on the installment plan.

Sales	Calendar Year 2014	Calendar Year 2015
Total volume of sales	$80,000	$100,000
Cost of Goods Sold	60,000	40,000
Gross Profit	$20,000	$ 60,000
Cash Collections		
From 2014 Sales	$18,000	$36,000
From 2015 Sales		22,000
Total Cash Collections	$18,000	$58,000

12. Using the deferred profit method of determining the income from installment sales, the   12._____
gross profit on sales for the calendar year 2014 was

    A. $4,500   B. $18,000   C. $20,000   D. None

13. Using the deferred profit method of determining the income from installment sales, the   13._____
gross profit on sales for the calendar year 2015 was

    A. $22,000   B. $22,200   C. $60,000   D. None

Questions 14-15.

DIRECTIONS: Answer Questions 14 through 15 based on the following data developed from an examination of the records of Ralston, Inc. for the month of April 2015.

Beginning inventory: 10,000 units @ $4.00 each

Purchases				sales			
April	10	20,000	units @ $5 each	April	13	15,000 units	@ $8 each
	17	60,000	units @ $6 each		21	50,000 units	@ $9 each
	26	40,000	units @ $7 each		27	50,000 units	@ $10 each

14. The gross profit on sales for the month of April, 2015, assuming that inventory is priced on the FIFO basis, is   14.____

     A. $330,000   B. $355,000   C. $395,000   D. $435,000'

15. The gross profit on sales for the month of April, 2015, assuming that inventory is priced on the LIFO basis, is   15.____

     A. $330,000   B. $355,000   C. $395,000   D. $435,000

Question 16.

DIRECTIONS: Answer Question 16 based on the data presented for June 30, 2015.

Balance per Bank Statement	$24,019.00
Balance per General Ledger	20,592.64
Proceeds of note collected by the bank which had not been recorded in the Cash account	4,000.00
Interest on note collected by the bank (no book entries made)	39.40
Debit memo for Bank charges for the month of May	23.50
Deposit in Transit (June 30, 2015)	2,144.00
Customer's check returned by the bank due to lack of funds	150.00
Outstanding checks - June 30, 2015	1,631.46
Error in recording check made by our bookkeeper - check cleared in the amount of $463.00 but entered in the bank book for $436.00	

16. If we wish to reconcile the bank and book balance so that the bank balance and the book balance are reconciled to a corrected balance, the corrected balance should be   16.____

     A. $20,592.64   B. $24,019.00   C. $24,531.54   D. $26,163.00

17. The Ateb Company has issued a $500,000 bond issue on January 1, 2014, at 8% interest, payable semi-annually, sold at par, with interest payable on June 30 and December 31.
On September 30, 2014, at the close of the fiscal year of the Ateb Company, the interest expense accrual should reflect interest payable of, approximately,   17.____

     A. $10,000   B. $20,000   C. $40,000   D. $50,000

18. Assume that a new procedure requires that a particular and unvarying sequence of steps be followed in order to yield the desired data. You are assigned to be in charge of subordinates working with this procedure.
Which one of the following is *most likely* to impress subordinates with the importance of following the sequence of steps exactly as given?   18.____

     A. *Explain* the consequences of error if the procedure is not followed
     B. *Suggest* how rewarding would be the feeling of finding errors before the supervisor catches them
     C. *Indicate* that independent verification of their work will be done by other staff members
     D. *Advise* that upward career mobility usually results from following instructions exactly

19. It is essential for an experienced accountant to know approximately how long it will take him to complete a particular assignment because

    19.___

    A. his supervisors will need to obtain this information only from someone planning to perform the assignment
    B. he must arrange his schedule to insure proper completion of the assignment consistent with agency objectives
    C. he must measure whether he is keeping pace with others performing similar assignments
    D. he must determine what assignments are essential and have the greatest priority within his agency

20. There are circumstances which call for special and emergency efforts by employees. You must assign your staff to make this type of effort.
Of the following, this special type of assignment is *most likely* to succeed if the

    20.___

    A. time schedule required to complete the assignment is precisely stated but is not adhered to
    B. employees are individually free to determine the work schedule
    C. assignment is clearly defined
    D. employees are individually free to use any procedure or method available to them

---

KEY (CORRECT ANSWERS)

1.	A	11.	A
2.	B	12.	A
3.	B	13.	B
4.	D	14.	C
5.	A	15.	B
6.	B	16.	C
7.	C	17.	A
8.	B	18.	A
9.	A	19.	B
10.	B	20.	C

EXAMINATION SECTION

TEST 1

DIRECTIONS: Each question or incomplete statement is followed by several suggested answers or completions. Select the one that BEST answers the question or completes the statement. *PRINT THE LETTER OF THE CORRECT ANSWER IN THE SPACE AT THE RIGHT.*

1. The private foundation status of an exempt organization will terminate if it   1._____
    A. does not distribute all of its net assets to one or more public charity
    B. qualifies as an exempt operating foundation
    C. becomes a public charity
    D. is governed by a charter that limits the organization's exempt purposes

2. In 2017, Aca Corp. adopted a plan of complete liquidation. Distributions   2._____
to stockholders in 2017, under this plan of complete liquidation, included
marketable securities purchased in 2010 with a basis of $100,000 and a
fair market value of $120,000 at the date of distribution. On June 30,
2017, the date this plan of complete liquidation was adopted, Aca had
100 equal stockholders, and the fair market value of all of Aca's
outstanding stock was $12,000,000.
In Aca's 2017 return, what amount should be reported as long-term
capital gain?
    A. $20,000   B. $10,000   C. $8,000   D. $0

3. With regard to corporate reorganizations, which one of the following   3._____
statements is CORRECT?
    A. A mere change in identity, form, or place of organization of one
       corporation does not qualify as a reorganization.
    B. The reorganization provisions cannot be used to provide tax-free
       treatment for corporate transactions.
    C. Securities in corporations not parties to a reorganization are
       always *boot*.
    D. A *party to the reorganization* does not include the consolidated
       company.

4. Mem Corp., which had earnings and profits of $500,000, made a   4._____
nonliquidating distribution of property to its stockholders in 2017 as a
dividend in kind. This property, which had an adjusted basis of $10,000
and a fair market value of $15,000 at the date of distribution, did not
constitute assets used in the active conduct of Mem's business.
How much gain did Mem have to recognize on this distribution?
    A. $0   B. $5,000   C. $10,000   D. $15,000

5. If an exempt organization is a corporation, the tax on unrelated business taxable income is
    A. computed at corporate income tax rates
    B. computed at rates applicable to trusts
    C. treated as a credit against the tax on recognized capital gains
    D. abated

5._____

6. In March, Lou Cole bought 100 shares of a listed stock for $10,000. In May, Cole sold this stock, for its fair market value of $16,000, to the partnership of Rook, Cole & Clive. Cole owned a one-third interest in this partnership.
In Cole's tax return, what amount should be reported as short-term capital gain as a result of this transaction?
    A. $6,000   B. $4,000   C. $2,000   D. $0

6._____

7. The following information pertains to land contributed by Bea Dott for a 30% interest in a new partnership:

Dott's adjusted basis	$42,000
Fair market value	150,000
Mortgage assumed by partnership	60,000

How much is Dott's basis for her partnership interest?
    A. $0   B. $24,000   C. $27,000   D. $42,000

7._____

8. Ben Krug, sole proprietor of Krug Dairy, hired Jan Karl in 2011 for an agreed salary and the promise of a 10% partnership capital interest if Karl continued in Krug's employ until the end of 2017. On January 1, 2018, when the fair value of the business was $300,000, the partnership was formed as agreed.
On what amount will Karl have to pay tax in 2018 for the partnership capital interest received by him?
    A. $0   B. $12,000   C. $18,000   D. $30,000

8._____

9. To qualify as an exempt organization, the applicant
    A. need not be specifically identified as one of the classes upon which exemption is conferred by the Internal Revenue Code, provided that the organization's purposes and activities are of a nonprofit nature
    B. must not be classified as a social club
    C. must file a written application with the Internal Revenue Service, even where no official forms are provided
    D. must meet the tests that permit donors to deduct their contributions on their individual or corporate tax returns

9._____

10. A corporation may reduce its income tax by taking a tax credit for
    A. accelerated depreciation
    B. state income taxes
    C. foreign income taxes
    D. dividends-received exclusion

10._____

11. For the first taxable year in which a corporation has qualifying research
and experimental expenditures, the corporation 11._____
    A. has a choice of either deducting such expenditures as current
business expenses or capitalizing these expenditures
    B. has to treat such expenditures in the same manner as they are
accounted for in the corporation's financial statements
    C. is required to deduct such expenditures currently as business
expenses or lose the deductions
    D. is required to capitalize such expenditures and amortize them
ratably over a period of not less than 60 months

Questions 12-14

DIRECTIONS: Questions 12 through 14 are to be answered on the basis of the
following data.

Ram Corp's operating for the year ended December 31 amounted to
$100,000. In addition, Ram received $2,000 in dividends from an unrelated
taxable domestic corporation during the year. Included in Ram's yearly operating
expenses is a $6,000 insurance premium on a policy insuring the life of Ram's
president. Ram is beneficiary of this policy. Also during the year, a machine
owned by Ram was completely destroyed in an accident. This machine's
adjusted basis immediately before the casualty was $15,000. The machine was
not insured and had no salvage value.

12. In Ram's tax return, what amount should be deducted for the casualty 12._____
loss?
    A. $5,000   B. $5,400   C. $14,900   D. $15,000

13. In Ram's tax return, what amount should be deducted for the $6,000 life 13._____
insurance premium?
    A. $6,000   B. $5,000   C. $1,000   D. $0

14. In Ram's tax return, what amount should be included in taxable income 14._____
for the dividends?
    A. $300   B. $400   C. $1,600   D. $1,700

15. Which one of the following is a capital asset? 15._____
    A. Delivery truck
    B. Goodwill
    C. Land used as a parking lot for customers
    D. Treasury stock, at cost

16. To qualify for tax-free incorporation, a sole proprietor must be in control of 16._____
the transferee corporation immediately after the exchange of the
proprietorship's assets for the corporation's stock.
Control for this purpose means ownership of stock amounting to AT
LEAST
    A. 80.00%   B. 75%   C. 66 2/3%   D. 51%

17. Kee Holding Corp. has 80 unrelated equal stockholders. For the year ended December 31, Kee's income comprised the following:

Net rental income	$1,000
Commissions earned on sales of franchises	3,000
Dividends from taxable domestic corporation	90,000

Deductible expenses for the year totaled $10,000. Kee paid no dividends for the past three years.
Kee's liability for personal holding company tax for the year will be based on

    A. $12,000   B. $11,000   C. $9,000   D. $0

17._____

18. Bow, Inc., an S corporation, has three equal stockholders. For the year ended December 31, 2018, Bow had taxable income and current earnings and profits of $300,000. Bow made cash distributions totaling $120,000 during 2018. For 2018, what amount from Bow should be included in each stockholder's gross income?

    A. $140,000   B. $100,000   C. $60,000   D. $40,000

18._____

19. For the year ended December 31, Sol Corp. had an operating income of $20,000. In addition, Sol had capital gains and losses resulting in a net short-term capital gain of $2,000 and a net long-term capital loss of $7,000. How much of the excess of net long-term capital loss over net short-term capital gain could Sol offset against ordinary income for the year?

    A. $5,000   B. $3,000   C. $1,500   D. $0

19._____

20. The accumulated earnings tax is NOT imposed on corporations that
    A. are personal holding companies
    B. are subsidiary corporations
    C. have assets with an aggregate book value of less than $1,000,000
    D. have more than 100 stockholders

20._____

21. Bart Co. adds materials at the beginning of the process in Department M. The following information pertains to Department M's work-in-process during April:

	Units
Work-in-process, April 1 (60% complete as to conversion cost)	3,000
Started in April	25,000
Completed	20,000
Work-in-process, April 30 (75% complete as to conversion cost)	8,000

Under the weighted average method, the equivalent units for conversion cost are

    A. 26,000   B. 25,000   C. 24,200   D. 21,800

21._____

22. Glo Co., a manufacturer of combs, budgeted sales of 125,000 units for the month of April. The following additional information is provided:

	Number of Units
Actual inventory at April 1	
Work-in-process	None
Finished goods	37,500
Budgeted inventory at April 30	
Work-in-process (75% processed)	8,000
Finished goods	30,000

How many equivalent units of production did Glo budget for April?
A. 126,500   B. 125,500   C. 123,500   D. 117,500

22._____

Questions 23-27

DIRECTIONS: Questions 23 through 27 are to be answered on the basis of the following selected data pertaining to Mar Co.'s Alo Division for the year.

Sales	$100,000
Variable costs	60,000
Traceable fixed costs	10,000
Average invested capital	20,000
Imputed interest rate on average invested capital	12%

In addition, consideration is being given to the possible purchase of a $30,000 machine for Alo, which is expected to result in a decrease of $12,000 per year in cash operating expenses. This machine, which has no residual value, has an estimated useful life of five years and will be depreciated on a straight-line basis.

23. If income taxes are ignored, the payback period for the new machine would be _____ years.
A. 1.67   B. 2.50   C. 4.17   D. 5.00

23._____

24. For the new machine, the accounting rate of return based on initial investment would be
A. 12%   B. 20%   C. 30%   D. 40%

24._____

25. Before the purchase of the $30,000 machine, Alo's residual income was
A. $27,600   B. $30,000   C. $32,400   D. $40,000

25._____

26. Before the purchase of the $30,000 machine, Alo's return on investment was
A. 60%   B. 75%   C. 138%   D. 150%

26._____

27. Before the purchase of the $30,000 machine, Alo's breakeven point in sales dollars was
A. $16,667   B. $25,000   C. $30,000   D. $70,000

27._____

Questions 28-29

DIRECTIONS: Questions 28 through 29 are to be answered on the basis of the
following data.

The following processing standards have been set for Duo Co.'s clerical
workers:

Number of hours per 1,000 papers processed	150
Normal number of papers processed per year	1,500,000
Wage rate per 1,000 papers	$600
Standard variable cost of processing	
1,500,000 papers	$900,000
Fixed costs per year	$150,000

The following information pertains to the 1,200,000 papers that were
processed during the year:

Total cost	$915,000
Labor cost	$760,000
Labor hours	190,000

28. For the year, Duo's labor rate variance would be   28._____
   A. $40,000 unfavorable   B. $32,000 favorable
   C. $10,000 unfavorable   D. $0

29. For the year, Duo's expected total cost to process the 1,200,000 papers,   29._____
assuming standard performance, should be
   A. $910,000   B. $900,000   C. $870,000   D. $840,000

30. Axe Co. produces joint products J and K from a process that yields   30._____
byproduct B. The cost assigned to byproduct B is its market value less
additional costs incurred after splitoff. Information concerning a batch
produced in April at a joint cost of $60,000 is as follows:

		After Splitoff	
	Units	Additional	Market
Product	produced	costs	values
J	1,000	$15,000	$50,000
K	2,000	10,000	40,000
B	4,000	2,000	5,000

How much of the joint cost should be allocated to the joint products?
   A. $53,000   B. $55,000   C. $57,000   D. $58,000

KEY (CORRECT ANSWERS)

1.	C	16.	A
2.	A	17.	D
3.	C	18.	B
4.	B	19.	D
5.	A	20.	A
6.	A	21.	A
7.	A	22.	C
8.	D	23.	B
9.	C	24.	B
10.	C	25.	A
11.	A	26.	D
12.	D	27.	B
13.	D	28.	D
14.	B	29.	C
15.	B	30.	C

TEST 2

1. The following data appeared in the accounting records of a retail store for the year ended December 31:

Sales	$150,000
Purchases	70,000
Inventories:	
January 1	35,000
December 31	50,000
Sales commissions	5,000

   How much was the gross margin?

   A. $65,000   B. $75,000   C. $90,000   D. $95,000

   1._____

2. During May, Roy Co. produced 10,000 units of Product X. Costs incurred by Roy during May were as follows:

Direct materials	$10,000
Direct labor	20,000
Variable manufacturing overhead	5,000
Variable selling and general	3,000
Fixed manufacturing overhead	9,000
Fixed selling and general	4,000
Total	$51,000

   Under absorption costing, Product X's unit cost was

   A. $5.10   B. $4.40   C. $3.80   D. $3.50

   2._____

3. Aba Caterers quotes a price of $30 per person for a dinner party. This price includes the 6% sales tax and the 15% service charge. Sales tax is computed on the food plus the service charge. The service charge is computed on the food only.
   At what amount does Aba price the food?

   A. $23.70   B. $24.61   C. $25.50   D. $28.20

   3._____

4. Meg Co. has developed a regression equation to analyze the behavior of its maintenance costs (Q) as a function of machine hours (Z). The following equation was developed by using 30 monthly observations with a related coefficient of determination of .90:

   $$Q = \$6,000 + \$5.25Z$$

   If 1,000 machine hours are worked in one month, the related point estimate of total maintenance costs would be

   A. $11,250   B. $10,125   C. $5,250   D. $4,725

   4._____

5. The following standard costs pertain to a component part manufactured   5._____
   by Bor Co.:

Direct materials	$ 4
Direct labor	10
Factory overhead	40
Standard cost per unit	$54

   Factory overhead is applied at $1 per standard machine hour. Fixed
   capacity cost is 60% of applied factory overhead, and is not affected by
   any *make or buy* decision. It would cost $49 per unit to buy the part from
   an outside supplier.
   In the decision to *make or buy*, what is the TOTAL relevant unit
   manufacturing cost?

   A. $54   B. $38   C. $30   D. $5

Questions 6-8

DIRECTIONS: Questions 6 through 8 are to be answered on the basis of the
            following data pertaining to Lam Co.'s manufacturing operations.

Inventories	4/1	4/30
Direct materials	$18,000	$15,000
Work-in-process	9,000	6,000
Finished goods	27,000	36,000

Additional information for the month of April:

Direct materials purchased	$42,000
Direct labor payroll	30,000
Direct labor rate per hour	$ 7.50
Factory overhead rate per direct labor hour	10.00

6. For the month of April, cost of goods manufactured was   6._____
   A. $118,000   B. $115,000   C. $112,000   D. $109,000

7. For the month of April, conversion cost incurred was   7._____
   A. $30,000   B. $40,000   C. $70,000   D. $72,000

8. For the month of April, prime cost incurred was   8._____
   A. $75,000   B. $69,000   C. $45,000   D. $39,000

9. Ral Co. sells 20,000 radios evenly throughout the year. The cost of   9._____
   carrying one unit in inventory for one year is $8, and the purchase order
   cost per order is $32.
   What is the economic order quantity?

   A. 625   B. 400   C. 283   D. 200

10. Joe Neil, CPA, has among his clientele a charitable organization that has   10._____
    a legal permit to conduct games of chance for fund-raising purposes.
    Neil's client derives its profit from admission fees and the sale of
    refreshments, and therefore wants to *break even* on the games of
    chance. In one of these games, the player draws one card from a
    standard deck of 52 cards. A player drawing any one of four *queens* wins
    $5, and a player drawing any one of 13 *hearts* wins $2. Neil is asked to
    compute the price that should be charged per draw so that the total
    amount paid out for winning draws can be expected to equal the total
    amount received from all draws.
    Which one of the following equations should Neil use to compute the
    price (P)?

$$A.\ 5 - 2 = \frac{35p}{52} \qquad\qquad B.\ \frac{4}{52}(5) + \frac{13}{52}(2) = \frac{35p}{52}$$

$$C.\ \frac{4}{52}(5 - P) + \frac{13}{52}(2 - P) = P \qquad D.\ \frac{4}{52}(5) + \frac{13}{52}(2) = P$$

11. Lin Co., a distributor of machinery, bought a machine from the   11._____
    manufacturer in November for $10,000. On December 30, Lin sold this
    machine to Zee Hardware for $15,000, under the following terms: 2%
    discount if paid within 30 days, 1% discount if paid after 30 days but
    within 60 days, or payable in full within 90 days if not paid within the
    discount periods. However, Zee had the right to return this machine to
    Lin if Zee was unable to resell the machine before expiration of the 90-
    day payment period, in which case Zee's obligation to Lin would be
    canceled.
    In Lin's net sales for the year ended December 31, how much should be
    included for the sale of this machine to Zee?
        A. $0   B. $14,700   C. $14,850   D. $15,000

12. In November and December 2018, Gee Co., a newly organized magazine   12._____
    publisher, received $36,000 for 1,000 three-year subscriptions at $12 per
    year, starting with the January 2019 issue of the magazine. Gee elected
    to include the entire $36,000 in its 2018 income tax return.
    How much should Gee have reported in its 2018 income statement for
    subscriptions revenue?
        A. $36,000   B. $12,000   C. $2,000   D. $0

13. On September 1, 2018, Ron Corp. issued 1,000 shares of its $25 par   13._____
    treasury common stock for a parcel of land to be held for a future plant
    site. The treasury shares were acquired by Ron at a cost of $30 per
    share. Ron's common stock had a fair market value of $40 per share on
    September 1, 2018. Ron received $5,000 from the sale of scrap when an
    existing structure on the site was razed.
    At what amount should the land be carried?
        A. $40,000   B. $35,000   C. $30,000   D. $25,000

Questions 14-16

DIRECTIONS: Questions 14 through 16 are to be answered on the basis of the following data.

Lake Corporation's accounting record showed the following investments at January 1, 2018:

Common stock:	
Kar Corp. (1,000 shares)	$ 10,000
Aub Corp. (5,000 shares)	100,000
Real estate:	
Parking lot (leased to Day Co.)	300,000
Other:	
Trademark (at cost, less accumulated amortization)	25,000
Total investments	$435,000

Lake owns 1% of Kar and 30% of Aub. Lake's directors constitute a majority of Aub's directors. The Day lease, which commenced on January 1, 2016, is for ten years, at an annual rental of $48,000. In addition, on January 1, 2016, Day paid a non-refundable deposit of $50,000, as well as a security deposit of $8,000 to be refunded upon expiration of the lease. The trademark was licensed to Barr Co. for royalties of 10% of sales of the trademarked items. Royalties are payable semiannually on March 1 (for sales in July through December of the prior year), and on September 1 (for sales in January through June of the same year).

During the year ended December 31, 2018, Lake received cash dividends of $1,000 from Kar, and $15,000 from Aub, whose 2018 net incomes were $75,000 and $150,000, respectively. Lake also received $48,000 rent from Day in 2018, and the following royalties from Barr:

	March 1	September 1
2017	$3,000	$5,000
2018	4,000	7,000

Barr estimated that sales of the trademarked items would total $20,000 for the last half of 2018.

14. In Lake's 2018 income statement, how much should be reported for rental revenue?

    A. $43,000   B. $48,000   C. $53,000   D. $53,800

14._____

15. In Lake's 2018 income statement, how much should be reported for royalty revenue?

    A. $14,000   B. $13,000   C. $11,000   D. $9,000

15._____

16. In Lake's 2018 income statement, how much should be reported for dividend revenue?

    A. $16,000   B. $2,400   C. $1,000   D. $150

16._____

17. James Lee, M.D., keeps his accounting records on a cash basis. During 2017, Dr. Lee collected $100,000 in fees from his patients. At December 31, 2016, Dr. Lee had accounts receivable of $20,000. At December 31, 2017, Dr. Lee had accounts receivable of $30,000 and unearned fees of $1,000.

On an accrual basis, how much was Dr. Lee's patient service revenue for 2017?

    A. $111,000   B. $109,000   C. $90,000   D. $89,000

17._____

18. On May 1, 2017, Lane Corp. bought a parcel of land for $100,000. Seven months later, Lane sold this land to a triple-A rated company for $150,000, under the following terms: 25% at closing, and a first mortgage note (at the market rate of interest) for the balance. The first payment on the note, plus accrued interest, is due December 1, 2018. Lane reported this sale on the installment basis in its 2017 tax return.

In its 2017 income statement, how much gain should Lane report from the sale of this land?

    A. $0   B. $12,500   C. $37,500   D. $50,000

18._____

19. In January 2017, Noll Corp. paid property taxes of $20,000 covering the calendar year 2017. Also in January 2017, Noll estimated that its year-end bonuses to factory workers would amount to $80,000 for 2017.

In Noll's quarterly income statement for the three months ended March 31, 2017, what is the TOTAL amount of expense related to these two items that should be reported?

    A. $25,000   B. $20,000   C. $5,000   D. $0

19._____

Questions 20-27

DIRECTIONS: Questions 20 through 27 are to be answered on the basis of the following data.

The separate condensed balance sheets and income statements of Par Corp. and its wholly-owned subsidiary, Sub Corp., are as follows:

BALANCE SHEETS
December 31, 2018

Assets	Par	Sub
Current		
Cash	$150,000	$ 50,000
Accounts receivable (net)	190,000	60,000
Inventories	90,000	40,000
Total current assets	430,000	150,000
Property, plant, and equipment (net)	365,000	200,000
Investment in Sub (equity method)	315,000	-----------
Total assets	$1,110,000	$350,000

Liabilities and Stockholders' Equity

	Par	Sub
Current liabilities		
Accounts payable	$100,000	$ 60,000
Accrued liabilities	30,000	20,000
Total current liabilities	130,000	80,000
Stockholders' equity		
Common stock ($10 par)	220,000	30,000
Additional paid-in capital	140,000	100,000
Retained earnings	620,000	140,000
Total stockholders' equity	980,000	270,000
Total liabilities and stockholders' equity	$1,110,000	$350,000

INCOME STATEMENTS
For the year ended December 31, 2018

	Par	Sub
Sales	$1,000,000	$300,000
Cost of goods sold	770,000	200,000
Gross margin	230,000	100,000
Other operating expenses	130,000	50,000
Operating income	100,000	50,000
Equity in earnings of Sub	25,000	--------
Income before income taxes	125,000	50,000
Provision for income taxes	40,000	20,000
Net income	$ 85,000	$ 30,000

Additional information:

- On January 1, 2018, Par purchased for $300,000 all of Sub's par, voting common stock. On January 1, 2018, the fair value of Sub's assets and liabilities equaled their carrying amount of $330,000 and $80,000, respectively. Par's policy is to amortize intangible assets over a 10-year period, unless a definite life is ascertainable.

- During 2018, Par and Sub paid cash dividends of $50,000 and $10,000, respectively. For tax purposes, Par receives the 100% exclusion for dividends received from Sub.

- There were no intercompany transactions except for Par's receipt of dividends from Sub, and Par's recording of its share of Sub's earnings.

- On June 30, 2018, Par issued 2,000 shares of common stock for $17 per share. There were no other changes in either Par's or Sub's common stock during 2018.

- Both Par and Sub paid income taxes at the rate of 40%.

20. In Par's 2018 income statement, what amount of deferred income taxes on Par's equity in Sub's earnings should be included in Par's provision for income taxes?
    A. $0   B. $2,000   C. $10,000   D. $12,000   20._____

21. Par's January 1, 2018 inventory was $110,000. Par's (parent only) 2005 inventory turnover ratio was
    A. 11.1   B. 10.0   C. 7.7   D. 7.0   21._____

22. In the December 31, 2018 consolidated balance sheet of Par and its subsidiary, Sub, how much should be reported as total current assets?
    A. $150,000   B. $280,000   C. $430,000   D. $580,000   22._____

23. In computing the consolidated earnings per share of Par and its subsidiary, Sub, the number of shares used should be
    A. 25,000   B. 24,000   C. 22,000   D. 21,000   23._____

24. In the consolidated income statement of Par and its subsidiary, Sub, how much expense should be reported for amortization of goodwill?
    A. $0   B. $3,000   C. $5,000   D. $10,000   24._____

25. The consolidated balance sheet of Par and its subsidiary, Sub, should report total retained earnings of
    A. $620,000   B. $640,000   C. $650,000   D. $760,000   25._____

26. The consolidated balance sheet of Par and its subsidiary, Sub, should   26._____
    report total consolidated assets of
        A. $1,110,000   B. $1,145,000
        C. $1,190,000   D. $1,460,000

27. In the 2018 consolidated income statement of Par and its subsidiary, Sub,   27._____
    what amount should be reported as consolidated net income?
        A. $60,000   B. $85,000   C. $90,000   D. $115,000

28. On January 1, 2018, Neu Co. sold equipment costing $380,000, with   28._____
    accumulated depreciation of $160,000 on the date of sale. Neu received
    as consideration for the sale a $400,000 noninterest bearing note due
    January 1, 2021. There was no established exchange price for the
    equipment, and the note had no ready market. The prevailing rate of
    interest for a note of this type at January 1, 2018 was 10%. The present
    value of 1 at 10% for three periods is 0.75.
    In Neu's 2018 income statement, how much should be included for
    interest income?
        A. $40,000   B. $33,333   C. $30,000   D. $13,500

Questions 29-30

DIRECTIONS: Questions 29 and 30 are to be answered on the basis of the
                 following data relating to a construction job started by Syl Co.
                 during 2018.

Total contract price	$100,000
Actual costs during 2018	20,000
Estimated remaining costs	40,000
Billed to customer during 2018	30,000
Received from customer during 2018	10,000

29. Under the percentage-of-completion method, how much should Syl   29._____
    recognize as gross profit for 2018?
        A. $0   B. $13,333   C. $26,667   D. $33,333

30. Under the completed contract method, how much should Syl recognize as   30._____
    gross profit for 2018?
        A. $0   B. $4,000   C. $10,000   D. $12,000

KEY (CORRECT ANSWERS)

1.	D	16.	C
2.	B	17.	B
3.	B	18.	D
4.	A	19.	A
5.	C	20.	A
6.	A	21.	C
7.	C	22.	D
8.	A	23.	D
9.	B	24.	C
10.	D	25.	A
11.	A	26.	C
12.	D	27.	B
13.	B	28.	C
14.	C	29.	B
15.	D	30.	A

EXAMINATION SECTION
TEST 1

DIRECTIONS: Each question or incomplete statement is followed by several suggested answers or completions. Select the one that BEST answers the question or completes the Statement. *PRINT THE LETTER OF THE CORRECT ANSWER IN THE SPACE AT THE RIGHT.*

1. Securities donated to a voluntary health and welfare organization should be recorded at the

    A. donor's recorded amount
    B. fair market value at the date of the gift
    C. fair market value at the date of the gift, or the donor's recorded amount, whichever is lower
    D. fair market value at the date of the gift, or the donor's recorded amount, whichever is higher

1.____

2. The current funds group of a not-for-profit private university includes which of the following?

	Annuity funds	Loan funds
A.	Yes	Yes
B.	Yes	No
C.	No	No
D.	No	Yes

2.____

3. The comprehensive annual financial report (CAFR) of a governmental unit should contain a combined statement of revenues, expenses, and changes in retained earnings for

	Governmental funds	Proprietary funds
A.	No	Yes
B.	No	No
C.	Yes	No
D.	Yes	Yes

3.____

4. Which of the following funds of a governmental unit could use the general fixed assets account group to account for fixed assets?

    A. Internal service   B. Enterprise
    C. Special assessment   D. Trust

4.____

5. Which type of fund can be either expendable or nonexpendable?

    A. Debt service   B. Enterprise
    C. Special revenue   D. Trust

5.____

6. Fixed assets of an enterprise fund should be accounted for in the

    A. general fixed asset account group but no depreciation on the fixed assets should be recorded
    B. general fixed asset account group and depreciation on the fixed assets should be recorded
    C. enterprise fund but no depreciation on the fixed assets should be recorded
    D. enterprise fund and depreciation on the fixed assets should be recorded

6.____

7. Fixed assets by a governmental unit should be accounted for in the   7._____

	Capital projects fund	General fund
A.	No	Yes
B.	No	No
C.	Yes	No
D.	Yes	Yes

8. The revenues control account of a governmental unit is debited when   8._____

    A. the budget is recorded at the beginning of the year
    B. the account is closed out at the end of the year
    C. property taxes are recorded
    D. property taxes are collected

9. Which of the following accounts of a governmental unit is credited when supplies previously ordered are received?   9._____

    A. Fund balance reserved for encumbrances
    B. Encumbrances control
    C. Expenditures control
    D. Appropriations control

10. Which of the following is an appropriate basis of accounting for a governmental fund of a governmental unit?   10._____

	Cash basis	Modified accrual basis
A.	Yes	No
B.	Yes	Yes
C.	No	Yes
D.	No	No

11. In the contribution margin approach to pricing, the price at which the income remains constant is equal to the price that covers   11._____

    A. prime costs
    B. variable costs
    C. fixed costs
    D. fixed and variable costs plus the desired profit

12. Assuming that sales and net income remain the same, a company's return on investment will   12._____

    A. increase if invested capital increases
    B. decrease if invested capital decreases
    C. decrease if the invested capital-employed turnover rate decreases
    D. decrease if the invested capital-employed turnover rate increases

13. The net present value capital budgeting technique can be used when cash flows from period to period are   13._____

	Uniform	Uneven
A.	No	Yes
B.	No	No
C.	Yes	No
D.	Yes	Yes

14. In using cost-volume-profit analysis to calculate an expected sales level expressed in units, which of the following should be subtracted from fixed costs in the numerator?   14.____

    A. Predicted operating loss
    B. Predicted operating profit
    C. Unit contribution margin
    D. Variable costs

15. A flexible budget is appropriate for a(n)   15.____

	Administrative budget	Direct material budget
A.	Yes	No
B.	Yes	Yes
C.	No	Yes
D.	No	No

16. In an income statement prepared as an internal report using the variable costing method, variable selling and administrative expenses would   16.____

    A. not be used
    B. be used in the computation of the contribution margin
    C. be used in the computation of operating income but not in the computation of the contribution margin
    D. be treated the same as fixed selling and administrative expenses

17. Which of the following is often subject to further processing in order to be salable?   17.____

	By-products	Scrap
A.	No	No
B.	No	Yes
C.	Yes	Yes
D.	Yes	No

18. When using the two-variance method for analyzing factory overhead, the difference between the budget allowance based on standard hours allowed and the factory overhead applied to production is the _____ variance.   18.____

    A. net overhead   B. controllable
    C. volume   D. efficiency

19. In the computation of manufacturing cost per equivalent unit, the weighted-average method of process costing considers   19.____

    A. current costs *only*
    B. current costs plus cost of ending work in process inventory
    C. current costs plus cost of beginning work in process inventory
    D. current costs less cost of beginning work in process inventory

20. Wages paid to a timekeeper in a factory are a   20.____

	Prime cost	Conversion cost
A.	Yes	No
B.	Yes	Yes
C.	No	No
D.	No	Yes

21. A development stage enterprise   21.____

    A. does not issue an income statement

    B. issues an income statement that only shows cumulative amounts from the enterprise's inception

    C. issues an income statement that is the same as an established operating enterprise, but does not show cumulative amounts from the enterprise's inception as additional information

    D. issues an income statement that is the same as an established operating enterprise and shows cumulative amounts from the enterprise's inception as additional information

22. How is the average inventory used in the calculation of each of the following?   22.____

	Acid test (quick ratio)	Inventory turnover rate
A.	Not used	Denominator
B.	Not used	Numerator
C.	Numerator	Numerator
D.	Numerator	Denominator

23. In financial reporting for segments of a business enterprise, the revenue of a segment should include   23.____

    A. intersegment sales of services similar to unaffiliated customers

    B. intersegment billings for the cost of shared facilities

    C. equity in income from unconsolidated subsidiaries

    D. extraordinary items

24. The accrual or deferral of interest costs to allocate cost to each period is appropriate for   24.____

	Interim financial reporting	Year-end financial reporting
A.	No	No
B.	No	Yes
C.	Yes	Yes
D.	Yes	No

25. Which of the following facts concerning inventories should be disclosed in the Summary of Significant Accounting Policies?   25.____

	Composition	Pricing
A.	Yes	Yes
B.	Yes	No
C.	No	Yes
D.	No	No

26. A nonmonetary asset received by Company Y in a nonreciprocal transfer from Company Z should be recorded by Y at   26.____

    A. Z's recorded amount

    B. Z's recorded amount or the fair value of the asset received, whichever is higher

    C. Z's recorded amount or the fair value of the asset received, whichever is lower

    D. the fair value of the asset received

27. A purchase of goods, denominated in a currency other than the entity's functional currency, resulted in a payable that was fixed in terms of the amount of foreign currency that would be paid. Exchange rates between the functional currency and the currency in which the transaction was denominated changed.
The resulting loss should be included as a(n)   27.____

   A. component of income from continuing operations
   B. separate component of stockholders' equity
   C. deferred asset
   D. extraordinary item

28. In a lease that is recorded as a sales-type lease by the lessor, unearned interest   28.____

   A. does not arise
   B. should be recognized in full as income at the lease's inception
   C. should be amortized over the period of the lease using the interest method
   D. should be amortized over the period of the lease using the straight-line method

29. A partnership is formed by two individuals who were previously sole proprietors. Property other than cash which is part of the initial investment in the partnership would be recorded for financial accounting purposes at the   29.____

   A. proprietors' book values or the fair value of the property at the date of the investment, whichever is higher
   B. proprietors' book values or the fair value of the property at the date of the investment, whichever is lower
   C. proprietors' book values of the property at the date of the investment
   D. fair value of the property at the date of the investment

30. Treasury stock was acquired for cash at more than its par value, and then subsequently sold for cash at more than its acquisition price.
Assuming that the cost method of accounting for treasury stock transactions is used, what is the effect of the subsequent sale of the treasury stock on each of the following?   30.____

	Additional Paid-in capital	Retained earnings
A.	Increase	Increase
B.	Increase	No effect
C.	No effect	No effect
D.	No effect	Increase

KEY (CORRECT ANSWERS)

1.	B	16.	B
2.	C	17.	D
3.	A	18.	C
4.	C	19.	C
5.	D	20.	D
6.	D	21.	D
7.	B	22.	A
8.	B	23.	A
9.	B	24.	C
10.	C	25.	C
11.	B	26.	D
12.	C	27.	A
13.	D	28.	C
14.	A	29.	D
15.	B	30.	B

TEST 2

DIRECTIONS: Each question or incomplete statement is followed by several suggested answers or completions. Select the one that BEST answers the question or completes the statement. *PRINT THE LETTER OF THE CORRECT ANSWER IN THE SPACE AT THE RIGHT.*

1. Interperiod income tax allocation should be used for

	Permanent differences	Timing differences
A.	Yes	Yes
B.	Yes	No
C.	No	Yes
D.	No	No

1.____

2. On February 1, authorized common stock was sold on a subscription basis at a price in excess of par value, and 20% of the subscription price was collected. On May 1, the remaining 80% of the subscription price was collected.
Additional paid-in capital would increase on

	February 1	May 1
A.	No	Yes
B.	No	No
C.	Yes	No
D.	Yes	Yes

2.____

3. Which of the following contingencies should generally be accrued on the balance sheet as a liability when the occurrence of the contingent event is reasonably possible and its amount can be reasonably estimated?

	Expropriation of assets	Product warranty obligation
A.	No	No
B.	No	Yes
C.	Yes	Yes
D.	Yes	No

3.____

4. A six-year capital lease entered into on December 31, 2007 specified equal minimum annual lease payments due on December 31 of each year.
The December 31, 2008 minimum annual lease payment consists of which of the following?

	Interest expense	Lease liability
A.	No	No
B.	No	Yes
C.	Yes	No
D.	Yes	Yes

4.____

5. Lease Y contains a bargain purchase option, and the lease term is equal to 75 percent of the estimated economic life of the leased property. Lease Z contains a bargain purchase option and the lease term is equal to less than 75 percent of the estimated economic life of the leased property.
How should the lessee classify these leases?

	Lease Y	Lease Z
A.	Operating lease	Operating lease
B.	Operating lease	Capital lease
C.	Capital lease	Capital lease
D.	Capital lease	Operating lease

5.____

6. Deferred income tax expense resulting from timing differences related to depreciation of plant assets should be presented in a statement of changes in financial position as a(n)   6.____

    A. source and a use of funds
    B. use of funds
    C. deduction from income from continuing operations
    D. addition to income from continuing operations

7. A stock split-up should be presented in a statement of changes in financial position as   7.____

	Source of funds	Use of funds
A.	No	Yes
B.	No	No
C.	Yes	No
D.	Yes	Yes

8. At the end of the most recent year, a company's deferred income tax credit related to a current asset exceeded a deferred income tax charge related to a noncurrent liability. Which of the following should be reported in the company's most recent year-end balance sheet?   8.____

    A. The excess of the deferred income tax credit over the deferred income tax charge as a current liability
    B. The excess of the deferred income tax credit over the deferred income tax charge as a noncurrent liability
    C. The deferred income tax credit as a current liability
    D. The deferred income tax credit as a noncurrent liability

9. A profitable company uses interperiod income tax allocation and has an effective income tax rate of 40%. At December 31, 40% of the excess of the accelerated cost recovery system deduction over the straight-line depreciation method expense should be reported in the balance sheet as a _____ deferred income tax _____.   9.____

    A. noncurrent; credit   B. current; credit
    C. noncurrent; debit   D. current; debit

10. A company using the composite depreciation method for its fleet of trucks, cars, and campers retired one of its trucks due to damage before the average service life of the composite group was reached. An insurance recovery was received.
Net book value of these composite asset accounts would be decreased by the   10.____

    A. insurance recovery received
    B. insurance recovery received less depreciation on the truck to the date of retirement
    C. original cost of the truck less the insurance recovery received
    D. original cost of the truck

11. A lessee incurred landscaping costs to improve leased property. The estimated useful life of the landscaping costs is six years. The remaining term of the nonrenewable lease is five years.
The landscaping costs should be   11.____

    A. capitalized as leasehold improvements and depreciated over five years
    B. capitalized as leasehold improvements and depreciated over six years
    C. expensed as incurred and included with rent expense
    D. expensed as incurred but not included with rent expense

12. The lessee should amortize the capitalizable cost of the leased asset in a manner consistent with the lessee's normal depreciation policy for owned assets for leases that   12.____

	Contain a bargain purchase option	Transfer ownership of the property to the lessee by the end of the lease term
A.	No	No
B.	No	Yes
C.	Yes	Yes
D.	Yes	No

13. A depreciable asset has an estimated 15% salvage value. At the end of its estimated useful life, the accumulated depreciation would equal the original cost of the asset under which of the following depreciation methods?   13.____

	Straight-line	Productive output
A.	Yes	Yes
B.	Yes	No
C.	No	No
D.	No	Yes

14. An asset is being constructed for an enterprise's own use. The asset has been financed with a specific new borrowing. The interest cost incurred during the construction period as a result of expenditures for the asset is   14.____

   A. interest expense in the construction period
   B. a prepaid asset to be written off over the estimated useful life of the asset
   C. a part of the historical cost of acquiring the asset to be written off over the estimated useful life of the asset
   D. a part of the historical cost of acquiring the asset to be written off over the term of the borrowing used to finance the construction of the asset

15. When computing fully diluted earnings per share, convertible securities that are NOT common stock equivalents are   15.____

   A. recognized only if they are dilutive
   B. recognized only if they are anti-dilutive
   C. recognized whether they are dilutive or anti-dilutive
   D. ignored

16. How would the declaration of a 10% stock dividend by a corporation affect each of the following on its books?   16.____

	Retained earnings	Total stockholders' equity
A.	Decrease	No effect
B.	Decrease	Decrease
C.	No effect	Decrease
D.	No effect	No effect

17. When a property dividend is declared and the book value of the property exceeds its market value, the dividend is recorded at the _____ value of the property at the date of _____.

    A. market; distribution
    B. market; declaration
    C. book; declaration
    D. book; distribution if it still exceeds the market value of the property at the date of declaration

17.____

18. A returnable cash deposit should be classified by the company as a liability when the deposit is received from

	A customer	An employee
A.	Yes	No
B.	Yes	Yes
C.	No	Yes
D.	No	No

18.____

19. Legal fees incurred in successfully defending a patent suit should be capitalized when the patent has been

	Internally developed	Purchased from an inventor
A.	Yes	No
B.	Yes	Yes
C.	No	Yes
D.	No	No

19.____

20. The weighted average for the year inventory cost flow method is applicable to which of the following inventory systems?

	Periodic	Perpetual
A.	Yes	Yes
B.	Yes	No
C.	No	Yes
D.	No	No

20.____

21. Theoretically, cash discounts permitted on purchased raw materials should be

    A. added to other income, whether taken or not
    B. added to other income, only if taken
    C. deducted from inventory, whether taken or not
    D. deducted from inventory, only if taken

21.____

22. The original cost of an inventory item is above the replacement cost and below the net realizable value.
The net realizable value less the normal profit margin is above the replacement cost and the original cost.
Using the lower of cost or market method, the inventory item should be priced at its

    A. original cost
    B. replacement cost
    C. net realizable value
    D. net realizable value less the normal profit margin

22.____

23. When the allowance method of recognizing bad debt expense is used, the entries at the time of collection of a small account previously written off would

    23.____

    A. increase net income
    B. decrease the allowance for doubtful accounts
    C. have no effect on the allowance for doubtful accounts
    D. increase the allowance for doubtful accounts

24. A 90-day 15% interest-bearing note receivable is sold to a bank with recourse after being held for 60 days. The proceeds are calculated using an 18% interest rate.
The amount credited to notes receivable at the date of the discounting transaction would be

    24.____

    A. the same as the cash proceeds
    B. less than the face value of the note
    C. the face value of the note
    D. the maturity value of the note

25. How will the investor's investment account be affected by the investor's share of the earnings of the investee after the date of acquisition under each of the following accounting methods?

    25.____

	Cost method	Equity method
A.	No effect	Increase
B.	Increase	Increase
C.	Increase	No effect
D.	No effect	No effect

26. An investor purchased a bond as a long-term investment on January 1. Annual interest was received on December 31.
The investor's interest income for the year would be HIGHEST if the bond was purchased at

    26.____

    A. par   B. face value
    C. a discount   D. a premium

27. The valuation allowance for a marketable equity securities portfolio included in current assets should be a component of

    27.____

    A. current liabilities   B. noncurrent liabilities
    C. noncurrent assets   D. current assets

28. A short-term marketable debt security was purchased on September 1, 2007 between interest dates. The next interest payment date was February 1, 2008. Because of a permanent decline in market value, the cost of the debt security substantially exceeded its market value at December 31, 2007.
On the balance sheet at December 31, 2007, the debt security should be carried at

    28.____

    A. cost
    B. cost plus the accrued interest paid
    C. market value
    D. market value plus the accrued interest paid

29. During a period of inflation, an account balance remains constant. 29.____
With respect to this account, a purchasing power gain
will be recognized if the account is a

    A. monetary liability
    B. monetary asset
    C. nonmonetary liability
    D. nonmonetary asset

30. According to Statements of Financial Accounting Concepts, neutrality is an ingredient of   30.____

	Relevance	Reliability
A.	Yes	Yes
B.	Yes	No
C.	No	No
D.	No	Yes

KEY (CORRECT ANSWERS)

1.	C	16.	A
2.	C	17.	B
3.	A	18.	B
4.	D	19.	B
5.	C	20.	B
6.	D	21.	C
7.	B	22.	A
8.	C	23.	D
9.	A	24.	C
10.	A	25.	A
11.	A	26.	C
12.	C	27.	D
13.	C	28.	C
14.	C	29.	A
15.	A	30.	D

EXAMINATION SECTION
TEST 1

DIRECTIONS: Each question or incomplete statement is followed by several suggested answers or completions. Select the one that BEST answers the question or completes the statement. *PRINT THE LETTER OF THE CORRECT ANSWER IN THE SPACE AT THE RIGHT.*

1. *Which one* of the following generalizations is *most likely* to be INACCURATE and lead to judgmental errors in communication?   1.____

    A. A supervisor must be able to read with understanding
    B. Misunderstanding may lead to dislike
    C. Anyone can listen to another person and understand what he means
    D. It is usually desirable to let a speaker talk until he is finished

2. Assume that, as a supervisor, you have been directed to inform your subordinates about the implementation of a new procedure which will affect their work. While communicating this information, you should do all of the following EXCEPT   2.____

    A. obtain the approval of your subordinates regarding the new procedure
    B. explain the reason for implementing the new procedure
    C. hold a staff meeting at a time convenient to most of your subordinates
    D. encourage a productive discussion of the new procedure

3. Assume that you are in charge of a section that handles requests for information on matters received from the public. One day, you observe that a clerk under your supervision is using a method to log-in requests for information that is different from the one specified by you in the past. Upon questioning the clerk, you discover that instructions changing the old procedure were delivered orally by your supervisor on a day on which you were absent from the office.
Of the following, the *most appropriate* action for you to take is to   3.____

    A. tell the clerk to revert to the old procedure at once
    B. ask your supervisor for information about the change
    C. call your staff together and tell them that no existing procedure is to be changed unless you direct that it be done
    D. write a memo to your supervisor suggesting that all future changes in procedure are to be in writing and that they be directed to you

4. At the first meeting with your staff after appointment as a supervisor, you find considerable indifference and some hostility among the participants.
Of the following, the *most appropriate* way to handle this situation is to   4.____

    A. disregard the attitudes displayed and continue to make your presentation until you have completed it
    B. discontinue your presentation but continue the meeting and attempt to find out the reasons for their attitudes
    C. warm up your audience with some good natured statements and anecdotes and then proceed with your presentation
    D. discontinue the meeting and set up personal interviews with the staff members to try to find out the reason for their attitude

5. In order to start the training of a new employee, it has been a standard practice to have him read a manual of instructions or procedures.
This method is currently being replaced by the _____ method.

   A. audio-visual   B. conference
   C. lecture   D. programmed instruction

5.___

6. Of the following subjects, the *one* that can usually be *successfully* taught by a first-line supervisor who is training his subordinates is:

   A. Theory and philosophy of manage-   B. Human relations
        ment
   C. Responsibilities of a supervisor   D. Job skills

6.___

7. Assume that as a supervisor you are training a clerk who is experiencing difficulty learning a new task.
Which one of the following would be the LEAST effective approach to take when trying to solve this problem? To

   A. ask questions which will reveal the clerk's understanding of the task
   B. take a different approach in explaining the task
   C. give the clerk an opportunity to ask questions about the task
   D. make sure the clerk knows you are watching his work closely

7.___

8. One school of management and supervision involves participation by employees in the setting of group goals and in the sharing of responsibility for the operation of the unit.
If this philosophy were applied to a unit consisting of professional and clerical personnel, one should expect

   A. the professional and clerical personnel to participate with equal effectiveness in operating areas and policy areas
   B. the professional personnel to participate with greater effectiveness than the clerical personnel in policy areas
   C. the clerical personnel to participate with greater effectiveness than the professional personnel in operating areas
   D. greater participation by clerical personnel but with less responsibility for their actions

8.___

9. With regard to productivity, high morale among employees *generally* indicates a

   A. history of high productivity
   B. nearly absolute positive correlation with high productivity
   C. predisposition to be productive under facilitating leadership and circumstances
   D. complacency which has little effect on productivity

9.___

10. Assume that you are going to organize the professionals and clerks under your supervision into work groups or teams of two or three employees.
Of the following, the step which is LEAST likely to foster the successful development of each group is to

   A. allow friends to work together in the group
   B. provide special help and attention to employees with no friends in their group
   C. frequently switch employees from group to group
   D. rotate jobs within the group in order to strengthen group identification

10.___

11. Following are four statements which might be made by an employee to his supervisor during a performance evaluation interview.
    Which of the statements BEST provides a basis for developing a plan to improve the employee's performance?

    A. *I understand that you are dissatisfied with my work and I will try harder in the future.*
    B. *I feel that I've been making too many careless clerical errors recently.*
    C. *I am aware that I will be subject to disciplinary action if my work does not improve within one month.*
    D. *I understand that this interview is simply a requirement of your job, and not a personal attack on me.*

11.____

12. Three months ago, Mr. Smith and his supervisor, Mrs. Jones, developed a plan which was intended to correct Mr. Smith's inadequate job performance. Now, during a follow-up interview, Mr. Smith, who thought his performance had satisfactorily improved, has been informed that Mrs. Jones is still dissatisfied with his work.
    Of the following, it is *most likely* that the disagreement occurred because, when formulating the plan ,they did NOT

    A. set realistic goals for Mr. Smith Is performance
    B. set a reasonable time limit for Mr. Smith to effect his improvement in performance
    C. provide for adequate training to improve Mr. Smith's skills
    D. establish performance standards for measuring Mr. Smith's progress

12.____

13. When a supervisor delegates authority to subordinates, there are usually many problems to overcome, such as inadequately trained subordinates and poor planning.
    All of the following are means of increasing the effectiveness of delegation EXCEPT:

    A. Defining assignments in the light of results expected
    B. Maintaining open lines of communication
    C. Establishing tight controls so that subordinates will stay within the bounds of the area of delegation
    D. Providing rewards for successful assumption of authority by a subordinate

13.____

14. Assume that one of your subordinates has arrived late for work several times during the current month. The last time he was late you had warned him that another unexcused lateness would result in formal disciplinary action.
    If the employee arrives late for work again during this month, the FIRST action you should take is to

    A. give the employee a chance to explain this lateness
    B. give the employee a written copy of your warning
    C. tell the employee that you are recommending formal disciplinary action
    D. tell the employee that you will give him only one more chance before recommending formal disciplinary action

14.____

15. In trying to decide how many subordinates a manager can control directly, one of the   15.___
determinants is how much the manager can reduce the frequency and time consumed in
contacts with his subordinates.
Of the following, the factor which LEAST influences the number and direction of these
contacts is:

    A. How well the manager delegates authority
    B. The rate at which the organization is changing
    C. The control techniques used by the manager
    D. Whether the activity is line or staff

16. Systematic rotation of employees through lateral transfer within a government organiza-   16.___
tion to provide for managerial development is

    A. *good,* because systematic rotation develops specialists who learn to do many jobs
       well
    B. *bad,* because the outsider upsets the status quo of the existing organization
    C. *good,* because rotation provides challenge and organizational flexibility
    D. *bad,* because it is upsetting to employees to be transferred within a service

17. Assume that you are required to provide an evaluation of the performance of your subor-   17.___
dinates.
Of the following factors, it is MOST important that the performance evaluation include a
rating of each employees

    A. initiative   B. productivity   C. intelligence   D. personality

18. When preparing performance evaluations of your subordinates, *one* way to help assure   18.___
that you are rating each employee fairly is to

    A. prepare a list of all employees and all the rating factors and rate all employees on
       one rating factor before going on to the next factor
    B. prepare a list of all your employees and all the rating factors and rate each
       employee on all factors before going on to the next employee
    C. discuss all the ratings you anticipate giving with another supervisor in order to
       obtain an unbiased opinion
    D. discuss each employee with his co-workers in order to obtain peer judgment of
       worth before doing any rating

19. A managerial plan which would include the GREATEST control is a plan which is   19.___

    A. spontaneous and geared to each new job that is received
    B. detailed and covering an extended time period
    C. long-range and generalized, allowing for various interpretations
    D. specific and prepared daily

20. Assume that you are preparing a report which includes statistical data covering   20.____
    increases in budget allocations of four agencies for the past ten years.
    For you to represent the statistical data pictorially or graphically within the report is a

   A. *poor idea*, because you should be able to make statistical data understandable
       through the use of words
   B. *good idea*, because it is easier for the reader to understand pictorial representation
       rather than quantities of words conveying statistical data
   C. *poor idea*, because using pictorial representation in a report may make the report
       too expensive to print
   D. *good idea*, because a pictorial representation makes the report appear more
       attractive than the use of many words to convey the statistical data

   _____

KEY (CORRECT ANSWERS)

1.	C	11.	A
2.	A	12.	B
3.	B	13.	C
4.	D	14.	A
5.	D	15.	D
6.	D	16.	C
7.	D	17.	B
8.	B	18.	A
9.	C	19.	B
10.	C	20.	B

_____

TEST 2

Each question or incomplete statement is followed by several suggested answers or completions. Select the one that BEST answers the question or completes the statement. *PRINT THE LETTER OF THE CORRECT ANSWER IN THE SPACE AT THE RIGHT.*

1. Research studies have shown that supervisors of groups with high production records USUALLY 1.____

 A. give detailed instructions, constantly check on progress, and insist on approval of all decisions before implementation
 B. do considerable paperwork and other work similar to that performed by subordinates
 C. think of themselves as team members on the same level as others in the work group
 D. perform tasks traditionally associated with managerial functions

2. Mr. Smith, a bureau chief, is summoned by his agency's head in a conference to discuss 2.____
Mr. Jones, an accountant who works in one of the divisions of his bureau. Mr. Jones has committed an error of such magnitude as to arouse the agency head's concern.
After agreeing with the other conferees that a severe reprimand would be the appropriate punishment, Mr. Smith should

 A. arrange for Mr. Jones to explain the reasons for his error to the agency head
 B. send a memorandum to Mr. Jones, being careful that the language emphasizes the nature of the error rather than Mr. Jones' personal faults
 C. inform Mr. Jones' immediate supervisor of the conclusion reached at the conference, and let the supervisor take the necessary action
 D. suggest to the agency head that no additional action be taken against Mr. Jones because no further damage will be caused by the error

3. Assume that Ms. Thomson, a unit chief, has determined that the findings of an internal 3.____
audit have been seriously distorted as a result of careless errors. The audit had been performed by a group of auditors in her unit and the errors were overlooked by the associate accountant in charge of the audit. Ms. Thomson has decided to delay discussing the matter with the associate accountant and the staff who performed the audit until she verifies certain details, which may require prolonged investigation.
Ms. Thomson's method of handling this situation is

 A. *appropriate;* employees should not be accused of wrongdoing until all the facts have been determined
 B. *inappropriate;* the employees involved may assume that the errors were considered unimportant
 C. *appropriate;* employees are more likely to change their behavior as a result of disciplinary action taken after a *cooling off* period
 D. *inappropriate;* the employees involved may have forgotten the details and become emotionally upset when confronted with the facts

4. After studying the financial situation in his agency, an administrative accountant decides   4.____
to recommend centralization of certain accounting functions which are being performed
in three different bureaus of the organization.
The one of the following which is *most likely* to be a DISADVANTAGE if this recom-
mendation is implemented is that

    A. there may be less coordination of the accounting procedure because central direc-
tion is not so close to the day-to-day problems as the personnel handling them in
each specialized accounting unit

    B. the higher management levels would not be able to make emergency decisions in
as timely a manner as the more involved, lower-level administrators who are closer
to the problem

    C. it is more difficult to focus the attention of the top management in order to resolve
accounting problems because of the many other activities top management is
involved in at the same time

    D. the accuracy of upward and inter-unit communication may be reduced because
centralization may require insertion of more levels of administration in the chain of
command

5. Of the following assumptions about the role of conflict in an organization, the *one* which   5.____
is the MOST accurate statement of the approach of modern management theorists is
that conflict

    A. can usually be avoided or controlled
    B. serves as a vital element in organizational change
    C. works against attainment of organizational goals
    D. provides a constructive outlet for problem employees

6. Which of the following is generally regarded as the BEST approach for a supervisor to fol-   6.____
low in handling grievances brought by subordinates?

    A. Avoid becoming involved personally
    B. Involve the union representative in the first stage of discussion
    C. Settle the grievance as soon as possible
    D. Arrange for arbitration by a third party

7. Assume that supervisors of similar-sized accounting units in city, state, and federal   7.____
offices were interviewed and observed at their work. It was found that the ways they
acted in and viewed their roles tended to be very similar, regardless of who employed
them.
Which of the following is the BEST explanation of this similarity?

    A. A supervisor will ordinarily behave in conformance to his own self-image
    B. Each role in an organization, including the supervisory role, calls for a distinct type
of personality
    C. The supervisory role reflects an exceptionally complex pattern of human response
    D. The general nature of the duties and responsibilities of the supervisory position
determines the role

8. Which of the following is NOT consistent with the findings of recent research about the characteristics of successful top managers?   8.___

   A. They are *inner-directed* and not overly concerned with pleasing others
   B. They are challenged by situations filled with high risk and ambiguity
   C. They tend to stay on the same job for long periods of time
   D. They consider it more important to handle critical assignments successfully than to do routine work well

9. As a supervisor you have to give subordinate operational guidelines.   9.___
   Of the following, the BEST reason for providing them with information about the overall objectives within which their operations fit is that the subordinates will

   A. be more likely to carry out the operation according to your expectations
   B. know that there is a legitimate reason for carrying out the operation in the way you have prescribed
   C. be more likely to handle unanticipated problems that may arise without having to take up your time
   D. more likely to transmit the operating instructions correctly to their subordinates

10. A supervisor holds frequent meetings with his staff.   10.___
    Of the following, the BEST approach he can take in order to elicit productive discussions at these meetings is for him to

    A. ask questions of those who attend
    B. include several levels of supervisors at the meetings
    C. hold the meetings at a specified time each week
    D. begin each meeting with a statement that discussion is welcomed

11. Of the following, the MOST important action that a supervisor can take to increase the productivity of a subordinate is to   11.___

    A. increase his uninterrupted work time
    B. increase the number of reproducing machines available in the office
    C. provide clerical assistance whenever he requests it
    D. reduce the number of his assigned tasks

12. Assume that, as a supervisor, you find that you often must countermand or modify your original staff memos. If this practice continues, *which one* of the following situations is MOST likely to occur? The   12.___

    A. staff will not bother to read your memos   B. office files will become cluttered
    C. staff will delay acting on your memos   D. memos will be treated routinely

13. In making management decisions the committee approach is often used by managers.   13.___
    Of the following, the BEST reason for using this approach is to

    A. prevent any one individual from assuming too much authority
    B. allow the manager to bring a wider range of experience and judgment to bear on the problem
    C. allow the participation of all staff members, which will make them feel more committed to the decisions reached
    D. permit the rapid transmission of information about decisions reached to the staff members concerned

14. In establishing standards for the measurement of the performance of a management   14.____
    project team, it is MOST important for the project manager to

    A. identify and define the objectives of the project
    B. determine the number of people who will be assigned to the project team
    C. evaluate the skills of the staff who will be assigned to the project team
    D. estimate fairly accurately the length of time required to complete each phase of the
       project

15. It is virtually impossible to tell an employee either that he is not so good as another   15.____
    employee or that he does not measure up to a desirable level of performance, without
    having him feel threatened, rejected, and discouraged.
    In accordance with the foregoing observation, a supervisor who is concerned about
    the performance of the less efficient members of his staff should realize that

    A. he might obtain better results by not discussing the quality and quantity of their
       work with them, but by relying instead on the written evaluation of their perfor-
       mance to motivate their improvement
    B. since he is required to discuss their performance with them, he should do so in
       words of encouragement and in so friendly a manner as to not destroy their morale
    C. he might discuss their work in a general way, without mentioning any of the specif-
       ics about the quality of their performance, with the expectation that they would
       understand the full implications of his talk
    D. he should make it a point, while telling them of their poor performance, to mention
       that their work is as good as that of some of the other employees in the unit

16. Some advocates of management-by-objectives procedures in public agencies have   16.____
    been urging that this method of operations be expanded to encompass all agencies of
    the government, for one or more of the following reasons, not all of which may be correct:
       I.   The MBO method is likely to succeed because it embraces the practice of
            setting near-term goals for the subordinate manager, reviewing accomplish-
            ments at an appropriate time, and repeating this process indefinitely
       II. Provision for authority to perform the tasks assigned as goals in the MBO
            method is normally not needed because targets are set in quantitative or
            qualitative terms and specific times for accomplishment are arranged in
            short-term, repetitive intervals
       III. Many other appraisal-of-performance programs failed because both super-
            visors and subordinates resisted them, while the MBO approach is not insti-
            tuted until there is an organizational commitment to it
       IV. Personal accountability is clearly established through the MBO approach
            because verifiable results are set up in the process of formulating the targets
    Which of the choices below includes ALL of the foregoing statements that are COR-
    RECT?

    A. I and III   B. II and IV
    C. I,II,III,IV   D. I,III,IV

101

17. In preparing an organizational structure, the PRINCIPAL guideline for locating staff units is to place them   17.___

    A. all under a common supervisor
    B. as close as possible to the activities they serve
    C. as close to the chief executive as possible without over-extending his span of control
    D. at the lowest operational level

18. The relative importance of any unit in a department can be LEAST reliably judged by the   18.___

    A. amount of office space allocated to the unit
    B. number of employees in the unit
    C. rank of the individual who heads the unit
    D. rank of the individual to whom the unit head reports directly

19. Those who favor Planning-Programming-Budgeting Systems (PPBS) as a new method of governmental financial administration emphasize that PPBS   19.___

    A. applies statistical measurements which correlate highly with criteria
    B. makes possible economic systems analysis, including an explicit examination of alternatives
    C. makes available scarce government resources which can be coordinated on a government-wide basis and shared between local units of government
    D. shifts the emphasis in budgeting methods to an automated system of data processing

20. The term applied to computer processing which processes data concurrently with a given activity and provides results soon enough to influence the selection of a course of action is   20.___

    A. realtime processing   B. batch processing
    C. random access processing   D. integrated data processing

---

KEY (CORRECT ANSWERS)

1.	D		11.	A
2.	C		12.	C
3.	B		13.	B
4.	D		14.	A
5.	B		15.	B
6.	C		16.	D
7.	D		17.	B
8.	C		18.	B
9.	C		19.	B
10.	A		20.	A

READING COMPREHENSION
UNDERSTANDING AND INTERPRETING WRITTEN MATERIAL
EXAMINATION SECTION
TEST 1

DIRECTIONS: Each question or incomplete statement is followed by several suggested answers or completions. Select the one that BEST answers the question or completes the statement. *PRINT THE LETTER OF THE CORRECT ANSWER IN THE SPACE AT THE RIGHT.*

Questions 1-4.

DIRECTIONS: Questions 1 through 4 are to be answered SOLELY on the basis of the following paragraph.

An annual leave allowance, which combines leaves previously given for vacation, personal business, family illness, and other reasons shall be granted members. Calculation of credits for such leave shall be on an annual basis beginning January 1st of each year. Annual leave credits shall be based on time served by members during preceding calendar year. However, when credits have been accrued and member retires during current year, additional annual leave credits shall, in this instance, be granted at accrual rate of three days for each completed month of service, excluding terminal leave. If accruals granted for completed months of service extend into following month, member shall be granted an additional three days accrual for completed month. This shall be the only condition where accruals in a current year are granted for vacation period in such year.

1. According to the above paragraph, if a fireman's wife were to become seriously ill so that he would take time off from work to be with her, such time off would be deducted from his _____ allowance.

    A. annual leave   B. vacation leave
    C. personal business leave   D. family illness leave

1.____

2. Terminal leave means leave taken

    A. at the end of the calendar year
    B. at the end of the vacation year
    C. immediately before retirement
    D. before actually earned, because of an emergency

2.____

3. A fireman appointed on July 1, 2007 will be able to take his first full or normal annual leave during the period

    A. July 1, 2007 to June 30, 2008
    B. Jan. 1, 2008 to Dec. 31, 2008
    C. July 1, 2008 to June 30, 2009
    D. Jan. 1, 2009 to Dec. 31, 2009

3.____

4. According to the above paragraph, a member who retires on July 15 of this year will be entitled to receive leave allowance based on this year of _____ days.   4.___

    A. 15   B. 18   C. 22   D. 24

5. Fire alarm boxes are electromechanical devices for transmitting a coded signal. In each box, there is a trainwork of wheels. When the box is operated, a spring-activated code wheel within begins to revolve. The code number of the box is notched on the circumference of the code wheel, and the latter is associated with the circuit in such a way that when it revolves it causes the circuit to open and close in a predetermined manner, thereby transmitting its particular signal to the central station. A fire alarm box is nothing more than a device for interrupting the flow of current in a circuit in such a way as to produce a coded signal that may be decoded by the dispatchers in the central office.
Based on the above, select the FALSE statement: 5.___

    A. Each standard fire alarm box has its own code wheel
    B. The code wheel operates when the box is pulled
    C. The code wheel is operated electrically
    D. Only the break in the circuit by the notched wheel causes the alarm signal to be transmitted to the central office

Questions 6-9.

DIRECTIONS: Questions 6 through 9 are to be answered SOLELY on the basis of the following paragraph.

Ventilation, as used in fire fighting operations, means opening up a building or structure in which a fire is burning to release the accumulated heat, smoke, and gases. Lack of knowledge of the principles of ventilation on the part of firemen may result in unnecessary punishment due to ventilation being neglected or improperly handled. While ventilation itself extinguishes no fires, when used in an intelligent manner, it allows firemen to get at the fire more quickly, easily, and with less danger and hardship.

6. According to the above paragraph, the MOST important result of failure to apply the principles of ventilation at a fire may be   6.___

    A. loss of public confidence
    B. waste of water
    C. excessive use of equipment
    D. injury to firemen

7. It may be inferred from the above paragraph that the CHIEF advantage of ventilation is that it   7.___

    A. eliminates the need for gas masks
    B. reduces smoke damage
    C. permits firemen to work closer to the fire
    D. cools the fire

8. Knowledge of the principles of ventilation, as defined in the above paragraph, would be LEAST important in a fire in a   8._____

    A. tenement house   B. grocery store
    C. ship's hold   D. lumberyard

9. We may conclude from the above paragraph that for the well-trained and equipped fire-man, ventilation is   9._____

    A. a simple matter   B. rarely necessary
    C. relatively unimportant   D. a basic tool

Questions 10-13.

DIRECTIONS: Questions 10 through 13 are to be answered SOLELY on the basis of the following passage.

Fire exit drills should be established and held periodically to effectively train personnel to leave their working area promptly upon proper signal and to evacuate the building, speedily but without confusion. All fire exit drills should be carefully planned and carried out in a serious manner under rigid discipline so as to provide positive protection in the event of a real emergency. As a general rule, the local fire department should be furnished advance information regarding the exact date and time the exit drill is scheduled. When it is impossible to hold regular drills, written instructions should be distributed to all employees.

Depending upon individual circumstances, fires in warehouses vary from those of fast development that are almost instantly beyond any possibility of employee control to others of relatively slow development where a small readily attackable flame may be present for periods of time up to 15 minutes or more during which simple attack with fire extinguishers or small building hoses may prevent the fire development. In any case, it is characteristic of many warehouse fires that at a certain point in development they flash up to the top of the stack, increase heat quickly, and spread rapidly. There is a degree of inherent danger in attacking warehouse type fires, and all employees should be thoroughly trained in the use of the types of extinguishers or small hoses in the buildings and well instructed in the necessity of always staying between the fire and a direct pass to an exit.

10. Employees should be instructed that, when fighting a fire, they MUST   10._____

    A. try to control the blaze
    B. extinguish any fire in 15 minutes
    C. remain between the fire and a direct passage to the exit
    D. keep the fire between themselves and the fire exit

11. Whenever conditions are such that regular fire drills cannot be held, then which one of the following actions should be taken?   11._____

    A. The local fire department should be notified.
    B. Rigid discipline should be maintained during work hours.
    C. Personnel should be instructed to leave their working area by whatever means are available.
    D. Employees should receive fire drill procedures in writing.

12. The above passage indicates that the purpose of fire exit drills is to train employees to

    A. control a fire before it becomes uncontrollable
    B. act as firefighters
    C. leave the working area promptly
    D. be serious

12.___

13. According to the above passage, fire exit drills will prove to be of UTMOST effectiveness if

    A. employee participation is made voluntary
    B. they take place periodically
    C. the fire department actively participates
    D. they are held without advance planning

13.___

Questions 14-16.

DIRECTIONS: Questions 14 through 16 are to be answered SOLELY on the basis of the following paragraph.

The heat output from unit heaters will depend on how fast and how completely dry hot steam fills the unit core. For complete and fast air removal and rapid drainage of condensate, use a trap actuated by water or vapor (inverted bucket trap) and not a trap operated by temperature only (thermostatic or bellows trap). A temperature-actuated trap will hold back the hot condensate until it cools to a point where the thermal element opens. When this happens, the condensate backs up in the heater and reduces the heat output. With a water-actuated trap, this will not happen as the water or condensate is discharged as fast as it is formed.

14. On the basis of the information given in the above paragraph, it can be concluded that the PROPER type of trap to use for a unit heater is a(n) _____ trap.

    A. thermostatic   B. bellows-type
    C. inverted bucket   D. temperature

14.___

15. According to the above paragraph, the MAIN reason for using the type of trap specified for a unit heater is to

    A. bring the condensate up to steam temperature
    B. prevent reduction in the heat output of the unit heater
    C. permit cycling of the heater
    D. maintain constant temperature of condensate in the trap

15.___

16. As used in the above paragraph, the word *actuated* means MOST NEARLY

    A. clogged   B. operated   C. cleaned   D. vented

16.___

Question 17 -25.

DIRECTIONS: Questions 17 through 25 are to be answered SOLELY on the basis of the following passage. Each question consists of a statement. You are to indicate whether the statement is TRUE (T) or FALSE (F).

MOVING AN OFFICE

An office with all its equipment is sometimes moved during working hours. This is a difficult task and must be done in an orderly manner to avoid confusion. The operation should be planned in such a way as not to interrupt the progress of work usually done in the office and to make possible the accurate placement of the furniture and records in the new location. If the office moves to a place inside the same building, the desks and files are moved with all their contents. If the movement is to another building, the contents of each desk and file are placed in boxes. Each box is marked with a letter showing the particular section in the new quarters to which it is to be moved. Also marked on each box is the number of the desk or file on which the box is to be placed. Each piece of equipment must have a numbered tag. The number of each piece of equipment is put in soft chalk on the floor in the new office to show the proper location, and several floor plans are made to show where each piece of equipment goes. When the moving is done, someone is stationed at each of the several exits of the old office to see that each box or piece of equipment has its destination clearly marked on it. At the new office, someone stands at each of the several entrances with a copy of the floor plan and directs the placing of the furniture and equipment according to the floor plan. No one should interfere at this point with the arrangements shown on the plan. Improvements in arrangement can be considered and made at a later date.

17. It is a hard job to move an office from one place to another during working hours.   17.____

18. Confusion cannot be avoided if an office is moved during working hours.   18.____

19. The work usually done in an office must be stopped for the day when the office is moved during working hours.   19.____

20. If an office is moved from one floor to another in the same building, the contents of a desk are taken out and put into boxes for moving.   20.____

21. If boxes are used to hold material from desks when moving an office, the box is numbered the same as the desk on which it is to be put.   21.____

22. Letters are marked in soft chalk on the floor at the new quarters to show where the desks should go when moved.   22.____

23. When the moving begins, a person is put at each exit of the old office to check that each box and piece of equipment has clearly marked on it where it to go.   23.____

24. A person stationed at each entrance of the new quarters to direct the placing of the furniture and equipment has a copy of the floor plan of the new quarters.   24.____

25. If, while the furniture is being moved into the new office, a person helping at a doorway gets an idea of a better way to arrange the furniture, he should change the planned arrangement and make a record of the change.   25.____

KEY (CORRECT ANSWERS)

1.	A		11.	D
2.	C		12.	C
3.	D		13.	B
4.	B		14.	C
5.	C		15.	B
6.	D		16.	B
7.	C		17.	T
8.	D		18.	F
9.	D		19.	F
10.	C		20.	F

21.	T
22.	F
23.	T
24.	T
25.	F

TEST 2

Questions 1-4.

DIRECTIONS: Questions 1 through 4 are to be answered SOLELY on the basis of the following paragraph.

In all cases of homicide, members of the Police Department who investigate will make
every effort to obtain statements from dying persons. Such statements are of the greatest
importance to the District Attorney. In many cases, there may be a failure to solve the crime if
they are not taken. The principal element to be considered in taking the declaration of a dying
person is his mental attitude. In order to be admissible in evidence, the person must have no
hope of recovery. The patient will be fully interrogated on that point before a statement is
taken.

1. In cases of homicide, according to the above paragraph, members of the police force will   1._____

    A. try to change the mental attitude of the dying person
    B. attempt to obtain a statement from the dying person
    C. not give the information they obtain directly to the District Attorney
    D. be careful not to injure the dying person unnecessarily

2. The mental attitude of the person making the dying statement is of GREAT importance   2._____
    because it can determine, according to the above paragraph, whether the

    A. victim should be interrogated in the presence of witnesses
    B. victim will be willing to make a statement of any kind
    C. statement will tell the District Attorney who committed the crime
    D. the statement can be used as evidence

3. District Attorneys find that statements of a dying person are important, according to the   3._____
    above paragraph, because

    A. it may be that the victim will recover and then refuse to testify
    B. they are important elements in determining the mental attitude of the victim
    C. they present a point of view
    D. it may be impossible to punish the criminal without such a statement

4. A well-known gangster is found dying from a bullet wound. The patrolman first on the   4._____
    scene, in the presence of witnesses, tells the man that he is going to die and asks, *Who
    shot you?* The gangster says, *Jones shot me, but he hasn't killed me. I'll live to get him.*
    He then falls back dead. According to the above paragraph, this statement is

    A. *admissible* in evidence; the man was obviously speaking the truth
    B. *not admissible* in evidence; the man obviously did not believe that he was dying
    C. *admissible* in evidence; there were witnesses to the statement
    D. *not admissible* in evidence; the victim did not sign any statement and the evidence
       is merely hearsay

Questions 5-7.

DIRECTIONS: Questions 5 through 7 are to be answered SOLELY on the basis of the following paragraph.

The factors contributing to crime and delinquency are varied and complex. The home and its immediate environment have been found to be crucial in determining the behavior patterns of the individual, and criminality can frequently be traced to faulty family relationships and a bad neighborhood. But in the search for a clearer understanding of the underlying causes of delinquent and criminal behavior, the total environment must be taken into consideration.

5. According to the above paragraph, family relationships 5.___

    A. tend to become faulty in bad neighborhoods
    B. are important in determining the actions of honest people as well as criminals
    C. are the only important element in the understanding of causes of delinquency
    D. are determined by the total environment

6. According to the above paragraph, the causes of crime and delinquency are 6.___

    A. not simple   B. not meaningless
    C. meaningless   D. simple

7. According to the above paragraph, faulty family relationships FREQUENTLY are 7.___

    A. responsible for varied and complex results
    B. caused when one or both parents have a criminal behavior pattern
    C. independent of the total environment
    D. the cause of criminal acts

Questions 8-10.

DIRECTIONS: Questions 8 through 10 are to be answered SOLELY on the basis of the following paragraph.

A change in the specific problems which confront the police and in the methods for dealing with them has taken place in the last few decades. The automobile is a two-way symbol of this change in policing. It menaces every city with a complicated traffic problem and has speeded up the process of committing a crime and making a getaway, but at the same time has increased the effectiveness of police operations. However, the major concern of police departments continues to be the antisocial or criminal actions and behavior of human beings.

8. On the basis of the above paragraph, it can be stated that, for the most part, in the past 8.___
few decades the specific problems of a police force

    A. have changed but the general problems have not
    B. as well as the general problems have changed
    C. have remained the same but the general problems have changed
    D. as well as the general problems have remained the same

9. According to the above paragraph, advances in science and industry have, in general, 9.___
made the police

    A. operations less effective from the overall point of view
    B. operations more effective from the overall point of view
    C. abandon older methods of solving police problems
    D. concern themselves more with the antisocial acts of human beings

10. The automobile is a *two-way symbol,* according to the above paragraph, because its use   10.____

    A. has speeded up getting to and away from the scene of a crime
    B. both helps and hurts police operations
    C. introduces a new antisocial act–traffic violation–and does away with criminals like horse thieves
    D. both increases and decreases speed by introducing traffic problems

Questions 11-14.

DIRECTIONS: Questions 11 through 14 are to be answered SOLELY on the basis of the following passage on INSTRUCTIONS TO COIN AND TOKEN CASHIERS.

INSTRUCTIONS TO COIN AND TOKEN CASHIERS

Cashiers should reset the machine registers to an even starting number before commencing the day's work. Money bags received directly from collecting agents shall be counted and receipted for on the collecting agent's form. Each cashier shall be responsible for all coin or token bags accepted by him. He must examine all bags to be used for bank deposits for cuts and holes before placing them in use. Care must be exercised so that bags are not cut in opening them. Each bag must be opened separately and verified before another bag is opened. The machine register must be cleared before starting the count of another bag. The amount shown on the machine register must be compared with the amount on the bag tag. The empty bag must be kept on the table for re-examination should there be a difference between the amount on the bag tag and the amount on the machine register.

11. A cashier should BEGIN his day's assignment by   11.____

    A. counting and accepting all money bags
    B. resetting the counting machine register
    C. examining all bags for cuts and holes
    D. verifying the contents of all money bags

12. In verifying the amount of money in the bags received from the collecting agent, it is BEST to   12.____

    A. check the amount in one bag at a time
    B. base the total on the amount on the collecting agent's form
    C. repeat the total shown on the bag tag
    D. refer to the bank deposit receipt

13. A cashier is instructed to keep each empty coin bag on. his table while verifying its contents CHIEFLY because, long as the bag is on the table,   13.____

    A. it cannot be misplaced
    B. the supervisor can see how quickly the cashier works
    C. cuts and holes are easily noticed
    D. a recheck is possible in case the machine count disagrees with the bag tag total

14. The INSTRUCTIONS indicate that it is NOT proper procedure for a cashier to   14.___

    A. assume that coin bags are free of cuts and holes
    B. compare the machine register total with the total shown on the bag tag
    C. sign a form when he receives coin bags
    D. reset the machine register before starting the day's counting

Questions 15-17.

DIRECTIONS: Questions 15 through 17 are to be answered SOLELY on the basis of the following passage.

The mass media are an integral part of the daily life of virtually every American. Among these media the youngest, television, is the most pervasive. Ninety-five percent of American homes have at least one T.V. set, and on the average that set is in use for about 40 hours each week. The central place of television in American life makes this medium the focal point of a growing national concern over the effects of media portrayals of violence on the values, attitudes, and behavior of an ever increasing audience.

In our concern about violence and its causes, it is easy to make television a scapegoat. But we emphasize the fact that there is no simple answer to the problem of violence – no single explanation of its causes, and no single prescription for its control. It should be remembered that America also experienced high levels of crime and violence in periods before the advent of television.

The problem of balance, taste, and artistic merit in entertaining programs on television are complex. We cannot <u>countenance</u> government censorship of television. Nor would we seek to impose arbitrary limitations on programming which might jeopardize television's ability to deal in dramatic presentations with controversial social issues. Nonetheless, we are deeply troubled by television's constant portrayal of violence, not in any genuine attempt to focus artistic expression on the human condition, but rather in pandering to a public preoccupation with violence that television itself has helped to generate.

15. According to the above passage, television uses violence MAINLY   15.___

    A. to highlight the reality of everyday existence
    B. to satisfy the audience's hunger for destructive action
    C. to shape the values and attitudes of the public
    D. when it films documentaries concerning human conflict

16. Which one of the following statements is BEST supported by the above passage?   16.___

    A. Early American history reveals a crime pattern which is not related to television.
    B. Programs should give presentations of social issues and never portray violent acts.
    C. Television has proven that entertainment programs can easily make the balance between taste and artistic merit a simple matter.
    D. Values and behavior should be regulated by governmental censorship.

17. Of the following, which word has the same meaning as *countenance,* as used in the above passage?   17.___

    A. Approve   B. Exhibit   C. Oppose   D. Reject

DIRECTIONS: Questions 18 through 21 are to be answered SOLELY on the basis of the following passage.

Maintenance of leased or licensed areas on public parks or lands has always been a problem. A good rule to follow in the administration and maintenance of such areas is to limit the responsibility of any lessee or licensee to the maintenance of the structures and grounds essential to the efficient operation of the concession, not including areas for the general use of the public, such as picnic areas, public comfort stations, etc.; except where such facilities are leased to another public agency or where special conditions make such inclusion practicable, and where a good standard of maintenance can be assured and enforced. If local conditions and requirements are such that public use areas are included, adequate safeguards to the public should be written into contracts and enforced in their administration, to insure that maintenance by the concessionaire shall be equal to the maintenance standards for other park property.

18. According to the above passage, when an area on a public park is leased to a concessionaire, it is usually BEST to

18.____

    A. confine the responsibility of the concessionaire to operation of the facilities and leave the maintenance function to the park agency
    B. exclude areas of general public use from the maintenance obligation of the concessionaire
    C. make the concessionaire responsible for maintenance of the entire area including areas of general public use
    D. provide additional comfort station facilities for the area

19. According to the above passage, a valid reason for giving a concessionaire responsibility for maintenance of a picnic area within his leased area is that

19.____

    A. local conditions and requirements make it practicable
    B. more than half of the picnic area falls within his leased area
    C. the concessionaire has leased picnic facilities to another public agency
    D. the picnic area falls entirely within his leased area

20. According to the above passage, a precaution that should be taken when a concessionaire is made responsible for maintenance of an area of general public use in a park is

20.____

    A. making sure that another public agency has not previously been made responsible for this area
    B. providing the concessionaire with up-to-date equipment, if practicable
    C. requiring that the concessionaire take out adequate insurance for the protection of the public
    D. writing safeguards to the public into the contract

KEY (CORRECT ANSWERS)

1.	B		11.	B
2.	D		12.	A
3.	D		13.	D
4.	B		14.	A
5.	B		15.	B
6.	A		16.	A
7.	D		17.	A
8.	A		18.	B
9.	B		19.	A
10.	B		20.	D

TEST 3

Questions 1-5.

DIRECTIONS: Questions 1 through 5 are to be answered SOLELY on the basis of the following paragraph.

Physical inspections are an important tool for the examiner because he will have to decide the case in many instances on the basis of the inspection report. Most proceedings in a rent office are commenced by the filing of a written application or complaint by an interested party; that is, either the landlord or the tenant. Such an application or complaint must be filed in duplicate in order that the opposing party may be served with a copy of the application or complaint and thus be given an opportunity to answer and oppose it. Sometimes, a further opportunity is given the applicant to file a written rebuttal or reply to his adversary's answer. Often an examiner can make a determination or decision based on the written application, the answer, and the reply to the answer; and, of course, it would speed up operations if it were always possible to make decisions based on written documents only. Unfortunately, decisions can't always be made that way. There are numerous occasions where disputed issues of fact remain which cannot be resolved on the basis of the written statements of the parties. Typical examples are the following: The tenant claims that the refrigerator or stove or bathroom fixture is not functioning properly and the landlord denies this. It is obvious that in such cases an inspection of the accommodations is almost the only means of resolving such disputed issues.

1. According to the above paragraph,

    A. physical inspections are made in all cases
    B. physical inspections are seldom made
    C. it is sometimes possible to determine the facts in a case without a physical inspection
    D. physical inspections are made when it is necessary to verify the examiner's determination

1.____

2. According to the above paragraph, in MOST cases, proceedings are started by a(n)

    A. inspector discovering a violation
    B. oral complaint by a tenant or landlord
    C. request from another agency, such as the Building Department
    D. written complaint by a tenant or landlord

2.____

3. According to the above paragraph, when a tenant files an application with the rent office, the landlord is

    A. not told about the proceeding until after the examiner makes his determination
    B. given the duplicate copy of the application
    C. notified by means of an inspector visiting the premises
    D. not told about the proceeding until after the inspector has visited the Premises

3.____

4. As used in the above paragraph, the word *disputed* means MOST NEARLY

    A. unsettled   B. contested
    C. definite   D. difficult

4.____

5. As used in the above paragraph, the word *resolved* means MOST NEARLY   5.___

    A. settled   B. fixed   C. helped   D. amended

Questions 6-10.

DIRECTIONS: Questions 6 through 10 are to be answered SOLELY on the basis of the following paragraph.

    The examiner should order or request an inspection of the housing accommodations. His request for a physical inspection should be in writing, identify the accommodations and the landlord and the tenant, and specify <u>precisely</u> just what the inspector is to look for and report on. Unless this request is specific and lists <u>in detail</u> every item which the examiner wishes to be reported, the examiner will find that the inspection has not served its purpose and that even with the inspector's report, he is still in no position to decide the case due to loose ends which have not been completely tied up. The items that the examiner is interested in should be separately numbered on the inspection request and the same number referred to in the inspector's report. You can see what it would mean if an inspector came back with a report that did not cover everything. It may mean a tremendous waste of time and often require a re-inspection.

6. According to the above paragraph, the inspector makes an inspection on the order of   6.___

    A. the landlord
    B. the tenant
    C. the examiner
    D. both the landlord and the tenant

7. According to the above paragraph, the reason for numbering each item that an inspector reports on is so that   7.___

    A. the report is neat
    B. the report can be easily read and referred to
    C. none of the examiner's requests for information is missed
    D. the report will be specific

8. The one of the following items that is NOT necessarily included in the request for inspection is   8.___

    A. location of dwelling   B. name of landlord
    C. item to be checked   D. type of building

9. As used in the above paragraph, the word precisely means MOST NEARLY   9.___

    A. exactly   B. generally   C. Usually   D. strongly

10. As used in the above paragraph, the words in detail mean MOST NEARLY   10.___

    A. clearly   B. item by item
    C. substantially   D. completely

Questions 11-13.

DIRECTIONS: Questions 11 through 13 are to be answered SOLELY on the basis of the following passage.

The agreement under which a tenant rents property from a landlord is known as a lease. Generally speaking, leases are classified as either short-term or long-term in duration. They are further subdivided according to the method used to determine the amount of periodic rent payments. Of the following types of lease in use, the more commonly used ones are the following:

1. The straight or fixed lease is one in which rent may be paid in equal amounts throughout the duration of the lease. These are usually restricted to short-term leasing, or somewhat longer-term if clauses in the lease provide for periodic escalation of payments as the economy shifts.
2. Percentage leasing, used for short-term commercial leasing, provides the landlord with a stipulated percentage of a tenant's gross sales from goods and services sold on the premises, in addition to a fixed amount of rent.
3. The net lease, generally long-term (ten years or more), requires the tenant to pay all operating costs, including real estate taxes and insurance. In a net-net lease, the tenant further agrees to meet mortgage interest and principal payments.
4. An escalated lease, which is a long-term lease, requires rent to be of a stipulated base amount which periodically is subject to escalation in accordance with cost-of-living index scales, or in direct proportion to taxes, insurance, and operating costs.

11. Based on the information given in the passage, which type of lease is MOST likely to be advantageous to a landlord if there is a high rate of inflation? _____ lease. 11._____

    A. Fixed   B. Percentage   C. Net   D. Escalated

12. On the basis of the above passage, which types of lease would generally be MOST suitable for a well-established textile company which requires permanent facilities for its large operations? 12._____
    _____ lease and _____ lease.

    A. Percentage; escalated   B. Escalated; net
    C. Straight; net   D. Straight; percentage

13. According to the above passage, the ONLY type of lease which assures the same amount of rent throughout a specified interval is the _____ lease. 13._____

    A. straight   B. percentage   C. net-net   D. escalated

Questions 14-15.

DIRECTIONS: Questions 14 and 15 are to be answered SOLELY on the basis of the following passage.

If you like people, if you seek contact with them rather than hide yourself in a corner, if you study your fellow men sympathetically, if you try consistently to contribute something to their success and happiness, if you are reasonably generous with your thought and your time, if you have a partial reserve with everyone but a seeming reserve with no one, you will get along with your superiors, your subordinates, and the human race.

By the scores of thousands, precepts and platitudes have been written for the guidance of personal conduct. The odd part of it is that, despite all of this labor, most of the frictions in modern society arise from the individual's feeling of inferiority, his false pride, his vanity, his unwillingness to yield space to any other man and his consequent urge to throw his own weight around. Goethe said that the quality which best enables a man to renew his own life, in his relation to others, is his capability of renouncing particular things at the right moment in order warmly to embrace something new in the next.

14. On the basis of the above passage, it may be INFERRED that   14.___

    A. a person should be unwilling to renounce privileges
    B. a person should realize that loss of a desirable job assignment may come at an opportune moment
    C. it is advisable for a person to maintain a considerable amount of reserve in his relationship with unfamiliar people
    D. people should be ready to contribute generously to a worthy charity

15. Of the following, the MOST valid implication made by the above passage is that   15.___

    A. a wealthy person who spends a considerable amount of money entertaining his friends is not really getting along with them
    B. if a person studies his fellow men carefully and impartially, he will tend to have good relationships with them
    C. individuals who maintain seemingly little reserve in their relationships with people have in some measure overcome their own feelings of inferiority
    D. most precepts that have been written for the guidance of personal conduct in relationships with other people are invalid

Questions 16-17.

DIRECTIONS: Questions 16 and 17 are to be answered SOLELY on the basis of the following passage.

When a design for a new bank note of the Federal Government has been prepared by the Bureau of Engraving and Printing and has been approved by the Secretary of the Treasury, the engravers begin the work of cutting the design in steel. No one engraver does all the work. Each man is a specialist. One works only on portraits, another on lettering, another on scroll work, and so on. Each engraver, with a steel tool known as a graver, and aided by a powerful magnifying glass, carefully carves his portion of the design into the steel. He knows that one false cut or a slip of his tool, or one miscalculation of width or depth of line, may destroy the merit of his work. A single mistake means that months or weeks of labor will have been in vain. The Bureau is proud of the fact that no counterfeiter ever has duplicated the excellent work of its expert engravers.

16. According to the above passage, each engraver in the Bureau of Engraving and Printing   16.___

    A. must be approved by the Secretary of the Treasury before he can begin work on the design for a new bank note
    B. is responsible for engraving a complete design of a new bank note by himself
    C. designs new bank notes and submits them for approval to the Secretary of the Treasury
    D. performs only a specific part of the work of engraving a design for a new bank note

17. According to the above passage,

    17.____

    A. an engraver's tools are not available to a counterfeiter
    B. mistakes made in engraving a design can be corrected immediately with little delay in the work of the Bureau
    C. the skilled work of the engravers has not been successfully reproduced by counterfeiter
    D. careful carving and cutting by the engravers is essential to prevent damage to equipment

Questions 18-21.

DIRECTIONS: Questions 18 through 21 are to be answered SOLELY on the basis of the following passage.

In the late fifties, the average American housewife spent $4.50 per day for a family of four on food and 5.15 hours in food preparation, if all of her food was *home prepared;* she spent $5.80 per day and 3.25 hours if all of her food was purchased *partially prepared;* and $6.70 per day and 1.65 hours if all of her food was purchased *ready to serve.*

Americans spent about 20 billion dollars for food products in 1941. They spent nearly 70 billion dollars in 1958. They spent 25 percent of their cash income on food in 1958. For the same kinds and quantities of food that consumers bought in 1941, they would have spent only 16% of their cash income in 1958. It is obvious that our food does cost more. Many factors contribute to this increase besides the additional cost that might be attributed to processing. Consumption of more expensive food items, higher marketing margins, and more food eaten in restaurants are other factors.

The Census of Manufacturers gives some indication of the total bill for processing. The value added by manufacturing of food and kindred products amounted to 3.5 billion of the 20 billion dollars spent for food in 1941. In the year 1958, the comparable figure had climbed to 14 billion dollars.

18. According to the above passage, the cash income of Americans in 1958 was MOST NEARLY _____ billion dollars.

    18.____

    A. 11.2   B. 17.5   C. 70   D. 280

19. According to the above passage, if Americans bought the same kinds and quantities of food in 1958 as they did in 1941, they would have spent MOST NEARLY _____ billion dollars.

    19.____

    A. 20   B. 45   C. 74   D. 84

20. According to the above passage, the percent increase in money spent for food in 1958 over 1941, as compared with the percentage increase in money spent for food processing in the same years,

    20.____

    A. was greater
    B. was less
    C. was the same
    D. cannot be determined from the passage

21. In 1958, an American housewife who bought all of her food ready-to-serve saved in time, as compared with the housewife who prepared all of her food at home

    21.___

    A. 1.6 hours daily
    B. 1.9 hours daily
    C. 3.5 hours daily
    D. an amount of time which cannot be determined from the above passage

Questions 22-25.

DIRECTIONS: Questions 22 through 25 are to be answered SOLELY on the basis of the following passage.

Any member of the retirement system who is in city service, who files a proper application for service credit and agrees to deductions from his compensation at triple his normal rate of contribution, shall be credited with a period of city service previous to the beginning of his present membership in the retirement system. The period of service credited shall be equal to the period throughout which such triple deductions are made, but may not exceed the total of the city service the member rendered between his first day of eligibility for membership in the retirement system and the day he last became a member. After triple contributions for all of the first three years of service credit claimed, the remaining service credit may be purchased by a single payment of the sum of the remaining payments. If the total time purchasable exceeds ten years, triple contributions may be made for one-half of such time, and the remaining time purchased by a single payment of the sum of the remaining payments. Credit for service acquired in the above manner may be used only in determining the amount of any retirement benefit. Eligibility for such benefit will, in all cases, be based upon service rendered after the employee's membership last began, and will be exclusive of service credit purchased as described below.

22. According to the above passage, in order to obtain credit for city service previous to the beginning of an employee's present membership in the retirement system, the employee must

    22.___

    A. apply for the service credit and consent to additional contributions to the retirement system
    B. apply for the service credit before he renews his membership in the retirement system
    C. have previous city service which does not exceed ten years
    D. make contributions to the retirement system for three years

23. According to the information in the above passage, credit for city service previous to the beginning of an employee's present membership in the retirement system, is

    23.___

    A. credited up to a maximum of ten years
    B. credited to any member of the retirement system
    C. used in determining the amount of the employee's benefits
    D. used in establishing the employee's eligibility to receive benefits

24. According to the information in the above passage, a member of the retirement system may purchase service credit for   24.____

    A. the period of time between his first day of eligibility for membership in the retirement system and the date he applies for the service credit
    B. one-half of the total of his previous city service if the total time exceeds ten years
    C. the period of time throughout which triple deductions are made
    D. the period of city service between his first day of eligibility for membership in the retirement system and the day he last became a member

25. Suppose that a member of the retirement system has filed an application for service credit for five years of previous city service.   25.____
Based on the information in the above passage, the employee may purchase credit for this previous city service by making

    A. triple contributions for three years
    B. triple contributions for one-half of the time and a single payment of the sum of the remaining payments
    C. triple contributions for three years and a single payment of the sum of the remaining payments
    D. a single payment of the sum of the payments

KEY (CORRECT ANSWERS)

1.	C		11.	D
2.	D		12.	B
3.	B		13.	A
4.	B		14.	B
5.	A		15.	C
6.	C		16.	D
7.	C		17.	C
8.	D		18.	D
9.	A		19.	B
10.	B		20.	B

21.	C
22.	A
23.	C
24.	D
25.	C

PREPARING WRITTEN MATERIAL

EXAMINATION SECTION
TEST 1

DIRECTIONS : Each of the sentences in the tests that follow may be classified under one of the following four categories:

    A. *Incorrect* because of faulty grammar or sentence structure
    B. *Incorrect* because of faulty punctuation
    C. *Incorrect* because of faulty capitalization
    D. *Correct*

      Examine each sentence carefully to determine under which of the above four options it is best classified. Then, in the space on the right, print the capital letter preceding the option which is the *BEST* of the four suggested above.
      (Each incorrect sentence contains but one type of error. Consider a sentence to be correct if it contains none of the types of errors mentioned, even though there may be other correct ways of expressing the same thought.)

1.   This fact, together with those brought out at the previous meeting, prove that the schedule is satisfactory to the employees.   1._____

2.   Like many employees in scientific fields, the work of bookkeepers and accountants requires accuracy and neatness.   2._____

3.   "What can I do for you," the secretary asked as she motioned to the visitor to take a seat.   3._____

4.   Our representative, Mr. Charles will call on you next week to determine whether or not your claim has merit.   4._____

5.   We expect you to return in the spring; please do not disappoint us.   5._____

6.   Any supervisor, who disregards the just complaints of his subordinates, is remiss in the performance of his duty.   6._____

7.   Because she took less than an hour for lunch is no reason for permitting her to leave before five o'clock.   7._____

8.   "Miss Smith," said the supervisor, "Please arrange a meeting of the staff for two o'clock on Monday."   8._____

9.   A private company's vacation and sick leave allowance usually differs considerably from a public agency.   9._____

10.   Therefore, in order to increase the efficiency of operations in the department, a report on the recommended changes in procedures was presented to the departmental committee in charge of the program.   10._____

11.   We told him to assign the work to whoever was available.   11._____

12.   Since John was the most efficient of any other employee in the bureau, he received the highest service rating.   12._____

13. Only those members of the national organization who resided in the middle West
attended the conference in Chicago.

13.____

14. The question of whether the office manager has as yet attained, or indeed can ever hope
to secure professional status is one which has been discussed for years.

14.____

15. No one knew who to blame for the error which, we later discovered, resulted in a considerable loss of time.

15.____

KEY (CORRECT ANSWERS)

1.	A		6.	B	
2.	A		7.	A	
3.	B		8.	C	
4.	B		9.	A	
5.	D		10.	D	

11. D
12. A
13. C
14. B
15. A

TEST 2

DIRECTIONS : Each of the sentences in the tests that follow may be classified under one of the following four categories:

      A. *Incorrect* because of faulty grammar or sentence structure
      B. *Incorrect* because of faulty punctuation
      C. *Incorrect* because of faulty capitalization
      D. *Correct*

1. The National alliance of Businessmen is trying to persuade private businesses to hire youth in the summertime.   1.____

2. The supervisor who is on vacation, is in charge of processing vouchers.   2.____

3. The activity of the committee at its conferences is always stimulating.   3.____

4. After checking the addresses again, the letters went to the mailroom.   4.____

5. The director, as well as the employees, are interested in sharing the dividends.   5.____

———

KEY (CORRECT ANSWERS)

1. C
2. B
3. D
4. A
5. A

TEST 3

DIRECTIONS: In each of the following groups of sentences, one of the four sentences is faulty in grammar, punctuation, or capitalization. Select the incorrect sentence in each case.

1.   A. Sailing down the bay was a thrilling experience for me.   1.____
      B. He was not consulted about your joining the club.
      C. This story is different than the one I told you yesterday.
      D. There is no doubt about his being the best player.

2.   A. He maintains there is but one road to world peace.   2.____
      B. It is common knowledge that a child sees much he is not supposed to see.
      C. Much of the bitterness might have been avoided if arbitration had been resorted to earlier in the meeting.
      D. The man decided it would be advisable to marry a girl somewhat younger than him.

3.   A. In this book, the incident I liked least is where the hero tries to put out the forest fire.   3.____
      B. Learning a foreign language will undoubtedly give a person a better understanding of his mother tongue.
      C. His actions made us wonder what he planned to do next.
      D. Because of the war, we were unable to travel during the summer vacation.

4.   A. The class had no sooner become interested in the lesson than the dismissal bell rang.   4.____
      B. There is little agreement about the kind of world to be planned at the peace conference.
      C. "Today," said the teacher, "we shall read 'The Wind in the Willows.' I am sure you'll like it.
      D. The terms of the legal settlement of the family quarrel handicapped both sides for many years.

5.   A. I was so suprised that I was not able to say a word.   5.____
      B. She is taller than any other member of the class.
      C. It would be much more preferable if you were never seen in his company.
      D. We had no choice but to excuse her for being late.

KEY (CORRECT ANSWERS)

1. C
2. D
3. A
4. C
5. C

TEST 4

DIRECTIONS: In each of the following groups of sentences, one of the four sentences is faulty in grammar, punctuation, or capitalization. Select the incorrect sentence in each case.

1. A. Please send me these data at the earliest opportunity.
    B. The loss of their material proved to be a severe handicap.
    C. My principal objection to this plan is that it is impracticable.
    D. The doll had laid in the rain for an hour and was ruined.

    1._____

2. A. The garden scissors, left out all night in the rain, were in a badly rusted condition.
    B. The girls felt bad about the misunderstanding which had arisen.
    C. Sitting near the campfire, the old man told John and I about many exciting adventures he had had.
    D. Neither of us is in a position to undertake a task of that magnitude.

    2._____

3. A. The general concluded that one of the three roads would lead to the besieged city.
    B. The children didn't, as a rule, do hardly anything beyond what they were told to do.
    C. The reason the girl gave for her negligence was that she had acted on the spur of the moment.
    D. The daffodils and tulips look beautiful in that blue vase.

    3._____

4. A. If I was ten years older, I should be interested in this work.
    B. Give the prize to whoever has drawn the best picture.
    C. When you have finished reading the book, take it back to the library.
    D. My drawing is as good as or better than yours.

    4._____

5. A. He asked me whether the substance was animal or vegetable.
    B. An apple which is unripe should not be eaten by a child.
    C. That was an insult to me who am your friend.
    D. Some spy must of reported the matter to the enemy.

    5._____

6. A. Limited time makes quoting the entire message impossible.
    B. Who did she say was going?
    C. The girls in your class have dressed more dolls this year than we.
    D. There was such a large amount of books on the floor that I couldn't find a place for my rocking chair.

    6._____

7. A. What with his sleeplessness and his ill health, he was unable to assume any responsibility for the success of the meeting.
    B. If I had been born in February, I should be celebrating my birthday soon.
    C. In order to prevent breakage, she placed a sheet of paper between each of the plates when she packed them.
    D. After the spring shower, the violets smelled very sweet.

    7._____

8. A. He had laid the book down very reluctantly before the end of the lesson.
    B. The dog, I am sorry to say, had lain on the bed all night.
    C. The cloth was first lain on a flat surface; then it was pressed with a hot iron.
    D. While we were in Florida, we lay in the sun until we were noticeably tanned.

    8._____

9. A. If John was in New York during the recent holiday season, I have no doubt he spent   9.___
      most of his time with his parents.
   B. How could he enjoy the television program; the dog was barking and the baby
      was crying.
   C. When the problem was explained to the class, he must have been asleep.
   D. She wished that her new dress were finished so that she could go to the party.

10. A. The engine not only furnishes power but light and heat as well.   10.___
    B. You're aware that we've forgotten whose guilt was established, aren't you?
    C. Everybody knows that the woman made many sacrifices for her children.
    D. A man with his dog and gun is a familiar sight in this neighborhood.

———

KEY (CORRECT ANSWERS)

1.	D	6.	D
2.	C	7.	B
3.	B	8.	C
4.	A	9.	B
5.	D	10.	A

———

TEST 5

DIRECTIONS: Each of Questions 1 to 15 consists of a sentence which may be classified appropriately under one of the following four categories:
   A.   *Incorrect* because of faulty grammar
   B.   *Incorrect* because of faulty punctuation
   C.   *Incorrect* because of faulty spelling
   D.   *Correct*

Examine each sentence carefully. Then, print, in the space on the right, the letter preceding the category which is the best of the four suggested above.

(Note: Each incorrect sentence contains only one type of error. Consider a sentence correct if it contains no errors, although there may be other correct ways of writing the sentence.)

1.   Of the two employees, the one in our office is the most efficient.   1._____

2.   No one can apply or even understand, the new rules and regulations.   2._____

3.   A large amount of supplies were stored in the empty office.   3._____

4.   If an employee is occassionally asked to work overtime, he should do so willingly.   4._____

5.   It is true that the new procedures are difficult to use but, we are certain that you will learn them quickly.   5._____

6.   The office manager said that he did not know who would be given a large allotment under the new plan.   6._____

7.   It was at the supervisor's request that the clerk agreed to postpone his vacation.   7._____

8.   We do not believe that it is necessary for both he and the clerk to attend the conference.   8._____

9.   All employees, who display perseverance, will be given adequate recognition.   9._____

10.   He regrets that some of us employees are dissatisfied with our new assignments.   10._____

11.   "Do you think that the raise was merited," asked the supervisor?   11._____

12.   The new manual of procedure is a valuable supplament to our rules and regulations.   12._____

13.   The typist admitted that she had attempted to pursuade the other employees to assist her in her work.   13._____

14.   The supervisor asked that all amendments to the regulations be handled by you and I. 14._____

15.   The custodian seen the boy who broke the window.   15._____

KEY (CORRECT ANSWERS)

1.	A		6.	D
2.	B		7.	D
3.	A		8.	A
4.	C		9.	B
5.	B		10.	D

11.	B
12.	C
13.	C
14.	A
15.	A

PREPARING WRITTEN MATERIAL

PARAGRAPH REARRANGEMENT
COMMENTARY

The sentences which follow are in scrambled order. You are to rearrange them in proper order and indicate the letter choice containing the correct answer at the space at the right.

Each group of sentences in this section is actually a paragraph presented in scrambled order. Each sentence in the group has a place in that paragraph; no sentence is to be left out. You are to read each group of sentences and decide upon the best order in which to put the sentences so as to form as well-organized paragraph.

The questions in this section measure the ability to solve a problem when all the facts relevant to its solution are not given.

More specifically, certain positions of responsibility and authority require the employee to discover connections between events sometimes, apparently, unrelated. In order to do this, the employee will find it necessary to correctly infer that unspecified events have probably occurred or are likely to occur. This ability becomes especially important when action must be taken on incomplete information.

Accordingly, these questions require competitors to choose among several suggested alternatives, each of which presents a different sequential arrangement of the events. Competitors must choose the MOST logical of the suggested sequences.

In order to do so, they may be required to draw on general knowledge to infer missing concepts or events that are essential to sequencing the given events. Competitors should be careful to infer only what is essential to the sequence. The plausibility of the wrong alternatives will always require the inclusion of unlikely events or of additional chains of events which are NOT essential to sequencing the given events.

It's very important to remember that you are looking for the best of the four possible choices, and that the best choice of all may not even be one of the answers you're given to choose from.

There is no one right way to solve these problems. Many people have found it helpful to first write out the order of the sentences, as they would have arranged them, on their scrap paper before looking at the possible answers. If their optimum answer is there, this can save them some time. If it isn't, this method can still give insight into solving the problem. Others find it most helpful to just go through each of the possible choices, contrasting each as they go along. You should use whatever method feels comfortable, and works, for you.

While most of these types of questions are not that difficult, we've added a higher percentage of the difficult type, just to give you more practice. Usually there are only one or two questions on this section that contain such subtle distinctions that you're unable to answer confidently, and you then may find yourself stuck deciding between two possible choices, neither of which you're sure about.

EXAMINATION SECTION
TEST 1

DIRECTIONS: The sentences that follow are in scrambled order. You are to rearrange them in proper order and indicate the letter choice containing the correct answer. *PRINT THE LETTER OF THE CORRECT ANSWER IN THE SPACE AT THE RIGHT.*

1. Below are four statements labeled W., X., Y., and Z.   1.____
    W.   He was a strict and fanatic drillmaster.
    X.   The word is always used in a derogatory sense and generally shows resentment and anger on the part of the user.
    Y.   It is from the name of this Frenchman that we derive our English word, martinet.
    Z.   Jean Martinet was the Inspector-General of Infantry during the reign of King Louis XIV.
    The *PROPER* order in which these sentences should be placed in a paragraph is:

    A. X, Z, W, Y   B. X, Z, Y, W   C. Z, W, Y, X   D. Z, Y, W, X

2. In the following paragraph, the sentences which are numbered, have been jumbled.   2.____
    1.   Since then it has undergone changes.
    2.   It was incorporated in 1955 under the laws of the State of New York.
    3.   Its primary purpose, a cleaner city, has, however, remained the same.
    4.   The Citizens Committee works in cooperation with the Mayor's Inter-departmental Committee for a Clean City.
    The order in which these sentences should be arranged to form a well-organized paragraph is:

    A. 2, 4, 1, 3   B. 3, 4, 1, 2   C. 4, 2, 1, 3   D. 4, 3, 2, 1

Questions 3-5.

DIRECTIONS: The sentences listed below are part of a meaningful paragraph but they are not given in their proper order. You are to decide what would be the *best order* in which to put the sentences so as to form a well-organized paragraph. Each sentence has a place in the paragraph; there are no extra sentences. You are then to answer questions 3 to 5 inclusive on the basis of your rearrangements of these scrambled sentences into a properly organized paragraph.

In 1887 some insurance companies organized an Inspection Department to advise their clients on all phases of fire prevention and protection. Probably this has been due to the smaller annual fire losses in Great Britain than in the United States. It tests various fire prevention devices and appliances and determines manufacturing hazards and their safeguards. Fire research began earlier in the United States and is more advanced than in Great Britain. Later they established a laboratory specializing in electrical, mechanical, hydraulic, and chemical fields.

3. When the five sentences are arranged in proper order, the paragraph starts with the sentence which begins   3.____

    A. "In 1887..."   B. "Probably this ..."   C. "It tests ..."
    D. "Fire research ..."   E. "Later they ..."

4. In the last sentence listed above, "they" refers to   4.____

    A. insurance companies
    B. the United States and Great Britain
    C. the Inspection Department
    D. clients
    E. technicians

5. When the above paragraph is properly arranged, it ends with the words   5.____

    A. "... and protection."   B. "... the United States."
    C. "... their safeguards."   D. "... in Great Britain."
    E. "... chemical fields."

KEY (CORRECT ANSWERS)

    1. C
    2. C
    3. D
    4. A
    5. C

TEST 2

DIRECTIONS: In each of the questions numbered 1 through 5, several sentences are given. For each question, choose as your answer the group of numbers that represents the *most logical* order of these sentences if they were arranged in paragraph form. *PRINT THE LETTER OF THE CORRECT ANSWER IN THE SPACE AT THE RIGHT.*

1. 1. It is established when one shows that the landlord has prevented the tenant's enjoyment of his interest in the property leased.
    2. Constructive eviction is the result of a breach of the covenant of quiet enjoyment implied in all leases.
    3. In some parts of the United States, it is not complete until the tenant vacates within a reasonable time.
    4. Generally, the acts must be of such serious and permanent character as to deny the tenant the enjoyment of his possessing rights.
    5. In this event, upon abandonment of the premises, the tenant's liability for that ceases.

    The CORRECT answer is:

    A. 2, 1, 4, 3, 5   B. 5, 2, 3, 1, 4   C. 4, 3, 1, 2, 5
    D. 1, 3, 5, 4, 2

1.____

2. 1. The powerlessness before private and public authorities that is the typical experience of the slum tenant is reminiscent of the situation of blue-collar workers all through the nineteenth century.
    2. Similarly, in recent years, this chapter of history has been reopened by anti-poverty groups which have attempted to organize slum tenants to enable them to bargain collectively with their landlords about the conditions of their tenancies.
    3. It is familiar history that many of the workers remedied their condition by joining together and presenting their demands collectively.
    4. Like the workers, tenants are forced by the conditions of modern life into substantial dependence on these who possess great political arid economic power.
    5. What's more, the very fact of dependence coupled with an absence of education and self-confidence makes them hesitant and unable to stand up for what they need from those in power.

    The CORRECT answer is:

    A. 5, 4, 1, 2, 3   B. 2, 3, 1, 5, 4   C. 3, 1, 5, 4, 2
    D. 1, 4, 5, 3, 2

2.____

3. 1. A railroad, for example, when not acting as a common carrier may contract away responsibility for its own negligence.
    2. As to a landlord, however, no decision has been found relating to the legal effect of a clause shifting the statutory duty of repair to the tenant.
    3. The courts have not passed on the validity of clauses relieving the landlord of this duty and liability.
    4. They have, however, upheld the validity of exculpatory clauses in other types of contracts.
    5. Housing regulations impose a duty upon the landlord to maintain leased premises in safe condition.

3.____

6. As another example, a bailee may limit his liability except for gross negligence, willful acts, or fraud.

The CORRECT answer is:

A. 2, 1, 6, 4, 3, 5   B. 1, 3, 4, 5, 6, 2   C. 3, 5, 1, 4, 2, 6
D. 5, 3, 4, 1, 6, 2

4. 1. Since there are only samples in the building, retail or consumer sales are generally eschewed by mart occupants, and in some instances, rigid controls are maintained to limit entrance to the mart only to those persons engaged in retailing.
    2. Since World War I, in many larger cities, there has developed a new type of property, called the mart building.
    3. It can, therefore, be used by wholesalers and jobbers for the display of sample merchandise.
    4. This type of building is most frequently a multi-storied, finished interior property which is a cross between a retail arcade and a loft building.
    5. This limitation enables the mart occupants to ship the orders from another location after the retailer or dealer makes his selection from the samples.

     4.____

The CORRECT answer is:

A. 2, 4, 3, 1, 5   B. 4, 3, 5, 1, 2   C. 1, 3, 2, 4, 5
D. 1, 4, 2, 3, 5

5. 1. In general, staff-line friction reduces the distinctive contribution of staff personnel.
    2. The conflicts, however, introduce an uncontrolled element into the managerial system.
    3. On the other hand, the natural resistance of the line to staff innovations probably usefully restrains over-eager efforts to apply untested procedures on a large scale.
    4. Under such conditions, it is difficult to know when valuable ideas are being sacrificed.
    5. The relatively weak position of staff, requiring accommodation to the line, tends to restrict their ability to engage in free, experimental innovation.

     5.____

The CORRECT answer is:

A. 4, 2, 3, 1, 3   B. 1, 5, 3, 2, 4   C. 5, 3, 1, 2, 4
D. 2, 1, 4, 5, 3

KEY (CORRECT ANSWERS)

1. A
2. D
3. D
4. A
5. B

TEST 3

DIRECTIONS: Questions 1 through 4 consist of six sentences which can be arranged in a logical sequence. For each question, select the choice which places the numbered sentences in the *most logical* sequence. *PRINT THE LETTER OF THE CORRECT ANSWER IN THE SPACE AT THE RIGHT.*

1.   1. The burden of proof as to each issue is determined before trial and remains upon the same party throughout the trial.   1.____
     2. The jury is at liberty to believe one witness' testimony as against a number of contradictory witnesses.
     3. In a civil case, the party bearing the burden of proof is required to prove his contention by a fair preponderance of the evidence.
     4. However, it must be noted that a fair preponderance of evidence does not necessarily mean a greater number of witnesses.
     5. The burden of proof is the burden which rests upon one of the parties to an action to persuade the trier of the facts, generally the jury, that a proposition he asserts is true.
     6. If the evidence is equally balanced, or if it leaves the jury in such doubt as to be unable to decide the controversy either way, judgment must be given against the party upon whom the burden of proof rests.
     The CORRECT answer is:

     A. 3, 2, 5, 4, 1, 6   B. 1, 2, 6, 5, 3, 4   C. 3, 4, 5, 1, 2, 6
     D. 5, 1, 3, 6, 4, 2

2.   1. If a parent is without assets and is unemployed, he cannot be convicted of the crime of non-support of a child.   2.____
     2. The term "sufficient ability" has been held to mean sufficient financial ability.
     3. It does not matter if his unemployment is by choice or unavoidable circumstances.
     4. If he fails to take any steps at all, he may be liable to prosecution for endangering the welfare of a child.
     5. Under the penal law, a parent is responsible for the support of his minor child only if the parent is "of sufficient ability."
     6. An indigent parent may meet his obligation by borrowing money or by seeking aid under the provisions of the Social Welfare Law.
     The CORRECT answer is:

     A. 6, 1, 5, 3, 2, 4   B. 1, 3, 5, 2, 4, 6   C. 5, 2, 1, 3, 6, 4
     D. 1, 6, 4, 5, 2, 3

3. 1. Consider, for example, the case of a rabble rouser who urges a group of twenty
        people to go out and break the windows of a nearby factory.
    2. Therefore, the law fills the indicated gap with the crime of inciting to riot.
    3. A person is considered guilty of inciting to riot when he urges ten or more per-
        sons to engage in tumultuous and violent conduct of a kind likely to create public
        alarm.
    4. However, if he has not obtained the cooperation of at least four people, he can-
        not be charged with unlawful assembly.
    5. The charge of inciting to riot was added to the law to cover types of conduct
        which cannot be classified as either the crime of "riot" or the crime of "unlawful
        assembly."
    6. If he acquires the acquiescence of at least four of them, he is guilty of unlawful
        assembly even if the project does not materialize.
    The CORRECT answer is:

    A. 3, 5, 1, 6, 4, 2   B. 5, 1, 4, 6, 2, 3   C. 3, 4, 1, 5, 2, 6
    D. 5, 1, 4, 6, 3, 2

4. 1. If, however, the rebuttal evidence presents an issue of credibility, it is for the jury to
        determine whether the presumption has, in fact, been destroyed.
    2. Once sufficient evidence to the contrary is introduced, the presumption disap-
        pears from the trial.
    3. The effect of a presumption is to place the burden upon the adversary to come
        forward with evidence to rebut the presumption.
    4. When a presumption is overcome and ceases to exist in the case, the fact or
        facts which gave rise to the presumption still remain.
    5. Whether a presumption has been overcome is ordinarily a question for the court.
    6. Such information may furnish a basis for a logical inference.
    The CORRECT answer is:

    A. 4, 6, 2, 5, 1, 3   B. 3, 2, 5, 1, 4, 6   C. 5, 3, 6, 4, 2, 1
    D. 5, 4, 1, 2, 6, 3

_____

KEY (CORRECT ANSWERS)

1. D
2. C
3. A
4. B

_____

INTERPRETING STATISTICAL DATA
GRAPHS, CHARTS AND TABLES
TEST 1

DIRECTIONS: Each question or incomplete statement is followed by several suggested answers or completions. Select the one that BEST answers the question or completes the statement. *PRINT THE LETTER OF THE CORRECT ANSWER IN THE SPACE AT THE RIGHT.*

Questions 1-5.

DIRECTIONS: Questions 1 through 5 are to be answered SOLELY on the basis of the following chart.

DUPLICATION JOBS

JOB. NO.	DATES Submitted	DATES Required	DATES Completed	PROCESS	NO. OF ORIGINALS	NO. OF COPIES OF EACH ORIGINAL	REQUEST- ING UNIT
324	6/22	6/25	6/25	Xerox	14	25	Research
325	6/25	6/27	6/28	Kodak	10	125	Training
326	6/25	6/25	6/25	Xerox	12	11	Budget
327	6/25	6/27	6/26	Press	17	775	Admin. Div. H
328	6/28	ASAP*	6/25	Press	5	535	Personnel
329	6/26	6/26	6/27	Xerox	15	8	Admin. Div. G

*ASAP - As soon as possible

1. The unit whose job was to be xeroxed but was NOT completed by the date required is   1.____

   A. Administrative Division H
   B. Administrative Division G
   C. Research
   D. Training

2. The job with the LARGEST number of original pages to be xeroxed is job number   2.____

   A. 324   B. 326   C. 327   D. 329

3. Jobs were completed AFTER June 26, for

    A. Training and Administrative Division G
    B. Training and Administrative Division H
    C. Research and Budget
    D. Administrative Division G *only*

3.____

4. Which one of the following units submitted a job which was completed SOONER than required?

    A. Training
    B. Administrative Division H
    C. Personnel
    D. Administrative Division G

4.____

5. The jobs which were submitted on different days but were completed on the SAME day and used the SAME process had job numbers

    A. 324 and 326   B. 327 and 328
    C. 324, 326, and 328   D. 324, 326, and 329

5.____

KEY (CORRECT ANSWERS)

1. B
2. D
3. A
4. B
5. A

TEST 2

Questions 1-10.

DIRECTIONS: Questions 1 through 10 are to be answered SOLELY on the basis of the Production Record table shown below for the Information Unit in Agency X for the work week ended Friday, December 6. The table shows, for each employee, the quantity of each type of work performed and the percentage of the work week spent in performing each type of work.

NOTE: Assume that each employee works 7 hours a day and 5 days a week, making a total of 35 hours for the work week.

PRODUCTION RECORD - INFORMATION UNIT IN AGENCY X
(For the work week ended Friday, December 6)

	NUMBER OF			
	Papers Filed	Sheets Proofread	Visitors Received	Envelopes Addressed
Miss Agar	3120	33	178	752
Mr. Brun	1565	59	252	724
Miss Case	2142	62	214	426
Mr. Dale	4259	29	144	1132
Miss Earl	2054	58	212	878
Mr. Farr	1610	69	245	621
Miss Glen	2390	57	230	790
Mr. Hope	3425	32	176	805
Miss Iver	3726	56	148	650
Mr. Joad	3212	55	181	495

	PERCENTAGE OF WORK WEEK SPENT ON				
	Filing Papers	Proof-reading	Receiving Visitors	Addressing Envelopes	Performing Miscellaneous Work
Miss Agar	30%	9%	34%	11%	16%
Mr. Brun	13%	15%	52%	10%	10%
Miss Case	23%	18%	38%	6%	15%
Mr. Dale	50%	7%	17%	16%	10%
Miss Earl	24%	14%	37%	14%	11%
Mr. Farr	16%	19%	48%	8%	9%
Miss Glenn	27%	12%	42%	12%	7%
Mr. Hope	38%	8%	32%	13%	9%
Miss Iver	43%	13%	24%	9%	11%
Mr. Joad	33%	11%	36%	7%	13%

1. For the week, the average amount of time which the employees spent in proofreading was MOST NEARLY _____ hours.   1._____

   A. 3.1   B. 3.6   C. 4.4   D. 5.1

2. The average number of visitors received daily by an employee was MOST NEARLY   2._____

   A. 40   B. 57   C. 198   D. 395

3. Of the following employees, the one who addressed envelopes at the FASTEST rate was   3._____

   A. Miss Agar   B. Mr. Brun   C. Miss Case   D. Mr. Dale

4. Mr. Farr's rate of filing papers was MOST NEARLY _____ pages per minute.   4._____

   A. 2   B. 1.7   C. 5   D. 12

5. The average number of hours that Mr. Brun spent daily on receiving visitors exceeded the average number of hours that Miss Iver spent daily on the same type of work by MOST NEARLY _____ hours.   5._____

   A. 2   B. 3   C. 4   D. 5

6. Miss Earl worked at a FASTER rate than Miss Glen in   6._____

   A. filing papers   B. proofreading sheets
   C. receiving visitors   D. addressing envelopes

7. Mr. Joad's rate of filing papers _____ Miss Iver's rate of filing papers by APPROXI-MATELY _____ .   7._____

   A. was less than; 10%   B. exceeded; 33%
   C. was less than; 16%   D. exceeded; 12%

8. Assume that in the following week Miss Case is instructed to increase the percentage of her time spent on filing papers to 35%.
   If she continued to file papers at the same rate as she did for the week ended December 6, the number of additional papers that she filed the following week was MOST NEARLY   8._____

   A. 3260   B. 5400   C. 250   D. 1120

9. Assume that in the following week Mr. Hope increased his weekly total of envelopes addressed to 1092.
   If he continued to spend the same amount of time on this assignment as he did for the week ended December 6, the increase in his rate of addressing envelopes the following week was MOST NEARLY _____ envelopes per hour.   9._____

   A. 15   B. 65   C. 155   D. 240

10. Assume that in the following week Miss Agar and Mr. Dale spent 3 and 9 hours less,   10._____
respectively, on filing papers than they had spent for the week ended December 6, without changing their rates of work.
The total number of papers filed during the following week by both Miss Agar and Mr.
Dale was MOST NEARLY

    A.   4235   B.   4295   C.   4315   D.   4370

KEY (CORRECT ANSWERS)

1. C
2. A
3. B
4. C
5. A
6. C
7. D
8. D
9. B
10. B

TEST 3

Questions 1-6.

DIRECTIONS: Questions 1 through 6 are to be answered SOLELY on the basis of the chart below.

EMPLOYMENT ERRORS

	Allan	Barry	Cary	David
July	5	4	1	7
Aug.	8	3	9	8
Sept.	7	8	7	5
Oct.	3	6	5	3
Nov.	2	4	4	6
Dec.	5	2	8	4

1. The clerk with the HIGHEST number of errors for the 6-month period was   1.___

   A. Allan   B. Barry   C. Cary   D. David

2. If the number of errors made by Allan in the six months shown represented one-eighth of   2.___
   the total errors made by the unit during the entire year, what was the TOTAL number of
   errors made by the unit for the year?

   A. 124   B. 180   C. 240   D. 360

3. The number of errors made by David in November was what fraction of the total errors   3.___
   made in November?

   A. 1/3   B. 1/6   C. 378   D. 3/16

4. The average number of errors made per month per clerk was MOST NEARLY   4.___

   A. 4   B. 5   C. 6   D. 7

5. Of the total number of errors made during the six-month period, the percentage made in   5.___
   August was MOST NEARLY

   A. 2%   B. 4%   C. 23%   D. 44%

6. If the number of errors in the unit were to decrease in the next six months by 30%, what   6.___
   would be MOST NEARLY the total number of errors for the unit for the next six months?

   A. 87   B. 94   C. 120   D. 137

KEY (CORRECT ANSWERS)

1. C
2. C
3. C
4. B
5. C
6. A

TEST 4

Questions 1-5.

DIRECTIONS: Questions 1 through 5 are to be answered SOLELY on the basis of the data given below. These data show the performance rates of the employees in a particular division for a period of six months.

Employee	Jan.	Feb.	Mar.	April	May	June
A	96	53	64	48	76	72
B	84	58	69	56	67	79
C	73	68	71	54	59	62
D	98	74	79	66	86	74
E	89	78	67	74	75	77

1. According to the above data, the average monthly performance for a worker is MOST NEARLY

    A. 66   B. 69   C. 72   D. 75

1.____

2. According to the above data, the mean monthly performance for the division is MOST NEARLY

    A. 350   B. 358   C. 387   D. 429

2.____

3. According to the above data, the employee who shows the LEAST month-to-month variation in performance is

    A. A   B. B   C. C   D. D

3.____

4. According to the above data, the employee who shows the GREATEST range in performance is

    A. A   B. B   C. C   D. D

4.____

5. According to the above data, the median employee with respect to performance for the six-month period is

    A. A   B. B   C. C   D. D

5.____

––––––––

KEY (CORRECT ANSWERS)

1. C
2. B
3. C
4. A
5. B

––––––––

TEST 5

Questions 1-5.

DIRECTIONS: Questions 1 through 5 are to be answered SOLELY on the basis of the chart below, which shows the absences in Unit A for the period November 1 through November 15.

ABSENCE RECORD - UNIT A
November 1-15

Date:	1	2	3	4	5	6	7	8	9	10	11	12	13	14	15
Employee:															
Ames	X	s	H					X			H			X	X
Bloom	X		H			X	X	S	s		H	S	S		X
Deegan	X	J	H	J	J	J	X	X			H				X
Howard	X		H					X			H			X	X
Jergens	X	M	H	M	M	M		X			H			X	X
Lange	X		H			S	X	X							X
Morton	X						X	X	V	V	H				X
O'Shea	X		H			0		X			H	X		X	X

CODE FOR TYPES OF ABSENCE
- X - Saturday or Sunday
- H - Legal Holiday
- P - Leave without pay
- M - Military Leave
- J - Jury duty
- V - Vacation
- S - Sick Leave
- O - Other leave of absence

NOTE: If there is no entry against an employee's name under a date, the employee worked on that date.

1. According to the above chart, NO employee in Unit A was absent on   1.____

   A. leave without pay
   C. other leave of absence
   B. military leave
   D. vacation

2. According to the above chart, all but one of the employees in Unit A were present on the   2.____

   A. 3rd   B. 5th   C. 9th   D. 13th

3. According to the above chart, the ONLY employee who worked on a legal holiday when the other employees were absent are   3.____

   A. Deegan and Morton
   C. Lange and Morton
   B. Howard and O'Shea
   D. Morton and O'Shea

4. According to the above chart, the employee who was absent ONLY on a day that was a Saturday, Sunday, or legal holiday was   4.____

    A. Bloom   B. Howard   C. G. Morton   D. O'Shea

5. The employees who had more absences than anyone else are   5.____

    A. Bloom and Deegan
    B. Bloom, Deegan, and Jergens
    C. Deegan and Jergens
    D. Deegan, Jergens, and O'Shea

KEY (CORRECT ANSWERS)

    1. A
    2. D
    3. C
    4. B
    5. B

TEST 6

Questions 1-7.

DIRECTIONS: Questions 1 through 7 are to be answered SOLELY on the basis of the time sheet and instructions given below.

	MON.	TUBS.	WED.	THURS .	FRI.
	IN OUT	IN OUT	IN OUT	IN OUT	IN OUT
Walker	8:45 5:02	9:20 5:00	9:00 5:02	Annual Lv.	9:04 5:05
Jones	9:01 5:00	9:03 5:02	9:08 5:01	8:55 5:04	9:00 5:00
Rubins	8:49 5:04	Sick Lv.	9:05 5:04	9:03 5:03	9:04 3:30(PB)
Brown	9:00 5:01	8:55 5:03	9:00 5:05	9:04 5:07	9:05 5:03
Roberts	9:30 5:08 (PA)	8:43 5:07	9:05 5:05	9:09 12:30 (PB)	8:58 5:04

The above time sheet indicates the arrival and leaving times of five telephone operators who punched a time clock in a city agency for the week of April 14. The times they arrived at work in the mornings are indicated in the columns labeled *IN* and the times they left work are indicated in the columns labeled *OUT*. The letters (PA) mean prearranged lateness, and the letters (PB) mean personal business. Time lost for these purposes is charged to annual leave.

The operators are scheduled to arrive at 9:00. However, they are not considered late unless they arrive after 9:05. If they prearrange a lateness, they are not considered late. Time lost through lateness is charged to annual leave. A full day's work is eight hours, from 9:00 to 5:00.

1. Which operator worked the entire week WITHOUT using any annual leave or sick leave time?   1.___

    A. Jones   B. Brown
    C. Roberts   D. None of the above

2. On which days was NONE of the operators considered late?   2.___

    A. Monday and Wednesday   B. Monday and Friday
    C. Wednesday and Thursday   D. Wednesday and Friday

3. Which operator clocked out at a different time each day of the week?   3.___

    A. Roberts   B. Jones   C. Rubins   D. Brown

4. How many of the operators were considered late on Wednesday?   4.___

    A. 0   B. 1   C. 2   D. 3

5. What was the TOTAL number of charged latenesses for the week of April 14?   5.___

    A. 1   B. 3   C. 5   D. 7

6. Which day shows the MOST time charged to all types of leave by all the operators?   6.___

    A. Monday   B. Tuesday   C. Wednesday   D. Thursday

7. What operators were considered ON TIME all week?　　　　　　　　　7._____

    A. Jones and Rubins　　　　　　　　B. Rubins and Brown
    C. Brown and Roberts　　　　　　　D. Walker and Brown

———

KEY (CORRECT ANSWERS)

    1. B
    2. B
    3. A
    4. B
    5. B
    6. D
    7. B

———

TEST 7

Questions 1-10.

DIRECTIONS: Questions 1 through 10 are to be answered SOLELY on the basis of the information and code tables given below.

In accordance with these code tables, each employee in the department is assigned a code number consisting of ten digits arranged from left to right in the following order:

    I.   Division in Which Employed
   II.   Title of Position
  III.   Annual Salary
  IV.   Age
   V.   Number of Years Employed in Department

EXAMPLE: A clerk is 21 years old, has been employed in the department for three years, and is working in the Supply Division at a yearly salary of $25,000. His code number is 90-115-13-02-2.

DEPARTMENTAL CODE

TABLE I		TABLE II		TABLE III		TABLE IV		TABLE V	
Code	Division No. in Which Employed	Code	Title No. of Position	Code	Annual No. Salary	Code	No. Age	Code	No. of No. Years Employee in Dept.
10	Accounting	115	Clerk	11	$18,000 or less	01	Under 20 yrs.	1	Less than 1 yr.
20	Construction	155	Typist			02	20 to 29 yrs.		
		175	Stenographer	12	$18,001 to $24,000			2	1 to 5 yrs.
30	Engineering					03	30 to 39 yrs.		
40	Information	237	Bookkeeper	13	$24,001 to $30,000			3	6 to 10 yrs.
50	Maintenance					04	40 to 49 yrs.		
60	Personnel	345	Statistician					4	11 to 15 yrs.
70	Record			14	$30,001 to $36,000	05	50 to 59 yrs.		
80	Research	545	Storekeeper					5	16 to 25 yrs.
90	Supply			15	$36,001 to $45,000	06	60 to 69 yrs.		
		633	Draftsman					6	26 to 35 yrs.
		665	Civil Engineer	16	$45,001 to $60,000	07	70 yrs. or over		
								7	36 yrs. or over
		865	Machinist	17	$60,001 to $70,000				
		915	Porter	18	$70,001 or over				

1. A draftsman employed in the Engineering Division at a yearly salary of $34,800 is 36   1.____
    years old and has been employed in the department for 9 years.
    He should be coded

    A. 20-633-13-04-3   B. 30-865-13-03-4
    C. 20-665-14-04-4   D. 30-633-14-03-3

2. A porter employed in the Maintenance Division at a yearly salary of $28,800 is 52 years   2.____
    old and has been employed in the department for 6 years.
    He should be coded

    A. 50-915-12-03-3   B. 90-545-12-05-3
    C. 50-915-13-05-3   D. 90-545-13-03-3

3. Richard White, who has been employed in the department for 12 years, receives $50,000   3.____
    a year as a civil engineer in the Construction Division. He is 38 years old.
    He should be coded

    A. 20-665-16-03-4   B. 20-665-15-02-1
    C. 20-633-14-04-2   D. 20-865-15-02-5

4. An 18-year-old clerk appointed to the department six months ago is assigned to the   4.____
    Record Division. His annual salary is $21,600.
    He should be coded

    A. 70-115-11-01-1   B. 70-115-12-01-1
    C. 70-115-12-02-1   D. 70-155-12-01-1

5. An employee has been coded 40-155-12-03-3.   5.____
    Of the following statements regarding this employee, the MOST accurate one is that
    he is

    A. a clerk who has been employed in the department for at least 6 years
    B. a typist who receives an annual salary which does not exceed $24,000
    C. under 30 years of age and has been employed in the department for at least 11
        years
    D. employed in the Supply Division at a salary which exceeds $18,000 per annum

6. Of the following statements regarding an employee who is coded 60-175-13-01-2, the   6.____
    LEAST accurate statement is that this employee

    A. is a stenographer in the Personnel Division
    B. has been employed in the department for at least one year
    C. receives an annual salary which exceeds $24,000
    D. is more than 20 years of age

7. The following are the names of four employees of the department with their code num-   7.____
    bers:
                    James Black, 80-345-15-03-4
                    William White, 30-633-14-03-4
                    Sam Green, 80-115-12-02-3
                    John Jones, 10-237-13-04-5
    If a salary increase is to be given to the employees who have been employed in the
    department for 11 years or more and who earn less than $36,001 a year, the two of the
    above employees who will receive a salary increase are

A. John Jones and William White
B. James Black and Sam Green
C. James Black and William White
D. John Jones and Sam Green

8. Code number 50-865-14-02-6, which has been assigned to a machinist, contains an obvious inconsistency.
This inconsistency involves the figures

   A. 50-865   B. 865-14   C. 14-02   D. 02-6

9. Ten employees were awarded merit prizes for outstanding service during the year. Their code numbers were:

      80-345-14-04-4   40-155-12-02-2
      40-155-12-04-4   10-115-12-02-2
      10-115-13-03-2   80-115-13-02-2
      80-175-13-05-5   10-115-13-02-3
      10-115-12-04-3   30-633-14-04-4

Of these outstanding employees, the number who were clerks employed in the Accounting Division at a salary ranging from $24,001 to $30,000 per annum is

   A. 1   B. 2   C. 3   D. 4

10. The MOST accurate of the following statements regarding the ten outstanding employees listed in the previous question is that

A. fewer than half of the employees were under 40 years of age
B. there were fewer typists than stenographers
C. four of the employees were employed in the department 11 years or more
D. two of the employees in the Research Division receive annual salaries ranging from $30,001 to $36,000

KEY (CORRECT ANSWERS)

  1. D
  2. C
  3. A
  4. B
  5. B
  6. D
  7. A
  8. D
  9. B
10. C

INTERPRETING STATISTICAL DATA
GRAPHS, CHARTS AND TABLES

TEST 1

DIRECTIONS: Each question or incomplete statement is followed by several suggested answers or completions. Select the one that BEST answers the question or completes the statement. *PRINT THE LETTER OF THE CORRECT ANSWER IN THE SPACE AT THE RIGHT.*

Questions 1-5.

DIRECTIONS: Questions 1 through 5 are to be answered SOLELY on the basis of the following table.

ANNUAL SALARIES PAID TO SELECTED CLERICAL TITLES IN FIVE MAJOR CITIES IN 2012 AND 2014				
2014				
			Legal	Computer
Clerk	Typist	Steno	Steno	Operator
Newton $33,900	$34,800	$36,300	$43,800	$35,400
Barton $32,400	$34,200	$35,400	$43,500	$34,200
Phelton $32,400	$32,400	$34,200	$42,000	$33,000
Washburn $33,600	$34,800	$35,400	$43,800	$34,800
Biltmore $33,000	$34,200	$35,100	$43,500	$34,500
2012				
			Legal	Computer
Clerk	Typist	Steno	Steno	Operator
Newtown $31,800	$33,600	$35,400	$41,400	$34,500
Barton $30,000	$31,500	$33,000	$39,600	$31,500
Phelton $29,400	$30,600	$31,800	$37,800	$31,200
Washburn $30,600	$32,400	$33,600	$40,200	$32,400
Biltmore $30,000	$31,800	$33,000	$39,600	$32,100

1. Assume that the value of the fringe benefits offered to clerical employees in 2014 amounted to 14% of their annual salaries in Newton, 17% in Barton, 18% in Phelton, 15% in Washburn, and 16% in Biltmore.
The total cost of employing a computer operator for 2014 was GREATEST in

    A. Newtown   B. Barton   C. Phelton   D. Washburn

1.____

2. During negotiations for their 2015 contract, the stenographers of Biltmore are demanding that their rate of pay be fixed at 85% of the legal stenographer salary.
If this demand is granted and if the legal stenographer salary increases by 7% in 2015, the 2015 stenographer salary will be MOST NEARLY

    A. $36,972   B. $37,560   C. $39,564   D. $40,020

2.____

3. Of the following, the GREATEST percentage increase in salary from 2012 to 2014 was gained by   3.____

    A. clerks in Newtown
    B. stenographers in Barton
    C. legal stenographers in Washburn
    D. computer operators in Biltmore

4. The title which achieved the SMALLEST average percentage increase in salary from 2012 to 2014 was   4.____

    A. clerk   B. typist
    C. stenographer   D. legal stenographer

5. Assume that, in 2014, clerks accounted for 60% of the clerical work force in Barton. The clerical work force consists of 140 employees. In 2012, the clerks accounted for 65% of the clerical work force in Barton. The clerical work force then consisted of 120 employees.   5.____
    The difference between the 2012 and 2014 payroll for clerks in Barton is MOST NEARLY

    A. $120,000   B. $240,000   C. $360,000   D. $480,000

KEY (CORRECT ANSWERS)

1. A
2. C
3. C
4. C
5. C

TEST 2

Questions 1-9.

DIRECTIONS: Questions 1 through 9 are to be answered SOLELY on the basis of the facts given in the table below, which contains certain information about employees in a city bureau.

RECORD OF EMPLOYEES IN A CITY BUREAU					
NAME	TITLE	AGE	ANNUAL SALARY	YEARS OF SERVICE	EXAMINATION RATING
Jones	Clerk	34	$20,400	10	82
Smith	Stenographer	25	19,200	2	72
Black	Typist	19	14,400	1	71
Brown	Stenographer	36	25,200	12	88
Thomas	Accountant	49	41,200	21	91
Gordon	Clerk	31	30,000	8	81
Johnson	Stenographer	26	26,400	5	75
White	Accountant	53	36,000	30	90
Spencer	Clerk	42	27,600	19	85
Taylor	Typist	24	21,600	5	74
Simpson	Accountant	37	50,000	11	87
Reid	Typist	20	12,000	2	72
Fulton	Accountant	55	55,000	31	100
Chambers	Clerk	22	15,600	4	75
Calhoun	Stenographer	48	28,800	16	80

1. The name of the employee whose salary would be the middle one if all the salaries were ranked in order of magnitude is   1.____

    A. White   B. Johnson   C. Brown   D. Spencer

2. The combined monthly salary of all the stenographers EXCEEDS the combined monthly salary of all the clerks by   2.____

    A. $6,000   B. $500   C. $22,800   D. $600

3. The age of the employee who received the HIGHEST rating in the examination among those who have less than 10 years of service is _____ years.   3.____

    A. 22   B. 31   C. 55   D. 34

4. The average examination rating of those employees who had 15 years of service or more as compared with the average examination rating of those employees who had 5 years of service or less is MOST NEARLY _____ points _____.   4.____

    A. 16; greater   B. 7; greater
    C. 10; less   D. 25; greater

5. The name of the youngest employee whose monthly salary is more than $1,000 per month and who has more than one year of service is   5.____

    A. Reid   B. Black   C. Chambers   D. Taylor

6. The name of the employee who received an examination rating of over 85%, who has more than 15 years of service, and who earns a yearly salary of more than $25,000 but less than $40,000 is   6.____

    A. Thomas   B. Spencer   C. Calhoun   D. White

7. The annual salary of the HIGHEST paid stenographer is

   7.____

   A. more than twice as great as the salary of the youngest employee
   B. greater than the salary of the oldest typist but not as great as the salary of the oldest clerk
   C. greater than the salary of the highest paid typist but not as great as the salary of the lowest paid accountant
   D. less than the combined salaries of the two youngest typists

8. The number of employees whose annual salary is more than $15,600 but less than $28,800 and who have at least 5 years of service is

   8.____

   A. 11   B. 8   C. 6   D. 5

9. Of the following, it would be MOST accurate to state that the

   9.____

   A. youngest employee is lowest with respect to number of years of service, examination rating, and salary
   B. oldest employee is highest with respect to number of years of service, examination rating, but not with respect to salary
   C. annual salary of the youngest clerk is $1,200 more than the annual salary of the youngest typist and $2,400 less than the annual salary of the youngest stenographer
   D. difference in age between the youngest and oldest typist is less than one-fourth the difference in age between the youngest and oldest stenographer

---

KEY (CORRECT ANSWERS)

1. B
2. B
3. B
4. A
5. C
6. D
7. C
8. D
9. D

TEST 3

Questions 1-10.

DIRECTIONS: Questions 1 through 10 are to be answered SOLELY on the basis of the Personnel Record of Division X shown below.

Employee	Bureau In Which Employed	Title	Annual Salary	No. of Days Absent On Vacation	No. of Days Absent On Sick Leave	No. of Times Late
Abbott	Mail	Clerk	$31,200	18	0	1
Barnes	Mail	Clerk	25,200	25	3	7
Davis	Mail	Typist	24,000	21	9	2
Adams	Payroll	Accountant	42,500	10	0	2
Bell	Payroll	Bookkeeper	31,200	23	2	5
Duke	Payroll	Clerk	27,600	24	4	3
Gross	Payroll	Clerk	21,600	12	5	7
Lane	Payroll	Stenographer	26,400	19	16	20
Reed	Payroll	Typist	22,800	15	11	11
Arnold	Record	Clerk	32,400	6	15	9
Cane	Record	Clerk	24,500	14	3	4
Fay	Record	Clerk	21,100	20	0	4
Hale	Record	Typist	25,200	18	2	7
Baker	Supply	Clerk	30,000	20	3	2
Clark	Supply	Clerk	27,600	25	6	5
Ford	Supply	Typist	22,800	25	4	22

Table title: DIVISION X — PERSONNEL RECORD - CURRENT YEAR

1. The percentage of the total number of employees who are clerks is MOST NEARLY   1.____

   A. 25%   B. 33%   C. 38%   D. 56%

2. Of the following employees, the one who receives a monthly salary of $2,100 is   2.____

   A. Barnes   B. Gross   C. Reed   D. Clark

3. The difference between the annual salary of the highest paid clerk and that of the lowest paid clerk is   3.____

   A. $6,000   B. $8,400   C. $11,300   D. $20,900

4. The number of employees receiving more than $25,000 a year but less than $40,000 a year is   4.____

   A. 6   B. 9   C. 12   D. 15

5. The TOTAL annual salary of the employees of the Mail Bureau is _____ the total annual salary of the employees of the _____.   5.____

   A. one-half of; Payroll Bureau
   B. less than; Record Bureau by $21,600
   C. equal to; Supply Bureau
   D. less than; Payroll Bureau by $71,600

6. The average annual salary of the employees who are not clerks is MOST NEARLY   6.____

    A. $23,700   B. $25,450   C. $26,800   D. $27,850

7. If all the employees were given a 10% increase in pay, the annual salary of Lane would   7.____
then be

    A. *greater* than that of Barnes by $1,320
    B. *less* than that of Bell by $4,280
    C. *equal* to that of Clark
    D. *greater* than that of Ford by $3,600

8. Of the clerks who earned less than $30,000 a year, the one who was late the FEWEST   8.____
number of times was late _____ time(s).

    A. 1   B. 2   C. 3   D. 4

9. The bureau in which the employees were late the FEWEST number of times on an aver-   9.____
age is the _____ Bureau.

    A. Mail   B. Payroll   C. Record   D. Supply

10. The MOST accurate of the following statements is that   10.____

    A. Reed was late more often than any other typist
    B. Bell took more time off for vacation than any other employee earning $30,000 or
more annually
    C. of the typists, Ford was the one who was absent the fewest number of times
because of sickness
    D. three clerks took no time off because of sickness

_____

KEY (CORRECT ANSWERS)

    1. D
    2. A
    3. C
    4. B
    5. C
    6. D
    7. A
    8. C
    9. A
  10. B

_____

TEST 4

DIRECTIONS: Questions 1 through 10 are to be answered SOLELY on the basis of the Weekly Payroll Record shown below of Bureau X in a public agency. In answering these questions, note that gross weekly salary is the salary before deductions have been made; take-home pay is the amount remaining after all indicated weekly deductions have been made from the gross weekly salary. In answering questions involving annual amounts, compute on the basis of 52 weeks per year.

BUREAU X
WEEKLY PAYROLL PERIOD

Unit In Which Employed	Employee	Title	Gross Weekly Salary (Before Deductions)	Weekly Deductions From Gross Salary		
				Medical Insurance	Income Tax	Pension System
Accounting	Allen	Accountant	$950	$14.50	$125.00	$53.20
Accounting	Barth	Bookkeeper	720	19.00	62.00	40.70
Accounting	Keller	Clerk	580	6.50	82.00	33.10
Accounting	Peters	Typist	560	6.50	79.00	35.30
Accounting	Simons	Stenographer	610	14.50	64.00	37.80
Information	Brown	Clerk	560	13.00	56.00	42.20
Information	Smith	Clerk	590	14.50	61.00	58.40
Information	Turner	Typist	580	13.00	59.00	62.60
Information	Williams	Stenographer	620	19.00	44.00	69.40
Mail	Conner	Clerk	660	13.00	74.00	55.40
Mail	Farrell	Typist	540	6.50	75.00	34.00
Mail	Johnson	Stenographer	580	19.00	36.00	37.10
Records	Dillon	Clerk	640	6.50	94.00	58.20
Records	Martin	Clerk	540	19.00	29.00	50.20
Records	Standish	Typist	620	14.50	67.00	60.10
Records	Wilson	Stenographer	690	6.50	101.00	75.60

1. Dillon's annual take-home pay is MOST NEARLY

   A. $25,000   B. $27,000   C. $31,000   D. $33,000

2. The difference between Turner's gross annual salary and his annual take-home pay is MOST NEARLY

   A. $3,000   B. $5,000   C. $7,000   D. $9,000

3. Of the following, the employee whose weekly take-home pay is CLOSEST to that of Keller's is

   A. Peters   B. Brown   C. Smith   D. Turner

4. The average gross annual salary of the typists is

   A. less than $27,500
   B. more than $27,500 but less than $30,000
   C. more than $30,000 but less than $32,500
   D. more than $32,500

5. The average gross weekly salary of the stenographers EXCEEDS the gross weekly salary of the clerks by   5._____

    A. $20   B. $30   C. $40   D. $50

6. Of the following employees in the Accounting Unit, the one who pays the HIGHEST percentage of his gross weekly salary for the Pension System is   6._____

    A. Barth   B. Keller   C. Peters   D. Simons

7. For all of the Accounting Unit employees, the total annual deductions for Medical Insurance are less than the total annual deductions for the Pension System by MOST NEARLY   7._____

    A. $6,000   B. $7,000   C. $8,000   D. $9,000

8. Of the following, the employee whose total weekly deductions are MOST NEARLY 27% of his gross weekly salary is   8._____

    A. Barth   B. Brown   C. Martin   D. Wilson

9. The total amount of the gross weekly salaries of all the employees in the Records Unit is MOST NEARLY   9._____

    A. 95% of the total amount of the gross weekly salaries of all the employees in the Information Unit
    B. 10% greater than the total amount of the gross weekly salaries of all the employees in the Mail Unit
    C. 75% of the total amount of the gross weekly salaries of all the employees in the Accounting Unit
    D. four times as great as the total amount deducted weekly for tax for all the employees in the Records Unit

10. For the employees in the Information Unit, the AVERAGE weekly deductions for Income Tax _____ the average weekly deduction for _____.   10._____

    A. exceeds; Income Tax for the employees in the Records Unit
    B. is less than; the Pension System for the employees in the Mail Unit
    C. exceeds; Income Tax for the employees in the Accounting Unit
    D. is less than; the Pension System for the employees in the Records Unit

KEY (CORRECT ANSWERS)

1. A
2. C
3. C
4. B
5. B
6. C
7. B
8. D
9. C
10. D

———

TEST 5

Questions 1-9.

DIRECTIONS: Questions 1 through 9 are to be answered SOLELY on the basis of the following information.

Assume that the following rules for computing service ratings are to be used experimentally in determining the service ratings of seven permanent city employees. (Note that these rules are hypothetical and are NOT to be confused with the existing method of computing service ratings for city employees.) The personnel record of each of these seven employees is given in Table II. You are to determine the answer to each of the questions on the basis of the rules given below for computing service ratings and the data contained in the personnel records of these seven employees.

All computations should be made as of the close of the rating period ending March 31, 2017.

Service Rating
The service rating of each permanent competitive class employee shall be computed by adding the following three scores: (1) a basic score, (2) the employee's seniority score, and (3) the employee's efficiency score.

Seniority Score
An employee's seniority score shall be computed by crediting him with 1/2% per year for each year of service starting with the date of the employee's entrance as a permanent employee into the competitive class, up to a maximum of 15 years (7 1/2%).

A residual fractional period of eight months or more shall be considered as a full year and credited with 1/2%. A residual fraction of from four to, but not including, eight months shall be considered as a half-year and credited with 1/4%. A residual fraction of less than four months shall receive no credit in the seniority score.

For example, a person who entered the competitive class as a permanent employee on August 1, 2014 would, as of March 31, 2017, be credited with a seniority score of 1 1/2% for his 2 years and 8 months of service.

Efficiency Score
An employee's efficiency score shall be computed by adding the annual efficiency ratings received by him during his service in his present position. (Where there are negative efficiency ratings, such ratings shall be subtracted from the sum of the positive efficiency ratings.) An employee's annual efficiency rating shall be based on the grade he receives from his supervisor for his work performance during the annual efficiency rating period.

Basic Score
A basic score of 70% shall be given to each employee upon permanent appointment to a competitive class position.

An employee shall receive a grade of A for performing work of the highest quality and shall be credited with an efficiency rating of plus (+) 3%. An employee shall receive a grade of F for performing work of the lowest quality and shall receive an efficiency rating of minus (-) 2%. Table I, entitled BASIS FOR DETERMINING ANNUAL EFFICIENCY RATINGS, lists the six grades of work performance with their equivalent annual efficiency ratings. Table I also lists the efficiency ratings to be assigned for service in a position for less than a year during the annual efficiency rating period.

The annual efficiency rating period shall run from April 1 to March 31, inclusive.

TABLE I – BASIS FOR DETERMINING ANNUAL EFFICIENCY RATINGS				
		Annual Efficiency Rating for Service in a Position For:		
Quality of Work Per-formed	Grade Assigned	8 months to a full year	At least 4 months but less than 8 months	Less than 4 months
Highest	A	+3%	+1 1/2%	0%
Good	B	+2%	+1%	0%
Standard	C	+1%	+1/2%	0%
Substandard	D	0%	0%	0%
Poor	E	-1%	-4%	0%
Lowest	F	-2%	-1%	0%

Appointment or Promotion During an Efficiency Rating Period

An employee who has been appointed or promoted during an efficiency rating period shall receive for that period an efficiency rating only for work performed by him during the portion of the period that he served in the position to which he was appointed or promoted. His efficiency rating for the period shall be determined in accordance with Table I.

Sample Computation of Service Rating

John Smith entered the competitive class as a permanent employee on December 1, 2012 and was promoted to his present position as a Clerk, Grade 3, on November 1, 2015. As a Clerk, Grade 3, he received a grade of B for work performed during the five-month period extending from November 1, 2015 to March 31, 2016 and a grade of C for work performed during the full annual period extending from April 1, 2016 to March 31, 2017.

On the basis of the RULES FOR COMPUTING SERVICE RATINGS, John Smith should be credited with:

    70%   Basic Score
    2 1/4%. Seniority Score - for 4 years and 4 months of service (from 12/1/12 to 3/31/17)
    2%   Efficiency Score - for 5 months of B service and a full _____ year of C service
    74 1/4%

TABLE II
PERSONNEL RECORD OF SEVEN PERMANENT
COMPETITIVE CLASS EMPLOYEES

Employee	Present Position	Date of Appointment or Promotion To Present Position	Date of Entry as Permanent Employee in Competitive Class
Allen	Clerk, Gr. 5	6-1-13	7-1-00
Brown	Clerk, Gr. 4	1-1-15	7-1-17
Cole	Clerk, Gr. 3	9-1-13	11-1-10
Fox	Clerk, Gr. 3	10-1-13	9-1-08
Green	Clerk, Gr. 2	12-1-11	12-1-11
Hunt	Clerk, Gr. 2	7-1-12	7-1-12
Kane	Steno, Gr. 3	11-16-14	3-1-11

GRADES RECEIVED ANNUALLY FOR WORK
PERFORMED IN PRESENT POSITION

Employee	4-1-11 to 3-31-12	4-1-12 to 3-31-13	4-1-13 to 3-31-14	4-1-14 to 3-31-15	4-1-15 to 3-31-16	4-1-16 to 3-31-17
Allen			C*	C	B	C
Brown				C*	C	B
Cole			A*	B	C	C
Fox			C*	C	D	C
Green	C*	D	C	D	C	C
Hunt		C*	C	E	C	C
Kane				B*	B	C

EXPLANATORY NOTES:
* Served in present position for less than a full year during this rating period. (Note date of appointment, or promotion, to present position.)
All seven employees have served continuously as permanent employees since their entry into the competitive class.

Questions 1 through 9 refer to the employees listed in Table II. You are to answer these questions SOLELY on the basis of the preceding RULES FOR COMPUTING SERVICE RATINGS and on the information concerning these seven employees given in Table II. You are reminded that all computations are to be made as of the close of the rating period ending March 31, 2017. Candidates may find it helpful to arrange their computations on their scratch paper in an orderly manner since the computations for one question may also be utilized in answering another question.

1. The seniority score of Allen is

    A. 7 1/2%   B. 8 1/2%   C. 8%   D. 8 1/4%

2. The seniority score of Fox EXCEEDS that of Cole by

    A. 1 1/2%   B. 2%   C. 1%   D. 3/4%

3. The seniority score of Brown is

    A. *equal* to Hunt's   B. *twice* Hunt's
    C. *move* than Hunt's by 1 1/2%   D. *less* than by Hunt's by 1/2%

1.___
2.___
3.___

4. Green's efficiency score is   4.____

    A. *twice* that of Kane
    B. *equal* to that of Kane
    C. *less* than Kane's by 1/2%
    D. *less* than Kane's by 1%

5. Of the following employees, the one who has the LOWEST efficiency score is   5.____

    A. Brown   B. Fox   C. Hunt   D. Kane

6. A comparison of Hunt's efficiency score with his seniority score reveals that his efficiency   6.____
score is

    A. *less* than his seniority score by 1/2%
    B. *less* than his seniority score by 3/4%
    C. *equal* to his seniority score
    D. *greater* than his seniority score by 1/2%

7. Fox's service rating is   7.____

    A. 72 1/2%   B. 74%   C. 76 1/2%   D. 76 3/4%

8. Brown's service rating is   8.____

    A. less than 78%   B. 78%
    C. 78 1/4%   D. more than 78 1/4%

9. Cole's service rating EXCEEDS Kane's by   9.____

    A. less than 2%   B. 2%
    C. 2 1/4%   D. more than 2 1/4%

KEY (CORRECT ANSWERS)

    1. A
    2. C
    3. B
    4. C
    5. B
    6. D
    7. D
    8. B
    9. A

ARITHMETICAL REASONING
EXAMINATION SECTION
TEST 1

DIRECTIONS: Each question or incomplete statement is followed by several suggested answers or completions. Select the one that BEST answers the question or completes the statement. *PRINT THE LETTER OF THE CORRECT ANSWER IN THE SPACE AT THE RIGHT.*

1. The ABC Corporation had a gross income of $125,500.00 in 2004. Of this, it paid 60% for overhead.
   If the gross income for 2005 increased by $6,500 and the cost of overhead increased to. 61% of gross income, how much MORE did it pay for overhead in 2005 than in 2004?

   A. $1,320   B. $5,220   C. $7,530   D. $8,052

    1.____

2. After one year, Mr. Richards paid back a total of $16,950 as payment for a $15,000 loan. All the money paid over $15,000 was simple interest.
   The interest charge was MOST NEARLY

   A. 13%   B. 11%   C. 9%   D. 7%

    2.____

3. A checking account has a balance of $253.36.
   If deposits of $36.95, $210.23, and $7.34 and withdrawals of $117.35, $23.37, and $15.98 are made, what is the NEW balance of the account?

   A. $155.54   B. $351.18   C. $364.58   D. $664.58

    3.____

4. In 2004, The W Realty Company spent 27% of its income on rent.
   If it earned $97,254 in 2004, the amount it paid for rent was

   A. $26,258.58   B. $26,348.58
   C. $27,248.58   D. $27,358.58

    4.____

5. Six percent simple annual interest on $2,436.18 is MOST NEARLY

   A. $145.08   B. $145.17   C. $146.08   D. $146.17

    5.____

6. H. Partridge receives a weekly gross salary (before deductions) of $397.50. Through weekly payroll deductions of $13.18, he is paying back a loan he took from his pension fund.
   If other fixed weekly deductions amount to $122.76, how much pay would Mr. Partridge take home over a period of 33 weeks?

   A. $7,631.28   B. $8,250.46   C. $8,631.48   D. $13,117.50

    6.____

7. Mr. Robertson is a city employee enrolled in a city retirement system. He has taken out a loan from the retirement fund and is paying it back at the rate of $14.90 every two weeks. In eighteen weeks, how much money will he have paid back on the loan?

   A. $268.20   B. $152.80   C. $134.10   D. $67.05

    7.____

8. In 2004, The Iridor Book Company had the following expenses: rent, $6,500; overhead, $52,585; inventory, $35,700; and miscellaneous, $1,275.
If all of these expenses went up 18% in 2005, what would they TOTAL in 2005?

    A. $17,290.80   B. $78,769.20
    C. $96,060.00   D. $113,350.80

8.____

9. Ms. Ranier had a gross salary of $710.72 paid once every two weeks.
If the deductions from each paycheck are $125.44, $50.26, $12.58, and $2.54, how much money would Ms. Ranier take home in eight weeks?

    A. $2,079.60   B. $2,842.88   C. $4,159.20   D. $5,685.76

9.____

10. Mr. Martin had a net income of $95,500 in 2004.
If he spent 34% on rent and household expenses, 3% on house furnishings, 25% on clothes, and 36% on food, how much was left for savings and other expenses?

    A. $980   B. $1,910   C. $3,247   D. $9,800

10.____

11. Mr. Elsberg can pay back a loan of $1,800 from the city employees' retirement system if he pays back $36.69 every two weeks for two full years.
At the end of the two years, how much more than the original $1,800 he borrowed will Mr. Elsberg have paid back?

    A. $53.94   B. $107.88   C. $190.79   D. $214.76

11.____

12. Mr. Nusbaum is a city employee receiving a gross salary (salary before deductions) of $20,800. Every two weeks the following deductions are taken out of his salary: Federal Income Tax, $162.84; FICA, $44.26; State Tax, $29.72; City Tax, $13.94; Health Insurance, $3.14.
If Mr. Nusbaum's salary and deductions remained the same for a full calendar year, what would his net salary (gross salary less deductions) be in that year?

    A. $6,596.20   B. $14,198.60
    C. $18,745.50   D. $20,546.30

12.____

13. Add: 8936
       7821
       8953
       4297
       9785
       <u>6579</u>

    A. 45,371   B. 45,381   C. 46,371   D. 46,381

13.____

14. Multiply: 987
           <u>867</u>

    A. 854,609   B. 854,729   C. 855,709   D. 855,729

14.____

15. Divide: $59\overline{)321439.0}$

    A. 5438.1   B. 5447.1   C. 5448.1   D. 5457.1

15.____

16. Divide: .052)‾721‾   16.____

    A. 12,648.0   B. 12,648.1   C. 12,649.0   D. 12,649.1

17. If the total number of employees in one city agency increased from 1,927 to 2,006 during   17.____
a certain year, the percentage increase in the number of employees for that year is
MOST NEARLY

    A. 4%   B. 5%   C. 6%   D. 7%

18. During a single fiscal year, which totaled 248 workdays, one account clerk verified 1,488   18.____
purchase vouchers. Assuming a normal work week of five days, what is the AVERAGE
number of vouchers verified by the account clerk in a one-week period during this fiscal
year?

    A. 25   B. 30   C. 35   D. 40

19. Multiplying a number by .75 is the same as   19.____

    A. multiplying it by 2/3   B. dividing it by 2/3
    C. multiplying it by 3/4   D. dividing it by 3/4

20. In City Agency A, 2/3 of the employees are enrolled in a retirement system. City Agency   20.____
B has the same number of employees as Agency A, and 60% of these are enrolled in a
retirement system.
If Agency A has a total of 660 employees, how many MORE employees does it have
enrolled in a retirement system than does Agency B?

    A. 36   B. 44   C. 56   D. 66

21. Net worth is equal to assets minus liabilities.   21.____
If, at the end of 2003, a textile company had assets of $98,695.83 and liabilities of
$59,238.29, what was its net worth?

    A. $38,478.54   B. $38,488.64
    C. $39,457.54   D. $48,557.54

22. Mr. Martin's assets consist of the following: 22.____

Cash on hand	$ 5,233.74
Automobile	3,206.09
Furniture	4,925.00
Government Bonds	5,500.00
House	36,690.85

What are his TOTAL assets?

    A. $54,545.68   B. $54,455.68
    C. $55,455.68   D. $55,555.68

23. If Mr. Mitchell has $627.04 in his checking account and then writes three checks for   23.____
$241.75, $13.24, and $102.97, what will be his new balance?

    A. $257.88   B. $269.08   C. $357.96   D. $369.96

24. An employee's net pay is equal to his total earnings less all deductions.
If an employee's total earnings in a pay period are $497.05, what is his net pay if he
has the following deductions: Federal income tax, $90.32; FICA, $28.74; State tax,
$18.79; City tax, $7.25; Pension, $1.88?

24.___

   A. $351.17   B. $351.07   C. $350.17   D. $350.07

25. A petty cash fund had an opening balance of $85.75 on December 1. Expenditures of
$23.00, $15.65, $5.23, $14.75, and $26.38 were made out of this fund during the first 14
days of the month. Then, on December 17, another $38.50 was added to the fund.
If additional expenditures of $17.18, $3.29, and $11.64 were made during the remain-
der of the month, what was the FINAL balance of the petty cash fund at the end of
December?

25.___

   A. $6.93   B. $7.13   C. $46.51   D. $91.40

KEY (CORRECT ANSWERS)

1. B		11. B
2. A		12. B
3. B		13. C
4. A		14. D
5. D		15. C
6. C		16. D
7. C		17. A
8. D		18. B
9. A		19. C
10. B		20. B

21. C
22. D
23. B
24. D
25. B

SOLUTIONS TO PROBLEMS

1. ($132,000)(.61)-($125,500)(.60) = $5220

2. Interest = $1950. As a percent, $1950÷15,000 = 13%

3. New balance = $253.36 + $36.95 + $210.23 + $7.34 - $117.35 -$23.37 - $15.98 = $351.18

4. Rent = ($97,254)(.27) = $26,258.58

5. ($2436.18)(.06) ≈ $146.17

6. ($397.50-$13.18-$122.76)(33) = $8631.48

7. ($14.90)($\frac{18}{2}$) = $134.10

8. ($6500+$52,585+$35,700+$1275)(1.18) = $113,350.80

9. ($710.72-$125.44-$50.26-$12.58-$2.54)($\frac{8}{2}$) = $2079.60

10. (1-.34-.03-.25-.36)($95,500) = $1910

11. ($36.69)(52) - $1800 = $107.88

12. $20,800 - (26)($162.84+$44.26+$29.72+$13.94+$3.14) = $14,198.60

13. 8936 + 7821 + 8953 + 4297 + 9785 + 6579 = 46,371

14. (987)(867) = 855,729

15. 321,439÷59 ≈ 5448.1

16. 721 ÷ .057 ≈ 12,649.1

17. (2006-1927)÷ 1927 ≈ 4%

18. Let x=number of vouchers. Then, $\frac{x}{5} = \frac{1488}{248}$. Solving, x=30

19. Multiplying by .75 is equivalent to multiplying by $\frac{3}{4}$

20. (660)($\frac{2}{3}$) - (660)(.60) = 44

21. Net worth = $98,695.83 - $59,238.29 = $39,457.54

22. Total assets = $5233.74 + $3206.09 + $4925.00 + $5500.00 + $36,690.85 = $55,555.68

23. New balance = $627.04 - $241.75 - $13.24 - $102.97 = $269.08

24. Net pay = $497.05 - $90.32 - $28,74 - $18.79 - $7.25 - $1.88 = $350.07

25. Final balance = $85.75 - $23.00 - $15.65 - $5.23 - $14.75 - $26.38 + $38.50 - $17.18 - $3.29 - $11.64 = $7.13

TEST 2

DIRECTIONS: Each question or incomplete statement is followed by several suggested answers or completions. Select the one that BEST answers the question or completes the statement. *PRINT THE LETTER OF THE CORRECT ANSWER IN THE SPACE AT THE RIGHT.*

1. The formula for computing base salary is: Earnings equals base gross plus additional gross.
   If an employee's earnings during a particular period are in the amounts of $597.45, $535.92, $639.91, and $552.83, and his base gross salary is $525.50 per paycheck, what is the TOTAL of the additional gross earned by the employee during that period?

   A. $224.11   B. $224.21   C. $224.51   D. $244.11   1.____

2. If a lump sum death benefit is paid by the retirement system in an amount equal to 3/7 of an employee's last yearly salary of $13,486.50, the amount of the death benefit paid is MOST NEARLY

   A. $5,749.29   B. $5,759.92   C. $5,779.92   D. $5,977.29   2.____

3. Suppose that a member has paid 15 installments on a 28-installment loan.
   The percentage of the number of installments paid to the retirement system is

   A. 53.57%   B. 53.97%   C. 54.57%   D. 55.37%   3.____

4. If an employee takes a 1-month vacation during a calendar year, the percentage of the year during which he works
   is MOST NEARLY

   A. 90.9%   B. 91.3%   C. 91.6%   D. 92.1%   4.____

5. Suppose that an employee took a leave of absence totaling 7 months during a calendar year.
   Assuming the employee did not take any vacation time during the remainder of that year, the percentage of the year in which he worked is MOST NEARLY

   A. 41.7%   B. 43.3%   C. 46.5%   D. 47.1%   5.____

6. A member has borrowed $4,725 from her funds in the retirement system.
   If $3,213 has been repaid, the percentage of the loan which is still outstanding is MOST NEARLY

   A. 16%   B. 32%   C. 48%   D. 68%   6.____

7. If an employee worked only 24 weeks during the year because of illness, the portion of the year he was out of work was MOST NEARLY

   A. 46%   B. 48%   C. 51%   D. 54%   7.____

8. If an employee purchased credit for a 16-week period of service which he had prior to rejoining the retirement system, the percentage of a year he purchased credit for was MOST NEARLY

   A. 27.9%   B. 28.8%   C. 30.7%   D. 33.3%   8.____

9. If an employee contributes 2/11 of his yearly salary to his pension fund account, the per-centage of his yearly salary which he contributes is MOST NEARLY

    A. 17.9%   B. 18.2%   C. 18.4%   D. 19.0%

9._

10. In 2005, the maximum amount of income from which social security tax could be with-held (base salary) was $70,500. In 2007, the base salary was $82,500.
The 2007 base salary represents a percentage increase over the 2005 base salary of approximately

    A. 15%   B. 16%   C. 17%   D. 18%

10._

11. If 17.5% of an employee's salary is withheld for taxes, the one of the following which is the fraction of the salary withheld is

    A. 3/20   B. 8/35   C. 7/40   D. 4/25

11._

12. If a person withdraws 42% of the funds from his account with the retirement system, the remaining balance represents a fraction of MOST NEARLY

    A. 7/13   B. 5/9   C. 7/12   D. 4/7

12._

13. A property decreases in value from $45,000 to $35,000. The percent of decrease is MOST NEARLY

    A. 20.5%   B. 22.2%   C. 25.0%   D. 28.6%

13._

14. The fraction $\dfrac{487}{101326}$ expressed as a decimal is MOST NEARLY

    A. .0482   B. .00481   C. .0049   D. .00392

14._

15. The reciprocal of the sum of 2/3 and 1/6 can be expressed as

    A. 0.83   B. 1.20   C. 1.25   D. 1.50

15._

16. Total land and building costs for a new commercial property equal $50 per square foot. If the investors expect a 10 percent return on their costs, and if total operating expenses average 5 percent of total costs, annual gross rentals per square foot must be AT LEAST

    A. $7.50   B. $8.50   C. $10.00   D. $12.00

16._

17. The formula for computing the amount of annual deposit in a compound interest bearing account to provide a lump sum at the end of a period of years is $X = \dfrac{r.L}{(1+r)^{n-1}}$ (X is the amount of annual deposit, r is the rate of interest, and n is the number of years) and L = lump sum)
Using the formula, the annual amount of the deposit at the end of each year to accu-mulate to $20,000 at the end of 3 years with interest at 2 percent on annual balances is

    A. $6,120.00   B. $6,203.33   C. $6,535.09   D. $6,666.66

17._

18. An investor sold two properties at $150,000 each. On one he made a 25 percent profit.   18.____
    On the other he suffered a 25 percent loss.
    The NET result of his sales was

    A. neither a gain nor a loss
    B. a $20,000 loss
    C. a $75,000 gain
    D. a $75,000 loss

19. A contractor decides to install a chain fence covering the perimeter of a parcel 75 feet   19.____
    wide and 112 feet in depth.
    Which one of the following represents the number of feet to be covered?

    A. 187   B. 364   C. 374   D. 8,400

20. A builder estimates he can build an average of 4 1/2 one-family homes to an acre. There   20.____
    are 640 acres to one square mile.
    Which one of the following CORRECTLY represents the number of one-family homes
    the builder would estimate he can build on one square mile?

    A. 1,280   B. 1,920   C. 2,560   D. 2,880

21. $.01059 deposited at 7 percent interest will yield $1.00 in 30 years.   21.____
    If a person deposited $1,059 at 7 percent interest on April 1, 1974, which one of the
    following amounts would represent the worth of this deposit on March 31, 2004?

    A. $100   B. $1,000   C. $10,000   D. $100,000

22. A building has an economic life of forty years. Assuming the building depreciates at a   22.____
    constant annual rate, which one of the following CORRECTLY represents the yearly per-
    centage of depreciation?

    A. 2.0%   B. 2.5%   C. 5.0%   D. 7.0%

23. A building produces a gross income of $200,000 with a   23.____
    net income of $20,000, before mortgage charges and capital recapture. The owner is
    able to increase the gross income 5 percent without a corresponding increase in oper-
    ating costs.
    The effect upon the net income will be an INCREASE of

    A. 5%   B. 10%   C. 12.5%   D. 50%

24. The present value of $1.00 not payable for 8 years, and at 10 percent interest, is $.4665.   24.____
    Which of the following amounts represents the PRESENT value of $1,000 payable 8
    years hence at 10 percent interest?

    A. $46.65   B. $466.50   C. $4,665.00   D. $46,650.00

25. The amount of real property taxes to be levied by a city is $100 million. The assessment   25.____
    roll subject to taxation shows an assessed valuation of $2 billion.
    Which one of the following tax rates CORRECTLY represents the tax rate to be levied
    per $100 of assessed valuation?

    A. $.50   B. $5.00   C. $50.00   D. $500.00

KEY (CORRECT ANSWERS)

1.	A	11.	C
2.	C	12.	C
3.	A	13.	B
4.	C	14.	B
5.	A	15.	B
6.	B	16.	A
7.	D	17.	C
8.	C	18.	B
9.	B	19.	C
10.	C	20.	D

21.	D
22.	B
23.	D
24.	B
25.	B

———

SOLUTIONS TO PROBLEMS

1. $597.45 + $535.92 + $639.91 + $552.83 = $2326.11 Then, $2326.11 - (4)($525.50) = $224.11

2. Death benefit = ($13,486.50)$(\frac{3}{7})$ ≈ $5779.92

3. $\frac{15}{28}$ ≈ 53.57%

4. $\frac{11}{12}$ ≈ 91.6% (closer to 91.7%)

5. $\frac{5}{12}$ ≈ 41.7%

6. ($4725-$3213) ÷ $4725 = 32%

7. $\frac{28}{52}$ ≈ 54%

8. $\frac{16}{52}$ ≈ 30.7% (closer to 30.8%)

9. $\frac{2}{11}$ ≈ 18.2%

10. ($82,500 -$70,500) ÷$70,500=17%

11. 17.5% $= \frac{175}{1000} = \frac{7}{40}$

12. 100%-42%=58%$=\frac{58}{100} = \frac{29}{50}$, closest to $\frac{7}{12}$ in selections

13. $\frac{\$10,000}{\$45,000}$ ≈ 22.2%

14. 487/101,326 ≈ .00481

15. $\dfrac{2}{3}+\dfrac{1}{6}=\dfrac{5}{6}$ Then, $1\div\dfrac{5}{6}=\dfrac{6}{5}=1.20$

16. $(.15)(\$50) = \$7.50$

17. $x = (.02)(\$20,000)/[(1+.02)^3-1] = 400 \div .061208 \approx \$6535.09$

18. Sold 150,000, 25% loss = paid 200,000, loss of 50,000 Sold 150,000, 25% profit = paid 120,000, profit of 30,000 - 50,000 + 30,000 = -20,000 (loss)

19. Perimeter = (2)(75) + (2)(112) = 374 ft.

20. (640)(4 1/2) = 2880 homes

21. $(1\div.01059)(1059) = \$100,000$

22. $1 \div 40 = .025 = 2.5\%$

23. New gross income = ($200,000)(X1.05) = $210,000.
    Then, ($210,000-$200,000) ÷ $20,000 = 50%

24. Let x = present value of $1000. Then, $\dfrac{\$1.00}{\$.4665}=\dfrac{\$1000}{x}$
    Solving, x = $466.50

25. Let x = tax rate. Then, $\dfrac{\$100,000,000}{\$2,000,000,000}=\dfrac{x}{\$100}$
    Solving, x = $5.00

TEST 3

DIRECTIONS: Each question or incomplete statement is followed by several suggested answers or completions. Select the one that BEST answers the question or completes the statement. *PRINT THE LETTER OF THE CORRECT ANSWER IN THE SPACE AT THE RIGHT.*

1. It is found that for the past three years the average weekly number of inspections per   1.____
   inspector ranged from 20 inspections to 40 inspections.
   On the basis of this information, it is MOST reasonable to conclude that

   A. on the average, 30 inspections per week were made
   B. the average weekly number of inspections never fell below 20
   C. the performance of inspectors deteriorated over the three-year period
   D. the range in average weekly inspections was 60

Questions 2-4.

DIRECTIONS: Questions 2 through 4 are to be answered on the basis of the following information.

The number of students admitted to University X in 2004 from High School Y was 268 students. This represented 13.7 percent of University X's entering freshman classes. In 2005, it is expected that University X will admit 591 students from High School Y, which is expected to represent 19.4 percent of the 2005 entering freshman classes of University X. t

2. Which of the following is the CLOSEST estimate of the size of University X's expected   2.____
   2005 entering freshman classes?
   _____ students.

   A. 2,000   B. 2,500   C. 3,000   D. 3,500

3. Of the following, the expected percentage of increase from 2004 to 2005 in the number   3.____
   of students graduating from High School Y and entering University X as freshmen is
   MOST NEARLY

   A. 5.7%   B. 20%   C. 45%   D. 120%

4. Assume that the cost of processing each freshman admission to University X from High   4.____
   School Y in 2004 was an average of $28. Also, that this was 1/3 more than the average
   cost of processing each of the other 2004 freshman admissions to University X.
   Then, the one of the following that MOST closely shows the total processing cost of all
   2004 freshman admissions to University X is

   A. $6,500   B. $20,000   C. $30,000   D. $40,000

5. Assume that during the fiscal year 2005-2006, a bureau produced 20% more work units   5.____
   than it produced in the fiscal year 2004-2005. Also assume that during the fiscal year
   2005-2006 that bureau's staff was 20% smaller than it was in the fiscal year 2004-2005.
   On the basis of this information, it would be MOST proper to conclude that the number
   of work units produced per staff member in that bureau in the fiscal year 2005-2006
   exceeded the number of work units produced per staff member in that bureau in the
   fiscal year 2004-2005 by which one of the following percentages?

   A. 20%   B. 25%   C. 40%   D. 50%

6. Assume that during the following five fiscal years (FY), a bureau has received the follow-   6.__
   ing appropriations:
   FY 2002-2003 - $200,000
   FY 2003-2004 - $240,000
   FY 2004-2005 - $280,000
   FY 2005-2006 - $390,000
   FY 2006-2007 - $505,000
   The bureau's appropriation for which one of the following fiscal years showed the
   LARGEST percentage of increase over the bureau's appropriation for the immediately
   previous fiscal year?

   A. FY 2003-2004   B. FY 2004-2005
   C. FY 2005-2006   D. FY 2006-2007

7. Assume that the number of buses (U_t) required for a given line-haul system serving the   7.__
   Central Business District depends upon roundtrip time (t), capacity of bus (c), and the
   total number of people to be moved in a peak hour (P) in the major direction, i.e., in the
   morning and out in the evening.
   The formula for the number of buses required is

   A. $U_t = Ptc$ B. $U_t = \dfrac{tP}{c}$ C. $U_t = \dfrac{cP}{t}$ D. $U_t = \dfrac{ct}{P}$

8. The area, in blocks, that can be served by a single stop for any maximum walking dis-   8.__
   tance is given by the following formula: $a = 2w^2$. In this formula, a = the area served by a
   stop, and w = maximum walking distance.
   If people will tolerate a walk of up to three blocks, how many stops would be needed to
   service an area of 288 square blocks?

   A. 9   B. 16   C. 18   D. 27

Questions 9-11.

DIRECTIONS: Questions 9 through 11 are to be answered on the basis of the following infor-
              mation.

   In 2006, a police precinct records 456 cases of car thefts which is 22.6 percent of all
grand larcenies. In 2007, there were 560 such cases, which constituted 35% of the broader
category.

9. The number of crimes in the broader category in 2007 was MOST NEARLY   9.__

   A. 1,600   B. 1,700   C. 1,960   D. 2,800

10. The change from 2006 to 2007 in the number of crimes in the broader category repre-   10.__
    sented MOST NEARLY a

    A. 2.5% decrease   B. 10.1% increase
    C. 12.5% increase   D. 20% decrease

11. In 2007, one out of every 6 of these crimes was solved. This represents MOST NEARLY   11.__
    what percentage of the total number of crimes in the broader category that year?

    A. 5.8   B. 6   C. 9.3   D. 12

12. Assume that a maintenance shop does 5 brake jobs to every 3 front-end jobs. It does 8,000 jobs altogether in a 240-day year. In one day, one worker can do 3 front-end jobs or 4 brake jobs.
About how many workers will be needed in the shop?

    A. 3   B. 5   C. 10   D. 18

12.____

13. Assume that the price of a certain item declines by 6% one year, and then increases by 5 and 10 percent, respectively, during the next two years.
What is the OVERALL increase in price over the three-year period?

    A. 4.2   B. 6   C. 8.6   D. 10.1

13.____

14. After finding the total percent change in a price (TO over a three-year period, as in the preceding question, one could compute the average annual percent change in the price by using the formula

    A. $(1 + TC)^{1/3}$
    B. $\dfrac{(1 + TC)}{3}$

    C. $(1 + TC)^{1/3 - 1}$
    D. $\dfrac{1}{(1+TC)^{1/3} - 1}$

14.____

15. 357 is 6% of

    A. 2,142   B. 5,950   C. 4,140   D. 5,900

15.____

16. In 2002, a department bought n pieces of a certain supply item for a total of $x. In 2003, the department bought k percent fewer of the item but had to pay a total of g percent more for it.
Which of the following formulas is CORRECT for determining the average price per item in 2003?

    A. $100\dfrac{xg}{nk}$
    B. $\dfrac{x(100+g)}{n(100-k)}$

    C. $\dfrac{x(100-g)}{n(100+k)}$
    D. $\dfrac{x}{n} - 100\dfrac{g}{k}$

16.____

17. A sample of 18 income tax returns, each with 4 personal exemptions, is taken for 2001 and for 2002. The breakdown is as follows in terms of income:

Average gross income (in thousands)	Number of returns 2001	2002
40	6	2
80	10	11
120	2	5

There is a personal deduction per exemption of $500.
There are no other expense deductions. In addition, there is an exclusion of $3,000 for incomes less than $50,000 and $2,000 for incomes from $50,000 to $99,999.99. From $100,000 upward there is no exclusion.

The average net taxable income for the samples in thousands) for 2001 is MOST NEARLY

    A. $67   B. $85   C. $10   D. $128

17.____

18. In the preceding question, the increase in average net taxable income for the sample (in thousands) between 2001 and 2002 is

    A. 16   B. 20   C. 24   D. 34

18.__

19. Assume that supervisor S has four subordinates - A, B, C, and D.
The MAXIMUM number of relationships, assuming that all combinations are included, that can exist between S and his subordinates is

    A. 28   B. 15   C. 7   D. 4

19.__

20. If the workmen's compensation insurance rate for clerical workers is 93 cents per $100 of wages, the total premium paid by a city whose clerical staff earns $8,765,000 is MOST NEARLY

    A. $8,150   B. $81,515   C. $87,650   D. $93,765

20.__

21. Assume that a budget of $3,240,000,000 for the fiscal year beginning July 1, 2003 has been approved. A city sales tax is expected to provide $1,100,000,000; licenses, fees and sundry revenues are expected to yield $121,600,000; the balance is to be raised from property taxes. A tax equalization board has appraised all property in the city at a fair value of $42,500,000,000. The council wishes to assess property at 60% of its fair value.
The tax rate would need to be MOST NEARLY _____ per $100 of assessed value.

    A. $12.70   B. $10.65   C. $7.90   D. $4.00

21.__

22. Men's white linen handkerchiefs cost $12.90 for 3. The cost per dozen handkerchiefs is

    A. $77.40   B. $38.70   C. $144.80   D. $51.60

22.__

23. Assume that it is necessary to partition a room measuring 40 feet by 20 feet into eight smaller rooms of equal size. Allowing no room for aisles, the MINIMUM amount of partitioning that would be needed is _____ feet.

    A. 90   B. 100   C. 110   D. 140

23.__

24. Assume that two types of files have been ordered: 200 of type A and 100 of type B.
When the files are delivered, the buyer discovers that 25% of each type is damaged.
Of the remaining files, 20% of type A and 40% of type B are the wrong color.
The total number of files that are the WRONG COLOR is

    A. 30   B. 40   C. 50   D. 60

24.__

25. In a unit of five inspectors, one inspector makes an average of 12 inspections a day, two inspectors make an average of 10 inspections a day, and two inspectors make an average of 9 inspections a day.
If in a certain week one of the inspectors who makes an average of nine inspections a day is out of work on Monday and Tuesday because of illness and all the inspectors do no inspections for half a day on Wednesday because of a special meeting, the number of inspections this unit can be expected to make in that week is MOST NEARLY

    A. 215   B. 225   C. 230   D. 250

25.__

KEY (CORRECT ANSWERS)

1.	B		11.	A
2.	C		12.	C
3.	D		13.	C
4.	D		14.	C
5.	D		15.	B
6.	C		16.	B
7.	B		17.	A
8.	B		18.	A
9.	A		19.	B
10.	D		20.	B

21. C
22. D
23. B
24. D
25. A

———

SOLUTIONS TO PROBLEMS

1. Since the number of weekly inspections ranged from 20 to 40, this implies that the average weekly number of inspections never fell below 20 (choice B).

2. $591 \div .194 \approx 3046$, closest to 3000 students

3. $(591-268) \div 268 = 120\%$

4. Total processing cost = $(268)(\$28)+(1688)(\$21) = \$42,952$, closest to \$40,000. [Note: Since 268 represents 13.7%, total freshman population = $268 \div .137 \approx 1956$. Then, $1956 - 268 = 1688$]

5. Let x = staff size in 2004-2005. Then, $.80x$ = staff size in 2005-2006. Since the 2005-2006 staff produced 20% more work, this is represented by 1.20. However, to measure the productivity per staff member, the factor $1/.80 = 1.25$ must also be used to equate the 2 staffs. Then, $(1.20)(1.25) = 1.50$. Thus, the 2005-2006 staff produced 50% more work than the 2004-2005 staff.

6. The respective percent increases are $\approx 20\%, 17\%, 39\%, 29\%$. The largest would be, over the previous fiscal year, for the current fiscal year 2005-2006.

7. $\dfrac{P}{c}$ = number of buses needed per hour. If t = time (in hrs.), then $U_t = tP/c$

8. $a = (2)(9) = 18$ for 1 stop. Then, $288 \div 18 = 16$ stops

9. $560 \div .35 = 1600$ grand larcenies

10. $456 \div .226 = 2018$; $560 .35 = 1600$. Then, $(1600-2018) \div 2018 = -20\%$, or a 20% decrease

11. $(\dfrac{1}{6})(560)=93\dfrac{1}{3}$.   Then, $93\dfrac{1}{3} \div 1600 = 5.8\%$

12. There are 5000 brake jobs and 3000 front-end jobs in one year.
    $5000 \div 4 = 1250$ days, and $1250 \div 240 \approx 5.2$. Also, $3000 \div 3 =$
    1000 days, and $1000 \div 240 \approx 4.2$. Total number of workers
    needed $\approx 5.2 + 4.2 \approx 10$

13. $(.94)(1.05)(1.10) = 1.0857$, which represents an overall increase by about 8.6%

14. Average annual % change = $(1+TC)^{\frac{1}{3}} - 1 = (1.0857)^{\frac{1}{3}} - 1 \approx 2.8\%$

15. $357 \div .06 = 5950$

16. In 2003, $(h)(1-\dfrac{k}{100})$ pieces $\text{cost}(x)(1+\dfrac{g}{100})$ dollars. To calculate the cost for 1 piece (average cost), find the value of $[(x)(1+\dfrac{G}{100})] \div [(n)(1-\dfrac{K}{100})] = [(x)(100+g)/100]$.

   $[100/\{n(100-k)\}] = [x(100+g)]/[n(100-k)]$

17.

	#	Deductions Up To 50,000		
40,000	6	2000	3000	$40,000-3,000-2,000 = 35,000 \times 6$
80,000	10	2000	2000	$80,000-2,000-2,000 = 76,000 \times 10$
20,000	2	2000		$= 118000 \times 2$

   $35,000 \times 6 = 210,000 = 210$
   $76,000 \times 10 = 760,000 = 760$
   $118,000 \times 2 = 236,000 = \underline{236}$
   1206

   $1206 \div 18 = 67$

18. 2002

		Deductions		
40,000	2	2000	3000	$35,000 \times 2 = \quad 70,000$
80,000	11	2000	2000	$76,000 \times 11 = \quad 836,000$
120,000	5	2000		$118,000 \times 5 = \quad \underline{590,000}$
				$1,496,000$

   $1,496,000 / 18 = 83,111$
   $83,111 - 67,000 = 16,111 =$ most nearly 16 (in thousands)

19. We are actually looking for the number of different groups of different sizes involving S. This reduces to $_4C_1 + {_4}C_2 + {_4}C_2 + {_4}C_4 = 4+6+4+1 = 15$. The notation nCr means combinations of n things taken R at a time $= [(n)(n-l)(n-2)(...)(n-R+l)]/[(R)(R-1)(...)(1)]$. The 15 groups are: SA, SB, SC, SD, SAB, SAC, SAD, SBC, SBD, SCD, SABC, SABD, SACD, SBCD, SABCD.

20. Let x = total premiums. Then, $\dfrac{.93}{100} = \dfrac{X}{8,765,000}$ Solving, x = \$81,515

21. The balance, raised from property taxes, = \$3,240,000,000 -\$1,100,000,000 - \$121,600,000 = \$2,018,400,000. Now, $(.60)(\$42,500,000,000) = \$25,500,000$. The tax rate per \$100 of assessed value = $(\$2,018,400,000)(\$100)/\$25,500,000,000 = \$7.90$

22. A dozen costs $(\$12.90)(\dfrac{12}{3}) = \$51.60$

23. $(40)(20) \div 8 = 100$ ft.

24.   Total number of wrong-color files = $(200)(.75)(.20)+(100)(.75)(.40) = 60$

25.   Weekly number of inspections = $(12 \times 5) + (10 \times 5) + (10 \times 5) + (9 \times 5) + (9 \times 5) = 250$
      Subtract: 9 Monday, 9 Tuesday, 25 Wednesday
      Total: $250 - 9 - 9 - 25 = 207$
      Closest entry is choice A

BASIC FUNDAMENTALS OF A FINANCIAL STATEMENT

TABLE OF CONTENTS

BASIC FUNDAMENTALS
OF A FINANCIAL STATEMENT

COMMENTARY

The ability to read and understand a financial statement is a basic requirement for the accountant, auditor, account clerk, bookkeeper, bank examiner. budget examiner, and, of course, for the executive who must manage and administer departmental affairs.

FINANCIAL REPORTS

Are financial reports really as difficult as all that? Well, if you know they are not so difficult because you have worked with them before, this section will be of auxiliary help for you. However, if you find financial statements a bit murky, but realize their great importance to you, we ought to get along fine together. For "mathematics," all we'll use is fourth-grade arithmetic.

Accountants, like all other professionals, have developed a specialized vocabulary. Sometimes this is helpful and sometimes plain confusing (like their practice of calling the income account, "Statement of Profit and Loss," when it is bound to be one or the other). But there are really only a score or so technical terms that you will have to get straight in mind. After that is done, the whole foggy business will begin to clear and in no time at all you'll be able to talk as wisely as the next fellow.

BALANCE SHEET

Look at the sample balance sheet printed on page 2, and we'll have an insight into how it is put together. This particular report is neither the simplest that could be issued, nor the most complicated. It is a good average sample of the kind of report issued by an up-to-date manufacturing company.

Note particularly that the *balance sheet* represents the situation as it stood on one particular day, December 31, not the record of a year's operation. This balance sheet is broken into two parts: on the left are shown *ASSETS* and on the right *LIABILITIES.* Under the asset column, you will find listed the value of things the company owns or are owed to the company. Under liabilities, are listed the things the company owes to others, plus reserves, surplus, and the stated value of the stockholders' interest in the company.

One frequently hears the comment, "Well, I don't see what a good balance sheet is anyway, because the assets and liabilities are always the same whether the company is successful or not."

It is true that they always balance and, by itself, a balance sheet doesn't tell much until it is analyzed. Fortunately, we can make a balance sheet tell its story without too much effort -- often an extremely revealing story, particularly, if we compare the records of several years. ASSETS The first notation on the asset side of the balance sheet is *CURRENT* ASSETS (item 1). In general, current assets include cash and things that can be turned into cash in a hurry, or that, in the normal course of business, will be turned into cash in the reasonably near future, usually within a year.

Item 2 on our sample sheet is *CASH.* Cash is just what you would expect -bills and silver in the till and money on deposit in the bank.

UNITED STATES GOVERNMENT SECURITIES is item 3. The general practice is to show securities listed as current assets at cost or market value, whichever is lower. The figure, for all reasonable purposes, represents the amount by which total cash could be easily increased if the company wanted to sell these securities.

The next entry is *ACCOUNTS RECEIVABLE* (item 4). Here we find the total amount of money owed to the company by its regular business creditors and collectable within the next year. Most of the money is owed to the company by its customers for goods that the company delivered on credit. If this were a department store instead of a manufacturer, what you owed the store on your charge account would be included here. Because some people fail to pay their bills, the company sets up a reserve for doubtful accounts, which it subtracts from all the money owed.

THE ABC MANUFACTURING COMPANY, INC.
CONSOLIDATED BALANCE SHEET – DECEMBER 31

Item		
1. CURRENT ASSETS		
2. Cash		
3. U.S. Government Securities		
4. Accounts Receivable (less reserves)	2,000,000	
5. Inventories (at lower of cost or market)	2,000,000	
6. Total Current Assets		$7,000,000
7. INVESTMENT IN AFFILIATED COMPANY Not consolidated (at cost, not in excess of net assets)		200,000
8. OTHER INVESTMENTS At cost, less than market		100,000
9. PLANT IMPROVEMENT FUND		550,000
10. PROPERTY, PLANT AND EQUIPMENT:		
Cost	$8,000,000	
11. Less Reserve for Depreciation	5,000,000	
12. NET PROPERTY		3,000,000
13. PREPAYMENTS		50,000
14. DEFERRED CHARGES		100,000
15. PATENTS AND GOODWILL		100,000
TOTAL		$11,100,000

Item		
16. CURRENT LIABILITIES		
17. Accts. Payable	$ 300,000	
18. Accrued Taxes	800,000	
19. Accrued Wages, Interest and Other Expenses	370,000	
20. Total Current Liabilities		$1,470,000
21. FIRST MORTGAGE SINKING FUND BONDS, 3 1/2% DUE 2002		2,000,000
22. RESERVE FOR CONTINGENCIES		200,000
23. CAPITAL STOCK:		
24. 5% Preferred Stock (authorized and issued 10,000 shares of $100 par value)	$1,000,000	
25. Common stock (authorized and issued 400,000 shares of no par value)	1,000,000	
		2,000,000
26. SURPLUS:		
27. Earned	3,530,000	
28. Capital (arising from sale of common capital stock at price in excess of stated value)	1,900,000	
		5,430,000
TOTAL		$11,100,000

Item 5, *INVENTORIES,* is the value the company places on the supplies it owns. The inventory of a manufacturer may contain raw materials that it uses in making the things it sells, partially finished goods in process of manufacture and, finally, completed merchandise that it is ready to sell. Several methods are used to arrive at the value placed on these various items. The most common is to value them at their cost or present market value, whichever is lower. You can be reasonably confident, however, that the figure given is an honest and significant one for the particular industry if the report is certified by a reputable firm of public accountants.

Next on the asset side is *TOTAL CURRENT ASSETS* (item 6). This is an extremely important figure when used in connection with other items in the report, which we will come to presently. Then we will discover how to make total current assets tell their story.

INVESTMENT IN AFFILIATED COMPANY (item 7) represents the cost to our parent company of the capital stock of its *subsidiary* or affiliated company. A subsidiary is simply one company that is controlled by another. Most corporations that own other companies outright, lump the figures in a *CONSOLIDATED BALANCE SHEET.* This means that, under cash, for example, one would find a total figure that represented *all* of the cash of the parent company and of its wholly owned subsidiary. This is a perfectly reasonable procedure because, in the last analysis, all of the money is controlled by the same persons.

Our typical company shows that it has *OTHER INVESTMENTS* (item 8), in addition to its affiliated company. Sometimes good marketable securities other than Government bonds are carried as current assets, but the more conservative practice is to list these other security holdings separately. If they have been bought as a permanent investment, they would always be shown by themselves. "At cost, less than market" means that our company paid $100,000 for these other investments, but they are now worth more.

Among our assets is a *PLANT IMPROVEMENT FUND* (item 9). Of course, this item does not appear in all company balance sheets, but is typical of *special funds* that companies set up for one purpose or another. For example, money set aside to pay off part of the bonded debt of a company might be segregated into a special fund. The money our directors have put aside to improve the plant would often be invested in Government bonds.

FIXED ASSETS

The next item (10), is *PROPERTY, PLANT AND EQUIPMENT,* but it might just as well be labeled *Fixed Assets* as these terms are used more or less interchangeably. Under item 10, the report gives the value of land, buildings, and machinery and such movable things as trucks, furniture, and hand tools. Historically, probably more sins were committed against this balance sheet item than any other.

In olden days, cattlemen used to drive their stock to market in the city. It was a common trick to stop outside of town, spread out some salt for the cattle to make them thirsty and then let them drink all the water they could hold. When they were weighed for sale, the cattlemen would collect cash for the water the stock had drunk. Business buccaneers, taking the cue from their farmer friends, would often "write up" the value of their fixed assets. In other words, they would increase the value shown on the balance sheet, making the capital stock appear to be worth a lot more than it was. *Watered stock* proved a bad investment for most stockholders. The practice has, fortunately, been stopped, though it took major financial reorganizations to squeeze the water out of some securities.

The most common practice today is to list fixed assets at cost. Often, there is no ready market for most of the things that fall under this heading, so it is not possible to give market value. A good report will tell what is included under fixed assets and how it has been valued. If the value has been increased by *write-up* or decreased by *write-down,* a footnote explanation is usually given. A *write-up* might occur, for instance, if the value of real estate increased substantially. A *write-down* might follow the invention of a new machine that put an important part of the company's equipment out of date.

DEPRECIATION

Naturally, all of the fixed property of a company will wear out in time (except, of course, non-agricultural land). In recognition of this fact, companies set up a *RESERVE FOR DEPRECIATION* (item 11). If a truck costs $4,000 and is expected to last four years, it will be depreciated at the rate of $1,000 a year.

Two other terms also frequently occur in connection with depreciation -*depletion* and *obsolescence*. Companies may lump depreciation, depletion, and obsolescence under a single title, or list them separately.

Depletion is a term used primarily by mining and oil companies (or any of the so-called extractive industries). Depletion means exhaust or use up. As the oil or other natural resource is used up, a reserve is set up, to compensate for the natural wealth the company no longer owns. This reserve is set up in recognition of the fact that, as the company sells its natural product, it must get back not only the cost of extracting but also the original cost of the natural resource.

Obsolescence represents the loss in value because a piece of property has gone out of date before it wore out. Airplanes are modern examples of assets that tend to get behind the times long before the parts wear out. (Women and husbands will be familiar with the speed at which ladies' hats "obsolesce.")

In our sample balance sheet we have placed the reserve for depreciation under fixed assets and then subtracted, giving us *NET PROPERTY* (item 12), which we add into the asset column. Sometimes, companies put the reserve for depreciation in the liability column. As you can see, the effect is just the same whether it is *subtracted* from assets or *added* to liabilities.

The manufacturer, whose balance sheet we use, rents a New York showroom and pays his rent yearly, in advance. Consequently, he has listed under assets *PREPAYMENTS* (item 13). This is listed as an asset because he has paid for the use of the showroom, but has not yet received the benefit from its use. The use is something coming to the firm in the following year and, hence, is an asset. The dollar value of this asset will decrease by one-twelfth each month during the coming year.

DEFERRED CHARGES (item 14) represents a type of expenditure similar to prepayment. For example, our manufacturer brought out a new product last year, spending $100,000 introducing it to the market. As the benefit from this expenditure will be returned over months or even years to come, the manufacturer did not think it reasonable to charge the full expenditure against costs during the year. He has *deferred* the charges and will write them off gradually.

INTANGIBLES

The last entry in our asset column is *PATENTS AND GOODWILL* (item 15). If our company were a young one, set up to manufacture some new patented prod uct, it would probably carry its patents at a substantial figure. In fact, *intangibles* of both old and new companies are often of great but generally unmeasurable worth.

Company practice varies considerably in assigning value to intangibles. Procter & Gamble, despite the tremendous goodwill that has been built up for IVORY SOAP, has reduced all of its intangibles to the nominal $1. Some of the big cigarette companies, on the contrary, place a high dollar value on the goodwill their brand names enjoy. Companies that spend a good deal for research and the development of new products are more inclined than others to reflect this fact in the value assigned to patents, license agreements, etc.

LIABILITIES

The liability side of the balance sheet appears a little deceptive at first glance. Several of the entries simply don't sound like liabilities by any ordinary definition of the term.

The first term on the liability side of any balance sheet is usually *CURRENT LIABILITIES* (item 16). This is a companion to the *Current Assets* item across the page and includes all debts that fall due within the next year. The relation between current assets and current liabilities is one of the most revealing things to be gotten from the balance sheet, but we will go into that quite thoroughly later on.

ACCOUNTS PAYABLE (item 17) represents the money that the company owes to its ordinary business creditors -- unpaid bills for materials, supplies, insurance, and the like. Many companies itemize the money they owe in a much more detailed fashion than we have done, but, as you will see, the totals are the most interesting thing to us.

Item 18, *ACCRUED TAXES,* is the tax bill that the company estimates it still owes for the past year. We have lumped all taxes in our balance sheet, as many companies do. However, sometimes you will find each type of tax given separately. If the detailed procedure is followed, the description of the tax is usually quite sufficient to identify the separate items.

Accounts Payable was defined as the money the company owed to its regular business creditors. The company also owes, on any given day, wages to its own employees; interest to its bondholders and to banks from which it may have borrowed money; fees to its attorneys; pensions, etc. These are all totaled under *ACCRUED WAGES, INTEREST AND OTHER EXPENSES* (item 19).

TOTAL CURRENT LIABILITIES (item 20) is just the sum of everything that the company owed on December 31 and which must be paid sometime in the next twelve months.

It is quite clear that all of the things discussed above are liabilities. The rest of the entries on the liability side of the balance sheet, however, do not seem at first glance to be liabilities.

Our balance sheet shows that the company, on December 31, had $2,000,000 of 3 1/2 percent First Mortgage *BONDS* outstanding (item 21). Legally, the money received by a company when it sells bonds is considered a loan to the company. Therefore, it is obvious that the company owes to the bondholders an amount equal to the face value or the *call price* of the bonds it has outstanding. The call price is a figure usually larger than the face value of the bonds at which price the company can *call* the bonds in from the bondholders and pay them off before they ordinarily fall due. The date that often occurs as part of the name of a bond is the date at which the company has promised to pay off the loan from the bondholders.

RESERVES

The next heading, *RESERVE FOR CONTINGENCIES* (item 22), sounds more like an asset than a liability. "My reserves," you might say, "are dollars in the bank, and dollars in the bank are assets."

No one would deny that you have something there. In fact, the corporation treasurer also has his reserve for contingencies balanced by either cash or some kind of unspecified investment on the asset side of the ledger. His reason for setting up a reserve on the liability side of the balance sheet is a precaution against making his financial position seem better than it is. He decided that the company might have to pay out this money during the coming year if certain things happened. If he did not set up the "reserve," his surplus would appear larger by an amount equal to his reserve.

A very large reserve for contingencies or a sharp increase in this figure from the previous year should be examined closely by the investor. Often, in the past, companies tried to hide their true earnings by transferring funds into a contingency reserve. As a reserve looks somewhat like a true liability, stockholders were confused about the real value of their securities. When a reserve is not set up for protection against some very probable loss or expenditure, it should be considered by the investor as part of surplus.

CAPITAL STOCK

Below reserves there is a major heading, *CAPITAL STOCK* (item 23). Companies may have one type of security outstanding, or they may have a dozen. All of the issues that represent shares of ownership are capital, regardless of what they are called on the balance sheet -- preferred stock, preference stock, common stock, founders' shares, capital stock, or something else.

Our typical company has one issue of 5 per cent *PREFERRED STOCK* (item 24). It is called *preferred* because those who own it have a right to dividends and assets before the *common* stockholders -- that is, the holders are in a preferred position as owners. Usually, preferred stockholders do not have a voice in company affairs unless the company fails to pay them dividends at the promised rate. Their rights to dividends are almost always *cumulative.* This simply means that all past dividends must be paid before the other stockholders can receive anything. Preferred stockholders are not creditors of the company so it cannot properly be said that the company *owes* them the value of their holdings. However, in case the company decided to go out of business, preferred stockholders would have a prior claim on anything that was left in the company treasury after all of the creditors, including the bondholders, were paid off. In practice, this right does not always mean much, but it does explain why the book value of their holdings is carried as a liability.

COMMON STOCK (item 25) is simple enough as far as definition is concerned it represents the rights of the ordinary owner of the company. Each company has as many owners as it has stockholders. The proportion of the company that each stockholder owns is determined by the number of shares he has. However, neither the book value of a no-par common stock, nor the par value of an issue that has a given par, can be considered as representing either the original sale price, the market value, or what would be left for the stockholders if the company were liquidated.

A profitable company will seldom be dissolved. Once things have taken such a turn that dissolution appears desirable, the stated value of the stock is generally nothing but a fiction. Even if the company is profitable as a going institution, once it ceases to function even its tangible assets drop in value because there is not usually a ready market for its inventory of raw materials and semi-finished goods, or its plant and machinery.

SURPLUS

The last major heading on the liability side of the balance sheet is *SURPLUS* (item 26). The surplus, of course, is not a liability in the popular sense at all. It represents, on our balance sheet, the difference between the stated value of our common stock and the net assets behind the stock.

Two different kinds of surplus frequently appear on company balance sheets, and our company has both kinds. The first type listed is *EARNED* surplus (item 27). Earned surplus is roughly similar to your own savings. To the corporation, earned surplus is that part of net income which has not been paid to stockholders as dividends. It still *belongs* to you, but the directors have decided that it is best for the company and the stockholders to keep it in the business. The surplus may be invested in the plant just as you might invest part of your savings in your home. It may also be in cash or securities.

In addition to the earned surplus, our company also has a *CAPITAL* surplus (item 28) of $1,900.00, which the balance sheet explains arose from selling the stock at a higher cost per share than is given as its stated value. A little arithmetic shows that the stock is carried on the books at $2.50 a share while the capital surplus amounts to $4.75 a share. From this we know that the company actually received an average of $7.25 net a share for the stock when it was sold.

WHAT DOES THE BALANCE SHEET SHOW?

Before we undertake to analyze the balance sheet figures, a word on just what an investor can expect to learn is in order. A generation or more ago, before present accounting standards had gained wide acceptance, considerable imagination went into the preparation of balance sheets. This, naturally, made the public skeptical of financial reports. Today, there is no substantial ground for skepticism. The certified public accountant, the listing requirements of the national stock exchanges, and the regulations of the Securities and Exchange Commission have, for all practical purposes, removed the grounds for doubting the good faith of financial reports.

The investor, however, is still faced with the task of determining the significance of the figures. As we have already seen, a number of items are based, to a large degree, upon estimates, while others are, of necessity, somewhat arbitrary.

NET WORKING CAPITAL

There is one very important thing that we can find from the balance sheet and accept with the full confidence that we know what we are dealing with. That is net working capital, sometimes simply called working capital.

On the asset side of our balance sheet we have added up all of the current assets and show the total as item 6. On the liability side, item 20 gives the total of current liabilities. *Net working capital* or *net current assets* is the difference left after subtracting current liabilities from current assets. If you consider yourself an investor rather than a speculator, you should always insist that any company in which you invest have a comfortable amount of working capital. The ability of a company to meet its obligations with ease, expand its volume as business expands and take advantage of opportunities as they present themselves, is, to an important degree, determined by its working capital.

Probably the question in your mind is: *"Just what does 'comfortable amount' of working capital mean?"* Well, there are several methods used by analysts to judge whether a particular company has a sound working capital position. The first rough test for an industrial company is to compare the working capital figure with the current liability total. Most analysts say that minimum safety requires that net working capital at least equal current liabilities. Or, put another way, that current assets should be at least twice as large as current liabilities.

There are so many different kinds of companies, however, that this test requires a great deal of modification if it is to be really helpful in analyzing companies in different industries. To help you interpret the *current position* of a company in which you are considering investing, the *current ratio* is more helpful than the dollar total of working capital. The current ratio is current assets divided by current liabilities.

In addition to working capital and current ratio, there are two other ways of testing the adequacy of the current position. *Net quick assets* provide a rigorous and important test of a company's ability to meet its current obligations. Net quick assets are found by taking total current assets (item 6) and subtracting the value of inventories (item 5). A well-fixed industrial company should show a reasonable excess of quick assets over current liabilities..

Finally, many analysts say that a good industrial company should have at least as much working capital (current assets less current liabilities) as the total book value of its bonds and preferred stock. In other words, current liabilities, bonded debt, and preferred stock *altogether* should not exceed the current assets.

INVENTORY AND INVENTORY TURNOVER

In the recent past, there has been much talk of inventories. Many commentators have said that these carry a serious danger to company earnings if management allows them to increase too much. Of course, this has always been true, but present high prices have made everyone more inventory-conscious than usual.

There are several dangers in a large inventory position. In the first place, a sharp drop in price may cause serious losses; also, a large inventory may indicate that the company has accumulated a big supply of unsalable merchandise. The question still remains, however: *"What do we mean by large inventory?"*

As you certainly realize, an inventory is large or small only in terms of the yearly turnover and the type of business. We can discover the annual turnover of our sample company by dividing inventories (item 5) into total annual sales (item "a" on the income account).

It is also interesting to compare the value of the inventory of a company being studied with total current assets. Again, however, there is considerable variation between different types of companies, so that the relationship becomes significant only when compared with similar companies.

NET BOOK VALUE OF SECURITIES

There is one other very important thing that can be gotten from the balance sheet, and that is the net book or equity value of the company's securities. We can calculate the net book value of each of the three types of securities our company has outstanding by a little very simple arithmetic. *Book value means the value at which something is carried on the books of the company.*

The full rights of the bondholders come before any of the rights of the stockholders, so, to find the net book value or net tangible assets backing up the bonds we add together the balance sheet value of the bonds, preferred stock, common stock, reserve, and surplus. This gives us a total of $9,630,000. (We would not include contingency reserve if we were reasonably sure the contingency was going to arise, but, as general reserves are often equivalent to surplus, it is, usually, best to treat the reserve just as though it were surplus.) However, part of this value represents the goodwill and patents carried at $100,000, which is not a tangible item, so, to be conservative, we subtract this amount, leaving $9,530,000 as the total net book value of the bonds. This is equivalent to $4,765 for each $1,000 bond, a generous figure. To calculate the net book value of the preferred stock, we must eliminate the face value of the bonds, and then, following the same procedure, add the value of the preferred stock, common stock, reserve, and surplus, and subtract goodwill. This gives us a total net book value for the preferred stock of $7,530,000 or $753 for each share of $100 par value preferred. This is also very good coverage for the preferred stock, but we must examine current earnings before becoming too enthusiastic about the *value* of any security.

The net book value of the common stock, while an interesting figure, is not so important as the coverage on the senior securities. In case of liquidation, there is seldom much left for the common stockholders because of the normal loss in value of company assets when they are put up for sale, as mentioned before. The book value figure, however, does give us a basis for comparison with other companies. Comparisons of net book value over a period of years also show us if the company is a soundly growing one or, on the other hand, is losing ground. Earnings, however, are our important measure of common stock values, as we will see shortly.

The net book value of the common stock is found by adding the stated value of the common stock, reserves, and surplus and then subtracting patents and goodwill. This gives us a total net book value of $6,530,000. As there are 400,000 shares of common outstanding, each share has a net book value of $16.32. You must be careful not to be misled by book value figures, particularly of common stock. Profitable companies (Coca-Cola, for example) often show a very low net book value and very substantial earnings. Railroads, on the other hand, may show a high book value for their common stock but have such low or irregular earnings that the market price of the stock is much less than its apparent book value. Banks, insurance companies, and investment -trusts are exceptions to what we have said about common stock net book value. As their assets are largely liquid (i.e., cash, accounts receivable, and marketable securities), the book value of their common stock sometimes indicates its value very accurately.

PROPORTION OF BONDS, PREFERRED AND COMMON STOCK

Before investing, you will want to know the proportion of each kind of security issued by the company you are considering. A high proportion of bonds reduces the attractiveness of both the preferred and common stock, while too large an amount of preferred detracts from the value of the common.

The *bond ratio* is found by dividing the face value of the bonds (item 21), or $2,000,000, by the total value of the bonds, preferred stock, common stock, reserve, and surplus, or $9,630,000. This shows that bonds amount to about 20 per cent of the total of bonds, capital, and surplus.

The *preferred stock ratio* is found in the same way, only we divide the stated value of the preferred stock by the total of the other five items. Since we have half as much preferred stock as we have bonds, the preferred ratio is roughly 10.

Naturally, the *common stock ratio* will be the difference between 100 per cent and the totals of the bonds and preferred, or 70 per cent in our sample company. You will want to remember that the most valuable method of determining the common stock ratio is in combination with reserve and surplus. The surplus, as we have noted, is additional backing for the common stock and usually represents either original funds paid in to the company in excess of the stated value of the common stock (capital surplus), or undistributed earnings (earned surplus).

Most investment analysts carefully examine industrial companies that have more than about a quarter of their capitalization represented by bonds, while common stock should total at least as much as all senior securities (bonds and preferred issues). When this is not the case, companies often find it difficult to raise new capital. Banks don't like to lend them money because of the already large debt, and it is sometimes difficult to sell common stock because of all the bond interest or preferred dividends that must be paid before anything is available for the common stockholder.

Railroads and public utility companies are exceptions to most of the rules of thumb that we use in discussing The ABC Manufacturing Company, Inc. Their situation is different because of the tremendous amounts of money they have invested in their fixed assets., their small inventories and the ease with which they can collect their receivables. Senior securities of railroads and utility companies frequently amount to more than half of their capitalization. Speculators often interest themselves in companies that have a high proportion of debt or preferred stock because of the *leverage factor*. A simple illustration will show why. Let us take, for example, a company with $10,000,000 of 4 per cent bonds outstanding. If the company is earning $440,000 before bond interest, there will be only $40,000 left for the common stock ($10,000,000 at 4% equals $400,000). However, an increase of only 10 per cent in earnings (to $484,000) will leave $84,000 for common stock dividends, or an increase of more than 100 per cent. If there is only a small common issue, the increase in earnings per share would appear very impressive.

You have probably already noticed that a decline of 10 per cent in earnings would not only wipe out everything available for the common stock, but result in the company being unable to cover its full interest on its bonds without dipping into surplus. This is the great danger of so-called high leverage stocks and also illustrates the fundamental weakness of companies that have a disproportionate amount of debt or preferred stock. Investors would do well to steer clear of them. Speculators, however, will continue to be fascinated by the market opportunities they offer.

THE INCOME ACCOUNT

The fundamental soundness of a company, as shown by its balance sheet, is important to investors, but of even greater interest is the record of its operation. Its financial structure shows much of its ability to weather storms and pick up speed when times are good. It is the income record, however, that shows us how a company is actually doing and gives us our best guide to the future.

The *Consolidated Income and Earned Surplus* account of our company is stated on the next page. Follow the items given there and we will find out just how our company earned its money, what it did with its earnings, and what it all means in terms of our three classes of securities. We have used a combined income and surplus account because that is the form most frequently followed by industrial companies. However, sometimes the two statements are given separately. Also, a variety of names are used to describe this same part of the financial report. Sometimes it is called profit and loss account, sometimes *record of earnings,* and, often, simply *income account.* They are all the same thing.

The details that you will find on different income statements also vary a great deal. Some companies show only eight or ten separate items, while others will give a page or more of closely spaced entries that break down each individual type of revenue or cost. We have tried to strike a balance between extremes; give the major items that are in most income statements, omitting details that are only interesting to the expert analyst.

The most important source of revenue always makes up the first item on the income statement. In our company, it is *Net Sales* (item "a"). If it were a railroad or a utility instead of a manufacturer, this item would be called *gross revenues.* In any case, it represents the money paid into the company by its customers. Net sales are given to show that the figure represents the amount of money actually received after allowing for discounts and returned goods.

Net sales or gross revenues, you will note, is given before any kind of miscellaneous revenue that might have been received from investments, the sale of company property, tax refunds, or the like. A well-prepared income statement is always set up this way so that the stockholder can estimate the success of the company in fulfilling its major job of selling goods or service. If this were not so, you could not tell whether the company was really losing or making money on its operations, particularly over the last few years when tax rebates and other unusual things have often had great influence on final net income figures.

COST OF SALES

A general heading, *Cost of Sales, Expenses and Other Operating Charges* (item "b") is characteristic of a manufacturing company, but a utility company or railroad would call all of these things *operating expenses.*

The most important subdivision is *Cost of Goods Sold* (item "c"). Included under cost of goods sold are all of the expenses that go directly into the manufacture of the products the company sells -- raw materials, wages, freight, power, and rent. We have lumped these expenses together, as many companies do. Sometimes, however, you will find each item listed separately. Analyzing a detailed income account is a pretty technical operation and had best be left to the expert.

The ABC Manufacturing Company, Inc.
CONSOLIDATED INCOME AND EARNED SURPLUS
For the Year Ended December 31

Item			
a.	Sales		$10,000,000
b.	COST OF SALES, EXPENSES AND OTHER OPERATING CHARGES:		
c.	Cost of Goods Sold	$7,000,000	
d.	Selling, Administrative & Gen. Expenses	500,000	
e.	Depreciation	200,000	
f.	Maintenance and Repairs	400,000	
g.	Taxes (Other than Federal Inc. Taxes)	300,000	8,400,000
h.	NET PROFIT FROM OPERATIONS		$ 1,600,000
i.	OTHER INCOME:		
j.	Royalties and Dividends	$ 250,000	
k.	Interest	25,000	275,000
l.	TOTAL		$ 1,875,000
m.	INTEREST CHARGES:		
n.	Interest on Funded Debt	$ 70,000	
o.	Other Interest	20,000	90,000
p.	NET INCOME BEFORE PROVISION FOR FED. INCOME TAXES		$ 1,785,000
q.	PROVISION FOR FEDERAL INCOME TAXES		678,300
r.	NET INCOME		$ 1,106,700
s.	DIVIDENDS:		
t.	Preferred Stock - $5.00 Per Share	$ 50,000	
u.	Common Stock - $1.00 Per Share	400,000	
v.	PROVISION FOR CONTINGENCIES	200,000	650,000
w.	BALANCE CARRIED TO EARNED SURPLUS		$ 456,700
x.	EARNED SURPLUS – JANUARY 1		3,073,000
y.	EARNED SURPLUS – DECEMBER 31		$ 3,530,000

We have shown separately, opposite "d," the *Selling, Administrative and General Expenses* of the past year. Unfortunately, there is little uniformity among companies in their treatment of these important non-manufacturing costs. Our figure includes the expenses of management; that is, executive salaries and clerical costs; commissions and salaries paid to salesmen; advertising expenses, and the like.

Depreciation ("e") shows us the amount that the company transferred from income during the year to the depreciation reserve that we ran across before as item "11" on the balance sheet (page 2). Depreciation must be charged against income unless the company is going to live on its own fat, something that no company can do for long and stay out of bankruptcy.

MAINTENANCE

Maintenance and Repairs (item "f") represents the money spent to keep the plant in good operating order. For example, the truck that we mentioned under depreciation must be kept running day by day. The cost of new tires, recharging the battery, painting and mechanical repairs are all maintenance costs. Despite this day-to-day work on the truck, the company must still provide for the time when it wears out -- hence, the reserve for depreciation.

You can readily understand from your own experience the close connection between maintenance and depreciation. If you do not take good care of your own car, you will have to buy a new one sooner than you would had you maintained it well. Corporations face the same problem with all of their equipment. If they do not do a good job of maintenance, much more will have to be set aside for depreciation to replace the abused tools and property.

Taxes are always with us. A profitable company always pays at least two types of taxes. One group of taxes are paid without regard to profits, and include real estate taxes, excise taxes, social security, and the like (item "g"). As these payments are a direct part of the cost of doing business, they must be included before we can determine the *Net Profit From Operations* (item "h").

Net Profit from Operations (sometimes called *gross profit)* tells us what the company made from manufacturing and selling its products. It is an interesting figure to investors because it indicates .how efficiently and successfully the company operates in its primary purpose as a creator of wealth. As a glance at the income account will tell you, there are still several other items to be deducted before the stockholder can hope to get anything. You can also easily imagine that for many companies these other items may spell the difference between profit and loss. For these reasons, we use net profit from operations as an indicator of progress in manufacturing and merchandising efficiency, not as a judge of the investment quality of securities.

Miscellaneous Income not connected with the major purpose of the company is generally listed after net profit from operations. There are quite a number of ways that corporations increase their income, including interest and dividends on securities they own, fees for special services performed, royalties on patents they allow others to use, and tax refunds. Our income statement shows *Other Income* as item "i," under which is shown income from *Royalties and Dividends* (item "j"), and, as a separate entry, *Interest* (item "k") which the company received from its bond investments. The *Total* of other income (item t1t?) shows us how much The ABC Manufacturing Company received from so-called *outside activities.* Corporations with diversified interests often receive tremendous amounts of *other income.*

INTEREST CHARGES

There is one other class of expenses that must be deducted from our income before we can determine the base on which taxes are paid, and that is *Interest Charges* (item "m"). As our company has $2,000,000 worth of 3 1/2 per cent bonds outstanding, it will pay *Interest on Funded Debt* of $70,000 (item "n"). During the year, the company also borrowed money from the bank, on which it, of course, paid interest, shown as *Other Interest* (item "o").

Net Income Before Provision for Federal Income Taxes (item "p") is an interesting figure for historical comparison. It shows us how profitable the company was in all of its various operations. A comparison of this entry over a period of years will enable you to see how well the company had been doing as a business institution before the Government stepped in for its share of net earnings. Federal taxes have varied so much in recent years that earnings before taxes are often a real help in judging business progress.

A few paragraphs back we mentioned that a profitable corporation pays two general types of taxes. We have already discussed those that are paid without reference to profits. *Provision for Federal Income Taxes* (item "q") is ordinarily figured on the total income of the company after normal business expenses, and so appears on our income account below these charges. Bond interest, for example, as it is payment on a loan, is deducted beforehand. Preferred and common stock dividends, which are *profits* that go to owners of the company, come after all charges and taxes.

NET INCOME

After we have deducted all of our expenses and income taxes from total income, we get *Net Income* (item "r"). Net income is the most interesting figure of all to the investor. Net income is the amount available to pay dividends on the preferred and common stock. From the balance sheet, we have learned a good deal about the company's stability and soundness of structure; from net profit from operations, we judge whether the company is improving in industrial efficiency. Net income tells us whether the securities of the company are likely to be a profitable investment.

The figure given for a single year is not nearly all of the story, however. As we have noted before, the historical record is usually more important than the figure for any given year. This is just as true of net income as any other item. So many things change from year to year that care must be taken not to draw hasty conclusions. During the war, Excess Profits Taxes had a tremendous effect on the earnings of many companies. In the next few years, *carryback tax credits* allowed some companies to show a net profit despite the fact that they had operated at a loss. Even net income can be a misleading figure unless one examines it carefully. A rough and easy way of judging how *sound* a figure it is would be to compare it with previous years.

The investor in stocks has a vital interest in *Dividends* (item "s"). The first dividend that our company must pay is that on its *Preferred Stock* (item "t"). Some companies will even pay preferred dividends out of earned surplus accumulated in the past if the net income is not large enough, but such a company is skating on thin ice unless the situation is most unusual.

The directors of our company decided to pay dividends totaling $400,000 on the *Common Stock,* or $1 a share (item "u"). As we have noted before, the amount of dividends paid is not determined by net income, but by a decision of the stockholders' representatives - the company's directors. Common dividends, just like preferred dividends, can be paid out of surplus if there is little or no net income. Sometimes companies do this if they have a long history of regular payments and don't want to spoil the record because of some special temporary situation that caused them to lose money. This occurs even less frequently and is more *dangerous* than paying preferred dividends out of surplus.

It is much more common, on the contrary, to *plough earnings back into the business* -- a phrase you frequently see on the financial pages and in company reports. The directors of our typical company have decided to pay only $1 on the common stock, though net income would have permitted them to pay much more. They decided that the company should *save* the difference.

The next entry on our income account, *Provision for Contingencies* (item "v"), shows us where our reserve for contingencies arose. The treasurer of our typical company has put the provision for contingencies after dividends. However, you will discover, if you look at very many financial reports, that it is sometimes placed above net income.

All of the net income that was not paid out as dividends, or set aside for contingencies, is shown as *Balance Carried to Earned Surplus* (item "w"). In other words, it is kept in the business. In previous years, the company had also earned more than it paid out so it had already accumulated by the beginning of the year an earned surplus of $3,073,000 (item "x"). When we total the earned surplus accumulated during the year to that which the company had at the first of the year, we get the total earned surplus at the end' of the year (item "y"). You will notice that the total here is the same as that which we ran across on the balance sheet as item 27.

Not all companies combine their income and surplus account. When they do not, you will find that *balance carried to surplus will* be the last item on the income account. The statement of consolidated surplus would appear as a third section of the corporation's financial report. A separate surplus account might be used if the company shifted funds for reserves to surplus during the year or made any other major changes in its method of treating the surplus account.

ANALYZING THE INCOME ACCOUNT

The income account, like the balance sheet, will tell us a lot more if we make a few detailed comparisons. The size of the totals on an income account doesn't mean much by itself. A company can have hundreds of millions of dollars in net sales and be a very bad investment. On the other hand, even a very modest profit in round figures may make a security attractive if there are only a small number of shares outstanding.

Before you select a company for investment, you will want to know something of its *margin of profit,* and how this figure has changed over the years. Finding the margin of profit is very simple. We just divide the net profit from operations (item "h") by net sales (item "a"). The figure we get (0.16) shows us that the company make a profit of 16 per cent from operations. By itself, though, this is not very helpful. We can make it significant in two ways.

In the first place, we can compare it with the margin of profit in previous years, and, from this comparison, learn if the company excels other companies that do a similar type of business. If the margin of profit of our company is very low in comparison with other companies in the same field, it is an unhealthy sign. Naturally, if it is high, we have grounds to be optimistic.

Analysts also frequently use *operating ratio* for the same purpose. The operating ratio is the complement of the margin of profit. The margin of profit of our typical company is 16. The operating ratio is 84. You can find the operating ratio either by subtracting the margin of profit from 100 or dividing the total of operating costs ($8,400,000) by net sales ($10,000,000).

The margin of profit figure and the operating ratio, like all of those ratios we examined in connection with the balance sheet, give us general information about the company, help us judge its prospects for the future. All of these comparisons have significance for the long term as they tell us about the fundamental economic condition of the company. But you still have the right to ask: *"Are the securities good investments for me now?"*

Investors, as opposed to speculators, are primarily interested in two things. The first is safety for their capital and the second, regularity of income. They are also interested in the rate of return on their investment but, as you will see, the rate of return will be affected by the importance placed on safety and regularity. High income implies risk. Safety must be bought by accepting a lower return.

The safety of any security is determined primarily by the earnings of the company that are available to pay interest or dividends on the particular issue. Again, though, round dollar figures aren't of much help to us. What we want to know is the relationship between the total money available and the requirements for each of the securities issued by the company.

INTEREST COVERAGE

As the bonds of our company represent part of its debt, the first thing we want to know is how easily the company can pay the interest. From the income account we see that the company had total income of $1,875,000 (item "1"). The interest charge on our bonds each year is $70,000 (3 1/2 per cent of $2,000,000 - item 21 on the balance sheet). Dividing total income by bond interest charges ($1,875,000 by $70,000) shows us that the company earned its bond interest 26 times over. Even after income taxes, bond interest was earned 17 times, a method of testing employed by conservative analysts. Before an industrial bond should be considered a safe investment, most analysts say that the company should earn interest charges several times over, so our company has a wide margin of safety.

To calculate the *preferred dividend coverage* (i.e., the number of times preferred dividends were earned), we must use net income as our base, as Federal Income Taxes and all interest charges must be paid before anything is available for stockholders. As we have 10,000 shares of $100 par value of preferred stock which pays a dividend of 5 per cent, the total dividend requirement for the preferred stock is $50,000 (items 24 on the balance sheet and "t" on the income account).

EARNINGS PER COMMON SHARE

The buyer of common stocks is often more concerned with the earnings per share of his stock than he is with the dividend. It is usually earnings per share or, rather, prospective earnings per share, that influence stock market prices. Our income account does not show the earnings available for the common stock, so we must calculate it ourselves. It is net income less preferred dividends (items "r" - "t"), or $1,056,700. From the balance sheet, we know that there are 400,000 shares outstanding, so the company earned about $2.64 per share.

All of these ratios have been calculated for a single year. It cannot be emphasized too strongly, however, that the *record* is more important to the investor than the report of any single year. By all the tests we have employed, both the bonds and the preferred stock of our typical company appear to be very good investments,, if their market prices were not too high. The investor would want to look back, however, to determine whether the operations were reasonably typical of the company.

Bonds and preferred stocks that are very safe usually sell at pretty high prices, so the yield to the investor is small. For example, if our company has been showing about the same coverage on its preferred dividends for many years and there is good reason to believe that the future will be equally kind, the company would probably replace the old 5 per cent preferred with a new issue paying a lower rate, perhaps 4 per cent.

STOCK PRICES

As the common stock does not receive a guaranteed dividend, its market value is determined by a great variety of influences in addition to the present yield of the stock measured by its dividends. The stock market, by bringing together buyers and sellers from all over the world, reflects their composite judgment of the present and future value of the stock. We cannot attempt here to write a treatise on the stock market. There is one important ratio, however, that every common stock buyer considers. That is the ratio of earnings to market price.

The so-called *price-earnings ratio is* simply the earnings per share on the common stock divided into the market price. Our typical company earned $2.64 a common share in the year, If the stock were selling at $30 a share, its price-earnings ratio would be about 11.4. This is the basic figure that you would want to use in comparing the common stock of this particular company with other similar stocks.

IMPORTANT TERMS AND CONCEPTS

LIABILITIES
    WHAT THE COMPANY OWES -- + RESERVES + SURPLUS + STOCKHOLDERS INTEREST IN THE COMPANY

ASSETS
    WHAT THE COMPANY OWNS -- + WHAT IS OWED TO THE COMPANY

FIXED ASSETS
    MACHINERY, EQUIPMENT, BUILDINGS, ETC.

EXAMPLES OF FIXED ASSETS
    DESKS, TABLES, FILING CABINETS, BUILDINGS, LAND, TIMBERLAND, CARS AND TRUCKS, LOCOMOTIVES AND FREIGHT CARS, SHIPYARDS, OIL LANDS, ORE DEPOSITS, FOUNDRIES

EXAMPLES OF:
    PREPAID EXPENSES
        PREPAID INSURANCE, PREPAID RENT, PREPAID ROYALTIES AND PREPAID INTEREST

    DEFERRED CHARGES
        AMORTIZATION OF BOND DISCOUNT, ORGANIZATION EXPENSE, MOVING EXPENSES, DEVELOPMENT EXPENSES

ACCOUNTS PAYABLE
    BILLS THE COMPANY OWES TO OTHERS

BONDHOLDERS ARE CREDITORS
    BOND CERTIFICATES ARE IOU'S ISSUED BY A COMPANY BACKED BY A PLEDGE

BONDHOLDERS ARE OWNERS
    A STOCK CERTIFICATE IS EVIDENCE OF THE SHAREHOLDER'S OWNERSHIP

EARNED SURPLUS
    INCOME PLOWED BACK INTO THE BUSINESS

NET SALES
    GROSS SALES MINUS DISCOUNTS AND RETURNED GOODS

NET INCOME
    = TOTAL INCOME MINUS ALL EXPENSES AND INCOME TAXES